Review copy
Please send a copy of the printed review to the address below

ASHGATE

First Communion

Ritual, Church and Popular Religious Identity

Peter McGrail

Liturgy, Worship & Society Series

May 2007	234 x 156 mm	212 pages
Hardback	978-0-7546-5741-5	£50.00

ASHGATE Gower House, Croft Road, Aldershot, Hampshire GU11 3HR, UK

Tel: 01252 331551 Fax: 01252 344405 email: info@ashgatepublishing.com

FIRST COMMUNION

One of the most carefully prepared liturgies of any Roman Catholic parish's year is the celebration of 'First Communion'. This is the ritual by which seven- or eight-year-old children are admitted to the Eucharist for the first time. It attracts the largest congregations of any parish liturgy, and yet is frequently marked by tension and dissent within the parish community. The same ritual holds very different meanings for the various parties involved – clergy, parish schools, regularly communicating parishioners, and the first communicants and their families. The tensions arise from dissonance between the parties on such key issues as expected patterns of Church attendance, Catholic identity, dress and expenditure, and family formation. The relationships and discontinuities between popular and 'official' religion is at the heart of these tensions. They touch upon deep-seated anxieties concerning the future viability of the very structures and patterns of parish life during the current period of falling Church attendance and parish closures.

For those within the Church who are concerned to understand and address the issues in its structural decline, this book will make sometimes uncomfortable but always stimulating reading. Peter McGrail examines the relationship between Church structures and popular religious identity, viewed through the lens of the first communion event. Drawing out hitherto unrecognized connections and significances for the future of the Catholic Church at local level, the insights into the decline of the parish as an institution present challenges to all with an interest in and concern for the future of the Church in the English-speaking world.

Bringing to the fore the relationship and tensions between liturgy and Church structures, both historically and at the present time, this book offers academics and students alike extensive material for reflection and future development.

LITURGY, WORSHIP AND SOCIETY

SERIES EDITORS

Dave Leal, Brasenose College, Oxford, UK
Bryan Spinks, Yale Divinity School, USA
Paul Bradshaw, University of Notre Dame, UK and USA
Gregory Woolfenden, St Mary's Orthodox Church, USA
Phillip Tovey, Ripon College Cuddesdon, UK

The Ashgate *Liturgy, Worship and Society* series forms an important new 'library' on liturgical theory at a time of great change in the liturgy and much debate concerning traditional and new forms of worship, suitability and use of places of worship, and wider issues concerning interaction of liturgy, worship and contemporary society. Offering a thorough grounding in the historical and theological foundations of liturgy, this series explores and challenges many key issues of worship and liturgical theology, currently in hot debate within academe and within Christian churches worldwide – issues central to the future of the liturgy, to public and private worship, and set to make a significant impact on changing patterns of worship and the place of the church in contemporary society.

Other titles in the series:

Early and Medieval Rituals and Theologies of Baptism
From the New Testament to the Council of Trent
Bryan D. Spinks

Reformation and Modern Rituals and Theologies of Baptism
From Luther to Contemporary Practices
Bryan D. Spinks

The Liturgies of Quakerism
Pink Dandelion

Inculturation of Christian Worship
Exploring the Eucharist
Phillip Tovey

First Communion
Ritual, Church and Popular Religious Identity

PETER McGRAIL
Liverpool Hope University, UK

ASHGATE

Published by
Ashgate Publishing Limited
Gower House
Croft Road
Aldershot
Hampshire GU11 3HR
England

Ashgate Publishing Company
Suite 420
101 Cherry Street
Burlington, VT 05401-4405
USA

Ashgate website: http://www.ashgate.com

British Library Cataloguing in Publication Data
McGrail, Peter
  First communion: ritual, church and popular religious
  identity. – (Liturgy, worship and society)
  1. Catholic Church – England 2. First communion
  I.Title
  264'.02036

Library of Congress Cataloging-in-Publication Data
McGrail, Peter, 1959-
  First communion: ritual, church, and popular religious identity / Peter McGrail.
    p. cm. – (Liturgy, worship, and society series)
  Includes index.
  ISBN-13: 978-0-7546-5741-5 (hardcover: alk. paper)
  1. First communion. I. Title. II. Series: Liturgy, worship, and society.
  BX2237.M37 2007
  264'.02036–dc22

                                                                    2006018033

ISBN 978-0-7546-5741-5

Printed and bound in Great Britain by TJ International Ltd, Padstow, Cornwall.

In Memoriam

John McGrail

Contents

Acknowledgements

In the almost ten years that have elapsed from the first beginnings of this project to its publication, very many people have in one way or another accompanied me along the way. They are too many to list individually, but I am grateful for the part each has played. It is, however, important to identify a few for special thanks because of the key contribution they have made. Preeminent among these are the Liverpool priests and their parishioners who kindly and willingly welcomed me into their first communion celebrations. My encounters with them have stimulated much of what is contained in this book. Martin Stringer of Birmingham University supervised the original doctoral thesis upon which this book is based. His unerring gift for asking the crucial question at just the right stage of the work proved invaluable. I am also endebted to two different sets of colleagues – the members of the Pastoral Formation Department of Liverpool Archdiocese and of the Department of Theology and Religious Studies at Liverpool Hope University. All have coped admirably with the demands created by my work on the project. Finally, two friends have played particularly significant roles in supporting and encouraging me across the length of this project. To Paul McPartlan, I owe a debt of gratitude for helping me decide to set out on the research path – as well as for his constant engagement with my work along its course. And without Ursula Leahy's help, the project could never have come to completion – not only because she has proved a most intelligent sounding-board, but also because of the hours she has spent in proofreading the text at all its stages and helping me negotiate the more complex areas of textual layout. She also very kindly prepared the Index. Thank you to both.

List of Abbreviations

AAS   *Acta Apostolicae Sedis* 1909-.

ADA   Acta et Documenta Concilio Oecumenici Vaticano II Apparando. Series Prima (Antepraeparatoria). 1960–61.

AS   Acta Synodalia Sacrosancti Concilii Oecumenici Vaticani II. 1970– .

ASS   *Acta Sancta Sedis*. 1865–1908.

CCC   *Catechism of the Catholic Church*. 1994.

CIC   *The Code of Canon Law in English Translation*. 1983.

DS   Denzinger, H. and A. Shönmetzer 1977: *Enchiridion Symbolorum, Definitionum et Declarationum de Rebus Fidei et Morum.*

Introduction

The *Catholic Times* of 26 August 1910 carried an article that welcomed a recent Vatican initiative in the following terms:

> Of a truth, this is a decree that future generations will bless, teaching us to set far above profound knowledge and reverential awe the babbling words of childish lips, the fearless love of childish hearts, the stretching out of childish hands to Him who opens wide his arms and cries: 'Suffer the little children to come unto me, for of such is the Kingdom of God.'[1]

The decree in question was *Quam Singulari,* promulgated on 8 August 1910.[2] This decree introduced a radical change into one of the most popular of all Roman Catholic (henceforth, 'Catholic') rituals – the admission of children for the first time to the eucharist. For centuries this ritual had been celebrated with children on the verge of adolescence, that is, generally at around twelve years of age. For generations of young Catholics the event had come to serve not only as the point of admission into the centre of the Church's liturgy, but also as a human rite of passage into adolescence. Now, at a stroke, the Vatican had changed all that. From now on the rite was to be detached from its previous association with the transition into adolescence and instead to be celebrated at a far younger age: around seven years. The practice that *Quam Singulari* established continues to this day, and the legislative norms contained in the decree remain in force throughout the Catholic Church. In a very real way, the 1910 reform of first communion has a continuing impact upon Catholic life today.

The weight of that impact can be recognized in the comments of a Catholic whom I interviewed in Liverpool in 1999. As in all interviews cited in this book, I have given her a pseudonym to respect her confidentiality: let us call her Annie. Annie was well in her eighties when I interviewed her. A retired schoolteacher, she had lived through the enormous changes experienced by the Catholic community during the twentieth century, and in many respects exhibited a mischievously subversive attitude towards authority – both in the Church and in society. She was a firm supporter of her somewhat unorthodox parish priest, yet when asked about the celebration of first communion in her parish she said:

> We put up with; we bear the six weeks of first communion. Oh, do we dread them. The church is a playground. And they're coming in, they're dressing children, and pulling their pants up and talking – you know – to the aunties at the back, and grandmas up

---

1   James Hughes, editorial in *The Catholic Times*, London edition, no. 2,246, 26 August 1910, p. 10.

2   Official text in *Acta Apostolicae Sedis* (henceforth AAS), vol. ii (1909), pp. 577–83. All English translations taken from Haggerty, 1973.

there who haven't a clue what to do – you know, they haven't been for years ... Mass is a torture, it really is. Some people stay away. They say, 'Uh-oh, we won't see you for six weeks, no way!' ... We have this ordeal every Sunday morning for six weeks. ... To me it's heartbreaking.

This is hardly the attitude of future generations that was so confidently predicated by the *Catholic Times* back in 1910. Yet, it is typical of the response of so many in the Catholic Church towards the event today. Far from 'blessing' the discipline that *Quam Singulari* introduced, they question it. Far from welcoming with open arms the Catholic children who pass through it, many church-going Catholics question the integrity of motive of the majority of families who present their children for the ritual even though they do not regularly attend church. Indeed, as those families approach the parish to seek admission for their children to the ritual, it is frequently a demanding gate-keeper rather than a warm welcome that they encounter. A ritual reform that was initially greeted so enthusiastically appears to have resulted in a celebration that ninety years on is a focus of conflict and anxiety. This book asks why that should be the case, and suggests some possible answers.

The desire to research this question grew from my experience as a Catholic priest working in three parishes of the Archdiocese of Liverpool between 1987 and 1999. In 1999 I moved out of parish work to assume archdiocesan responsibilities for parish catechesis, as well as to begin the part-time PhD research upon which this book is based. From an archdiocesan vantage point it became quickly clear that conflict around the event was widespread. Across the archdiocese the annual celebration of the ritual catalysed tensions throughout the Catholic community. These tensions arose from strong dissonances among the various outcomes expected for the ritual by the different parties involved – the clergy, parish schools, active parishioners, and first communicants and their families. The dissonances were to do with expected patterns of church-attendance, dress and expenditure, and family formation. They tapped – as they still tap – into deep-seated anxieties concerning the future viability of the very structures and patterns of parish life. What inherent potential does this ritual possess to bring this range of issues to the surface? Why is it endowed with such divergent meanings and expectations? And why do so many Catholics who otherwise choose not to practise their faith invest such emotional energy and expenditure in it?

These questions raise broader issues than simply those around liturgical performance, because the tensions catalysed by the event are profoundly structural in nature. The fracture-lines that become visible during the celebration run through the Catholic community, and relate to much wider issues than the first communion event alone. First communion thus serves as a lens through which the current condition of the community at its most local level, the parish, is brought into focus. Through that lens, the parish is seen not as a monolithic faith bloc, but as a complex of individually negotiated positions around family formation and worshipping practices. The first communion lens consequently reveals how disputes over religious meaning and Catholic identity are enacted within that complex. These disputes translate into power-play and gate-keeping between members of the community. This power-play is accentuated by the current structural crisis in the Catholic community in Liverpool, as the system of parishes that has been built up across 150 years proves increasingly unsustainable in the face of falling numbers of church-goers and priests alike.

My interest in the ritual has gone further than seeking to understand its history or analysing theological texts. I wanted to know why it has such power to catalyse tension within the Catholic community at this time, and to identify the roots of the problem. In order to do this a number of very different disciplines needed to be brought into a creative dialogue. The formal theological and disciplinary position of the Catholic Church needed to be explored alongside the informal discourses of participants in the ritual on the ground. Current conflicts needed to be seen in the light of historical developments. Educational texts and approaches needed to be considered in the light of institutional and structural ambitions. And all this needed to be explored in the light of the crisis generated when the very parish structure itself fails. Otherwise, a highly complex and fluid reality risked being reduced to single-issue perspectives that invite simplistic and ultimately futile responses.

Before outlining how the book draws these various disciplines together, it is useful to map the academic field with regard to first communion, as this will identify a number of unanswered questions that feed directly into my own research.

Previous Research

Given the elevated profile the first communion event enjoys within the parish, the ritual, as opposed to the catechetical, aspect of it has received surprisingly little academic attention. (For an overview of the catechetical issues, cf. Gallagher (2001). Williamson (1999) provides a thorough critique of the late twentieth-century catechetical material.) In terms of liturgical studies, this neglect may be due to the relatively late date of the rite's creation. Within liturgical-historical scholarship, a fault line runs through the study of the admission of children to the eucharist, broadly separating the pre- and post-Reformation periods. Since the late nineteenth century, Catholic academic focus has tended to be upon the early centuries of Christian history. The period stretching from the Council of Trent (1545–63) until the twentieth century has been seen as of relatively little interest, and is usually presented as an era of ritual calcification (Jungmann, 1959; Klauser, 1979; Cabié, 1986; Pecklers, 1997). As a consequence, liturgical studies generally discuss the first communion ritual only briefly (Cabié, 1987) or ignore it altogether (Nocent, 1986; Johnson, 1999). A possible reason for this omission is the fact that Catholic liturgical historians of the Reformation and post-Reformation period have been primarily concerned with the study of formally promulgated liturgical texts. First communion does not fall into that category because no formal Ordo for the ceremony has ever been produced for universal use in the Church. It was, however, precisely during the generally neglected post-Reformation period that the ritualization of first communion developed, as a response to the catechetical processes set in hand after the Council of Trent (Goubet-Mahé, 1987).

The Catholic scholarly bias towards affording normative status to the early liturgy is directly reflected in the current formal theological perspective on the ritual. Since the Second Vatican Council (1962–65) a theology of Christian initiation based upon studies of early liturgical texts has been mapped onto the first communion event. Consequently, the ritual is now understood as one of a sequence of three sacraments (the others being baptism and confirmation) by which the individual is fully initiated into the Catholic community. As will be discussed (in Chapter 5) this approach is seriously flawed, since it adequately acknowledges neither the very particular origins of the ritual nor the expectations and experience of its participants.

Since the mid-1980s, the scholarly neglect has been redressed, but only partially. Several studies of first communion have been published, and three unpublished doctoral theses have been successfully defended. These works explore the ritual from a number of perspectives: historical (Gaupin, 1985; Delumeau, 1987; Turner 2000), ethnographic (Hérault, 1996 and 1999; McCallion, Maines and Wolfel, 1996; Lodge, 1999; Bales 2005) and educational (Tozzi, 1994; Williamson, 1999). However, with the exception of the last-mentioned, none of the studies engages directly with the ritual in England. Nor do any of them bring together in a sustained manner the findings of the various academic disciplines with which they engage. Several significant unanswered questions thus remain.

Unanswered Questions

No detailed academic study of the history of the ritual of first communion in England has been carried out. This is a significant lacuna that raises a number of questions of an historical nature. At what stage and under what circumstances was the ritual introduced into England? What understanding of the event was in circulation among English Catholics before and at the time of *Quam Singulari*? What were the expectations of the event that fed into the *Catholic Times'* optimistic forecast that we saw at the start of this Introduction – and how were they communicated to the Catholic community, and to the participants in particular?

A response to the last two questions is of particular significance because the decree did not emerge as an isolated piece of legislation. None of the previous studies around first communion offers an in-depth contextualization of the 1910 reform within the legislative programme of the Catholic Church at the time. However, *Quam Singulari* was promulgated within a sequence of significant reforms that impacted upon every aspect of Catholic life and established the structural shape of the Catholic community that endured through the rest of the twentieth century. It is essential, therefore, to establish whether there was any correlation between the reduction in the age of first communicants – frequently portrayed in somewhat sentimental terms (cf. Dal-Gal, 1954) – and legislative reforms contemporary to it that imposed a uniform system of canon law on the Church, severely restricted the marriage options of Catholics, and silenced dissent among the clergy and intellectuals. If such a correlation exists, it raises questions as to whether the reform of the first communion ritual, too, was understood as fulfilling a structural role within the Catholic community. My perception is that it was very much understood in this way. Hence that understanding contributes significantly to explaining the power that the ritual has today to excite such powerful emotions, at a time in which the entire structure of the local parish has come under sustained threat in England, as elsewhere.

This last point can only be fully explored if we address a further lacuna, this time with regard to the current celebration of the ritual in England. No ethnographically based study of the celebration of the ritual itself has been reported. In any event, such a study would itself be incomplete unless it was underpinned by the (as yet missing) historical information. If the conflicts that today erupt around first communion turn on expectations regarding the meaning of the ritual and the structure of the Catholic community, then we need to ask how the playing-out of those issues today relates to and, indeed, is fed by expectations relating to structure and meaning that were operative in the past. To deal adequately with these two lacunae, then two very different types of study need to be brought into dialogue – historical research and ethnography.

The Argument of this Book

The first five chapters of the book are largely historical, and the second five largely ethnographic. We begin with examining the development of the ritual event, both generally and in England. Chapter 1 offers an overview of the history of first communion, and ends by suggesting the broad outlines of an answer to the lacuna over the history of the ritual in England. Chapter 2 explores English catechetical texts published from the Council of Trent up to *Quam Singulari*, and uses them to establish what may be learnt about the meaning that English Catholics brought to the event during the late eighteenth and nineteenth centuries. Chapter 3 then analyses in depth the almost entirely unexamined archival material and newspaper accounts relating to the first English celebrations of first communion after the 1910 reform. In Chapter 4 we examine the broader context within which that reform was situated. Chapter 5 moves on through the twentieth century, considering the liturgical reforms instituted by the Second Vatican Council, and scrutinizing the way in which the discourse of initiation emerged and became dominant within the formal ecclesial setting.

The second five chapters address the ethnographic issues, and are based upon fieldwork that I carried out in a number of locations in the Liverpool Archdiocese between 1998 and 2000. Chapter 6 sets the ethnographic research into context, describing the locations for the fieldwork and briefly outlining the methodology I followed in gathering data. Chapter 7 then picks up where Chapter 5 ended, and considers how the discourses of meaning that emerged in that chapter actually operate on the ground – if indeed they do. It begins to identify discourses of meaning very different from the formal ecclesial discourses. Chapter 8 examines the first arena in which these different discourses enter into conflict – the preparation process for first communion – and analyses the issues around power that emerged in that arena. Chapter 9 does the same, but this time for the ritual event itself. Finally, Chapter 10 examines in greater depth one of the most hotly contested areas of conflict, that of display and consumption, in which deep issues of identity validation, if not construction, come to the fore. A theoretical social-scientific framework is proposed for understanding the significance of consumer-related behaviour in the event.

First Communion until the Eve of *Quam Singulari*

Each time the ritual of first communion is celebrated today its participants are invited to enter into a condition of liturgical amnesia. Since the Second Vatican Council a false memory has been mapped onto this event through the Church's presentation of it as a rite of Christian initiation. This mapping detaches the ritual as celebrated today from the systems of meaning that underpinned it in the past. Such detachment does not operate simply at a theoretical level – rather it risks devaluing the memories and experiences of earlier generations. The insistence upon an initiatory understanding of first communion can therefore open a rift within the event itself, between the formal discourse of the Church and the residual power of the generations of experience within the popular consciousness of Catholics today.

From an academic perspective, it is essential that there be a recovery of the earlier discourses of meaning associated with the ritual, for two reasons. First, it is impossible to measure the extent to which the initiation discourse has penetrated into the collective consciousness of the Catholic community unless those earlier discourses are properly acknowledged. Second, the relationship between formal ecclesial and popular discourses within the ritual today cannot be understood unless we at least consider the extent to which those popular approaches to the rite reflect earlier approaches that were once formally endorsed. These still remain – albeit in altered form – generating resistance to ritual change. This opening chapter lays the groundwork for this task of recovery; it presents an overview of the true history of this ritual, resisting the tendency to leap from the third century to the twentieth that is inherent in the Sacrament of Initiation discourse. Most of this overview will comprise a review of recent scholarship in the field. The chapter will conclude with my own hypotheses in a possible reconstruction of the early history of the ritual in England. The three chapters that follow will then build upon this overview by exploring English textual and archival material.

The Linkage of First Communion and Human Development

The potential for mismatch between the current theology of initiation and the ritual as celebrated becomes evident when we consider the origins of the ritual of first communion. The primary theological reference point for today's discourse of Christian initiation is the patristic marriage of educational and ritual processes that together made up the classic catechumenate – as described, for example, by Ambrose of Milan or Cyril of Jerusalem (see Yarnold, 1994a). Within this perspective, today's children are presented as modern-day catechumens, completing on their first communion day an extended initiatory process that began at their baptism. The internal inconsistencies of this approach will be discussed in detail in Chapter 5. However, even at the surface level of ritual history, the mapping of the early catechumenate onto today's celebration of first communion cannot succeed with any real integrity. The catechetico-ritual complex for first communion is not at all a creation of the patristic era. Rather, the stimuli that eventually led to its development were a series of theological and educational questions that only emerged at the onset of the second millennium, and that then progressively preoccupied Church authorities through the medieval scholastic, Reformation and Enlightenment periods. The question that eventually led to the creation of the formal first communion in France during the final decade of the sixteenth century was not one of Christian initiation. Instead, the ritual took concrete form thanks to a long-standing concern to correlate an understanding of the human life-course – and in particular of the processes of intellectual development – with sacramental theology. The twin questions that underpin the origins of the ritual were how to ensure on the one hand that a child possessed the intellectual capacity to properly understand what he or she was doing in receiving communion, and on the other that the experience of the event would remain with them through life.

For most of the first millennium this linkage of the reception of first communion to a defined stage of human development was not an issue. Children were generally admitted to the eucharist at baptism (Fisher, 1965; Cabié, 1987; Johnson, 1999). In that sense, it can legitimately be argued that admission to the eucharist did indeed form part of the complex of initiation during that period. The *Gelasian Sacramentary* testifies to the adaptation of an early Roman ritual process for adult initiation for use with children, and that culminated in their admission to the eucharist (Mohlberg et al., 1981). However, two developments that took place towards the end of the first millennium compromised this early practice and produced a very different sacramental regime, one that still underpins today's Catholic practice – the formal initiatory discourse notwithstanding.

The first of these developments was the gradual fragmentation of the initiatory process. This was precipitated by the success of the Church's growth and initially came about through focus not on admission to the eucharist, but on the contribution of the Bishop to the original initiatory complex. The early Western Church orders for baptism – such as that found in the much-disputed *Apostolic Tradition* of Hippolytus (Botte, 1963), or the earlier liturgical strands that underpin the Gelasian Ordo (Mohlberg et al., 1981) – presume the presence of the Bishop at the final sequence of initiation rituals. His specific role in the entire complex occurred between the candidates' water immersion and their admission to the eucharist – the anointing with chrism that reflects the remote origins of today's confirmation ritual. As the number of candidates for admission into the Church increased and dioceses spread beyond towns and cities, it became impossible for all to be gathered in one place at one time for the initiation rituals. The solution that was generally adopted saw the Bishop's presence at baptism become optional. Presbyters baptized candidates and immediately admitted them to the eucharist. The Bishop retained his chrismating role, but generally exercised it outside the baptismal liturgy – sometimes years after a person had been admitted to the eucharist. The beginnings of a free-floating episcopal ritual that crystallized into 'confirmation' were thus set in place.

The second development brought about a further fragmentation of the original initiatory complex, setting in motion a progressive severance of admission to the eucharist from baptism. The primary impetus for this was a significant shift in the focus of eucharistic theology that took place towards the end of the first millennium. This shift moved from a generally symbolic approach to the eucharist towards the adoption of an increasingly realistic understanding of Christ's presence in the sacrament; that the substance of bread and wine was inwardly and effectively changed into the body and blood of Christ (Fisher, 1965, pp. 101–102). The eucharist gradually began to be thought of almost entirely from the viewpoint of the Real Presence (Jungmann, 1959, p. 89), and the response of the Magisterium to the anti-realism of Berengarius of Tours (d. 1088) reinforced the position (Cabié, 1986, p. 247; McPartlan, 1995, p. 38). This super-realistic perspective impacted upon the question of the admission of children to the eucharist because it placed increasing emphasis upon the responsibility of the communicant to understand exactly what he or she was receiving. This in turn introduced the question as to when somebody possessed the necessary intellectual capacity to make an informed assent to the Church's teaching on the sacrament. This question, which had not arisen during the patristic period, assumed increasing importance. If a capacity to understand and believe was a prerequisite for reception of the eucharist, then two things became necessary: first, a process of education that preceded the admission to the sacrament, and second, an ability to recognize the point at which a child's developing natural reasoning powers were sufficiently formed to permit the intellectual response that the new realistic approach required. It was this preoccupation with human development that increasingly came to dominate second-millennium thinking on admission to the eucharist. The concern directly contributed to the development of the ritual of first communion, fed into many of the discourses associated with it, and finally precipitated a crisis at the turn of the nineteenth and twentieth centuries that the reform of *Quam Singulari* sought definitively to resolve.

The introduction into the formal corpus of Church teaching of a direct relationship between the reception of first communion and the question of age took place in an almost accidental, tangential manner. Concern around the appropriate age for the onset of communicating became confused with another age-related issue that flanked it. This was the question of the age at which children acquired sufficient discretionary powers to become morally culpable for their actions. This question, too, carried implications for sacramental practice, because with culpability came the requirement for formal confession of sins to a priest. But when was this 'age of discretion' attained? Turner (2000) cites a number of texts that evidence a broad range of opinion, locating it at different points between the ages of seven and fourteen. Canon 21 of the Fourth Lateran Council of 1215 drew the issue into the formal Magisterium (Turner, 2000, 8, 5). This canon required penitents to confess their sins at least annually after the 'years of discretion' (*annos discretionis*) had been attained. That requirement does not in itself impact upon the age for first admission to the eucharist. However, the demand for annual penance is followed in the canon by the phrase, 'reverently receiving at least in Eastertide the sacrament of the eucharist'.

Whatever the intentions of the council fathers, the inclusion of this phrase in a text primarily concerned with confession had the long-term effect of linking the start of communicating with the 'years of discretion'.

In pastoral terms, however, vagueness remained as to what exactly those 'years' were. Lateran IV did not offer a specific age, leaving the question open to continued debate in future centuries (cf. Turner, 2000, 8, 5). There is evidence from French rituals that, Lateran IV notwithstanding, the administration of communion to infants continued in parts of France into the seventeenth century (Lemaitre, 1987, pp. 18–19). However, the general age drift was upwards, and in 1562 the twenty-fourth Session of the Council of Trent reinforced the link between the start of communion and a stage in human development. As had been the case for Lateran IV, the inclusion of material on the admission of children to the eucharist was caught up in a debate on a different matter – in this case, the reception of communion under two species (Lemaitre, 1987, p. 29). The issue at Trent was, of course, contextualized within the sacramental debates of the Reformation period; if the medieval super-realistic position on the eucharist is called into doubt, then the requirement for a delay in admission to the eucharist similarly loses its importance. The decision of the Council was – as in most cases – to reaffirm the traditional Roman perspective. The response was phrased in juridical terms by Canon 4 of the session: 'If anyone says that the communion of the eucharist is necessary for children before they have reached the years of discretion, let him be anathema' (Denzinger and Shönmetzer, 1977, section 1734; hereafter DS).

This decree, together with Canon 21 of Lateran IV, thus laid down the legal foundations for the admission of children to the eucharist that remain in force today: children are not required to receive holy communion until they attain the 'age of discretion'. Once they have reached that age, however, they are obliged to receive it.

Trent, like Lateran IV, did not offer a clear definition of what exactly was intended by those 'years of discretion'. The Catechism of the Council of Trent (published in England as *The Catechism of the Curats* in 1687) similarly drew back from defining the 'ages of discretion' too closely – recognizing that different children enjoyed different abilities to understand:

> But at what age the Sacred Mysteries are to be given to Children, no one can better determine than the Father and Priest, to whom they confess their sins, for it belongs to Them to try, and examine the Children, whether they have learn'd the knowledge of this admirable Sacrament, and any rellish to it. [p. 230]

A similar reticence is found over too closely defining the age at which confession was to begin (p. 263). This reticence introduces a common-sense insight that was repeated in 1910, namely that different children mature at different stages. The discipline, therefore, that Trent envisaged was that children would be educated in faith by their parish clergy. Along the way a decision would be made for each individual as to whether he or she had attained the use of reason sufficiently to understand the sacrament, and at that stage the child would begin to communicate. This highly nuanced and personal approach was, however, undermined by three related developments that very quickly moved first preparation for, and then the act of receiving, first communion into a group context and at a more absolutely defined age.

From Individual Accession to the Eucharist to the Ritual of First Communion

In preferring not to define too closely the 'age of discretion', the Council of Trent left open an area of ambiguity that later generations felt a need to resolve. The origins of this ambiguity lay, as we have seen, in the tendency for the Tridentine corpus to speak of both an 'age of reason' and an 'age of discretion'; indeed, Trent appears use the two interchangeably. However, Catholic tradition instinctively prefers clear definition to more open systems of meaning, and it is not surprising that the co-existence of the two terms invited debate as to whether the two were identical in practice. The situation that emerged was described in 1910 by the decree *Quam Singulari*:

> In the course of time many errors and deplorable abuses have crept in in deciding what is meant by the 'age of reason and discretion'. For some would maintain that the age of discretion for receiving the Sacrament of Penance is not the same as that for the reception of the Holy Eucharist. They feel that for Confession the age of discretion is reached when children can distinguish between right and wrong, and so can sin; but that for receiving the Holy Eucharist a more mature age is requisite, one at which they can have a fuller knowledge of the truths of faith and may better prepare themselves. Consequently, owing to varying local practices and views, in some places the age of ten years, in others, twelve, fourteen or even more are required, and until that age children are not allowed to receive Holy Communion. [AAS, vol. ii, p. 579]

An example of this distinction between the ages of 'reason' and 'discretion' can be found in the writings of the English Vicar Apostolic, Richard Challoner (1681–1781), who worked in London. Challoner (1737) distinguished between the two ages, holding that the age of reason was 'commonly presumed after seven years' whilst the age of discretion was arrived at 'seldom earlier than ten years' (pp. 74–5). Challoner associated the latter with admission to the eucharist, but linked the age of reason with confirmation (p. 23). By the mid-nineteenth century, the discourse of the age of discretion, cited as around the age of twelve, emerges in the early first communion material published in England. However, and significantly, this material relates the age of twelve not to confirmation but to first communion (*A Catechism for First Communicants*, 1781, p. 6). This appears to have remained the normal age at which first communion was administered in England, whilst an earlier start was made to confessing – usually around the age of seven.

The second factor that led – albeit unintentionally – towards a more regimented and corporate approach to admission to the eucharist was the post-Tridentine development of broad catechetical structures that articulated a child's education in faith from early childhood to the admission to the eucharist in the early teens. A key figure in this development was Charles Borromeo (1538–84), Archbishop of Milan. His 1574 *Instructions* to the confessors of his diocese outlined a detailed process by which each local priest should instruct the children in his pastoral care (Goubet-Mahé, 1987, pp. 54–6). Borromeo divided catechetical instruction into three age-related stages. The first ran from the ages of five to six, when a child was taught to examine its conscience and to distinguish between right and wrong. The ages of seven and eight were described as the 'Little Catechism'. During this period a more complete religious instruction was given, leading to the sacraments of confession and confirmation. The third stage, the 'Grand Catechism', led to first communion between the ages of ten and twelve. Borromeo's clearly articulated system was gradually adapted in France.

The third development flowed naturally from the second. It is a relatively short step from preparing the children together to admitting them to the eucharist as a cohort in a single ceremony. This step appears to have been taken in France towards the end of the sixteenth century, with the first recorded event taking place in 1593 under Jaques Gallemant (1559–1630) in the parish of Aumale in the diocese of Rouen (Goubet-Mahé, 1987, p. 63; Turner, 2000, 7, 10). The event acquired its definitive shape in the Latin Quarter of Paris during the first two decades of the seventeenth century. This was initially under the ministry of Adrien Bourdoise (1559–1630) at the church of St Nicholas of Chardonnet (Goubet-Mahé, 1987, pp. 65–9; Turner, 2000, 6, 10), and then at the nearby and far more important church of St Sulpice. From these local beginnings the ritual appears to have spread rapidly across France and beyond – a genuine example of a popular religious development that quickly received local episcopal sanction.

The pace at which the ritual spread is partly due to the early support it received from major players in the French Catholic community at the time – not least Jean Jacques Olier and Vincent de Paul. However, its rapid take-up must reflect a positive perception of its effectiveness – an effectiveness that extended beyond the potential impact that the event had on the individual child. The development of a special 'Mass of First Communion' at which all the children of a given age-determined cohort were admitted to the eucharist together, considerably raised the public profile of the event. This was no longer simply an intensely personal and essentially private moment, linked to an individual child's human development; instead, it could become a highly visible spectacle of faith and devotion for the parish community as a whole. This could extend the range of ends that the ritual served – from the spiritual maturation of the individual to strengthening the devotion, identity and institutional strength of the broader Catholic community.

The process for first communion that was developed in early sixteenth-century Paris thus articulated a remarkable marriage between catechetical process and ritual event in the service of a clear aim: to stimulate in participants an emotional and intellectual response that would ensure an allegiance to the Church which would then be sustained through life. A desired secondary effect was that the touching spectacle of childhood piety would also move the hearts of adult spectators. The event provided an annual opportunity for the re-education and revitalization of the entire parish community (Sauzet, 1987, p. 38f; Robert, 1987, p. 99f).

For this to happen two things were necessary. First, the ritual of first communion needed to be sufficiently dramatic both to form a life-long impression on the child and to evoke an emotional response from adults present. Second, the process of preparation needed to be thorough and to impress firmly upon the children the importance of the event for which they were preparing. The genius of the French first communion ritual – and particularly the approach that was codified at St Sulpice – was to unite these in a clearly articulated programme of catechesis that extended over a number of years and culminated in an elaborate sequence of rituals. The traditions of St Sulpice reached their final form in the early nineteenth century under the Sulpician Faillon (*The Method of S. Sulpice*, 1896; Colomb, 1958). They offer a meticulously detailed process of preparation for first communion. The intense ambitions for life-course formation embedded in the preparatory system found their ritual expression in the ceremonies that closed the process. The Mass of first communion itself was augmented by a sequence of other rituals. These opened on the evening before the first communion, when the children asked pardon of their parents for wrongs they had committed against them and in return received their parents' blessing. This exchange could take place either in private or within a public ceremony in the parish church (*Method*, 1896, p. 292; cf. also the 1666 Bourges ritual cited in Turner, 2000, 10, 7). The following day the children attended two rituals in the church; the morning Mass during which they received their first communion, and an extended form of Vespers (evening prayers), during which they renewed their baptismal promises at the font before consecrating themselves to the Virgin Mary (*Method*, 1896, pp. 285–7; Robert, 1987, p. 78). Turner (ibid.) notes eighteenth-century French variants in which the children processed with lighted candles during the first communion Mass itself (Bayeaux, 1700; Boulogne, 1750). The Boulogne ritual further extended the Vespers service by concluding it with a procession around the church as the *Te Deum* was sung. Inside a brief time-frame, then, the children were immersed in a sequence of rituals marked by high emotive content and rich symbolism that formed a closure to their previous life and propelled them towards a future rooted in adherence to Christ and his mother.

However, whilst the event was intended to reinforce a child's adherence to the Church and its priorities, this ambition began to be subverted from at least the eighteenth century onwards as a number of non-ecclesial elements were assimilated into the event (Robert, 1987). The church event was prolonged by a festal family meal, and increasing care was lavished upon the appearance of the communicants. The white dresses worn by the girls may have been variously interpreted as a counter-sign to the elaborate dress of court society (Turner, 2000), or as the traditional garb of nubile girls (Hérault, 1996), but they themselves became fashion items (Robert, 1987). Meanwhile, the white veil was deliberately introduced in the early eighteenth century at St Sulpice, to counter the tendency to spending several hours immediately before the event dressing the girls' hair (Robert, 1987, p. 110).

That the ritual should have attracted such elements can be partly understood in terms of the age of reason discourse. The linkage of the start of eucharistic participation to a particular point in the life-course invites the assimilation into the event of elements marking that point in its broader social context. The age of reason discourse had located first communion at the onset of adolescence; it is not surprising, therefore, that its celebration should have so quickly become associated with social elements that made first communion in its pre-*Quam Singulari* form serve as a rite of passage into adolescence. This, in turn associated the ritual with ecclesial preoccupations concerning the pubescent onset of sexual awareness that surface in the texts published in England and that as we shall see fed into the reform of 1910.

The Ritual in England

The translation and publication in England of both continental first communion texts and homegrown books by the mid-nineteenth century bear witness to the arrival of the ritual in England. But when and how did it arrive there? The recent tracing of the origins of the rite in France has been facilitated by a wealth of archival documents, including contemporary biographies, published catechisms and local diocesan regulations. For England the task is far more complex because throughout the period of the ritual's initial development and extension the life of English Catholics was subject to the penal laws issued in the wake of the Protestant Reformation in that country. It was not until the First Catholic Relief Act of 1778 (18 George III, c 60) that bishops, priests and schoolmasters were finally freed from the risk of prosecution and arrest. With the passing of the Second Catholic Relief Act of 1791 (31 George III, c 32), those Catholics who took the oath of allegiance to the British Crown were no longer liable for prosecution for hearing Mass or for building churches. Finally, the 1829 Catholic Emancipation Act (10 George IV, c 7) removed virtually all remaining bars on Catholics (see Norman, 1984, pp. 29–68). The circumscribed nature of recusant English Catholic life until the passing of these Relief Acts did not favour the exuberant spectacle that marked the continental ritual. Moreover, that ritual presupposed a tightly controlled ecclesial and catechetical framework that would have been impossible to maintain in most of pre-nineteenth-century England. The only possible exception might have been the Catholic schools that were introduced in late penal times by Challoner. Catechisms were almost certainly produced for use in those schools (Pickering, 1980), but there is no evidence as to how first communion would have been celebrated there. Moreover, the general character of English Catholic worship at this period was extremely restrained.

The post-Reformation English Catholic community only slowly developed a visibly structured life. The first significant step forward was taken in 1688, the last year of the brief reign of the Catholic James II, when for Catholic purposes England and Wales was divided into four ecclesiastical districts (Bossy, 1975, pp. 70, 214). Over the next two centuries this system was gradually expanded and in 1850 it was transmuted into a formal hierarchy of bishops, each of whom was responsible for a properly constituted diocese. None the less, until 1908 England and Wales retained dependence upon the Sacred Congregation of Propaganda, the arm of the Papal bureaucracy responsible for territories which were non-Catholic in government.

The earliest known text on first communion in England is a catechism published anonymously towards the end of the eighteenth century (*Catechism*, 1781). This gives no details of the ritual of first communion itself, apart from suggesting that it takes place at some time after Lent (p. 4). This catechism includes a number of discourses that can be found both in French and in later English catechetical material.

For example, the catechism states that the importance of first communion lies in an understanding that:

> ... the Effects of it reach through their whole Life; it is generally speaking a Source of Happiness, or Misery, for the rest of their Days, according as it is performed with due or undue Dispositions'. [p. 1]

This is close in spirit to the 1764 *Instructions for First Communion* by Voile de Villarnou:

> You cannot doubt, my brothers and sisters, that First Communion is the most important action of life. It is this First Communion which usually determines all the others, and on which most often depends salvation or eternal punishment. It is for all life either a source of goodness if it is well made, or a source of evil if it is poorly made. [cited in Turner, 2000, 10, 6]

The evidence of catechetical material that is at least similar to that in use in France does not of itself establish that the full French form of the rite had also taken hold. Indeed, the earliest firm evidence of the celebration of the elaborate first communion ritual in England comes almost two decades after the 1781 *Catechism*. It does not refer to the practice of the indigenous population, but rather to the ambit of the French émigrés who from 1792 onwards had sought refuge in England from the Revolution in their own country. In 1799 the homilies preached by the exiled Archbishop of Aix in the Catholic chapel in King St, Portman Square, London at a ceremony of first communion and subsequent renewal of baptismal promises were published (Boisgelin de Cucé, 1799). These highly politicized sermons indicate a certain process of preparation (p. 3), immediate preparation by confession (p. 8), and a sense that the age at which the children now stood was appropriate to the event because of their continued innocence – 'quand les semences des bonnes dispositions ont senti la rosée du ciel, & ne sont point encore atteintes des exhalaisons de la terre' (p. 9). There is a sense that the reception of communion renewed in each participant the grace of their baptism, but there is no discourse of the completion of initiation.

It would, of course, be tempting to see in the French émigrés the conduit through which the ritual of first communion passed into the English Catholic community. However, their impact upon English Catholic life is the subject of debate. Haile and Bonney (1912) suggest that the introduction of their lavish liturgical practices marked a turning point in previously restrained Catholic devotional practice. However, Bellenger (1981; 1986) draws upon contemporary accounts to argue that the contact with French patterns remained superficial, and that it was only around the mid-nineteenth century that continental devotional practices were more widely embraced.

If, therefore, we look forward a few years to the mid-nineteenth century, it is possible to identify a number of factors that would have combined to favour the diffusion of the continental pattern of first communion. The first of these was the establishment of a Catholic infrastructure, well-organized at local level, that was permitted by the relaxation of penal laws and Catholic Emancipation on the one hand and by the 1850 restoration of the Catholic hierarchy on the other. A second significant factor was the rapid numerical expansion and sociological change within the Catholic community in the wake of Irish immigration, especially during the period of the Irish famine 1848–53. The early nineteenth century also witnessed the energetic activity in England of foreign – chiefly Italian – missionaries, who introduced and fostered continental devotional practices. Two further, frequently interrelated factors would also have had a bearing on the establishment of the ritual: the growing presence of continental congregations of apostolic sisters, and the development of parish schools, many of which were entrusted to such sisters. The introduction of the lavish first communion ritual can thus be understood in terms of the broader changes that were taking place as a Catholicism lived discreetly under the patronage of a largely country gentry was transformed into an urban and increasingly working-class phenomenon (Bossy, 1975; Rowlands, 1999).

Above all, the evolution of the ritual is likely to have been linked to the gradual abandonment of the earlier restrained recusant devotional tradition in favour of the more colourful continental Catholic practices, a process that took place from the 1830s onwards. The work of new missionary orders in England during that time may be part of this. The two mid-nineteenth-century first communion texts published in England which most closely reflect the French style of celebration, *Letters* (1848) and *A Catechism for First Communion* (1850), are associated with Luigi Gentili (1801–48) and Giovanni Battisti Pagani, members of the Institute of Charity, usually referred to as the Rosminians. This institute was founded in Italy in 1828 by Antonio Rosmini Serbati (1797–1855), and the first Rosminians, including Gentili and Pagani, arrived in England in 1835. Gentili acquired an almost national fame (Leetham, 1965, p. 1), chiefly thanks to his work as an itinerant missionary during the 1840s. He led a series of parish missions, especially among the working classes in the industrial towns of northern England, and retreats to clergy and religious (Pagani, 1851, p. 228; Leetham, 1965, p. 376). Most significantly, Gentili actively used his missions to introduce continental devotional practices into the world of English Catholicism, whose devotional life was still formed in the sober and somewhat reticent Challoner mode. Thus, from his arrival in England he set himself against the English custom by which the Catholic clergy never wore distinctive dress, in accordance with the penal laws. By all accounts he was the first Catholic priest consistently to wear the Roman collar in England (Gwynn, 1951, pp. 105, 115–16; Leetham, 1965, p. 1; cf. also Bellenger, 1999, p. 157). His parish missions were exuberant, public manifestations of Catholic piety, particularly centred upon devotion to the eucharist. They included the practice of forty hours' prayer before the Blessed Sacrament exposed ('*Quarant' ore*') and even elaborate outdoor eucharistic processions. Gentili's biographers accredit him with introducing such practices into England, and more besides – for example, May devotions to Mary and the use of scapulars and blessed medals (Leetham, 1965, p. 1). This may be somewhat exaggerated: there is a full form of Benediction in Challoner, 1759b, pp. 152–6. However, it is significant that a major element of the missions was the dedication of an hour each day to the preparation of the parish's children for first confession and communion (Leetham, 1965, pp. 209, 342). The missions were also used as an opportunity to bring to the eucharist many adult Catholics who had yet to receive their first communion (ibid., pp. 215, 243). It is not surprising, then, that in the wake of Gentili's missions his colleagues should have been making available translations of French catechetical texts for first communion to English Catholics.

In addition to male missionaries such as Gentili, a further, and ultimately even more enduring, foreign influence came through the rapid introduction into England of female religious congregations during the second quarter of the nineteenth century. Before 1840 there were fewer than twenty convents in England (Leetham, 1965, p. 1; O'Brien, 1999, pp. 112–13), all but two of which had previously existed as English foundations in France and the Low Countries, populated by the daughters of the English recusant gentry. These continental foundations had been closed during the Revolution and were re-established in England. These had been enclosed orders, and upon establishment in England the nuns resumed their enclosed life. However, from the 1830s onwards, a different kind of female religious congregation began to be present in England. These were the continental and Irish orders of apostolic sisters, who were not enclosed within their convents, but became involved in the social and educational welfare of the increasing and ever more predominately urban working-class Catholic population. By 1887 there were sixty-two such congregations in England, of which thirty-two had come from France and five from Belgium (O'Brien, 1999, p. 114). O'Brien summarizes the influence of these religious sisters on the English Catholic Church as establishing 'standards and patterns which were all the more powerful in the context of the relatively open and rapidly developing Catholic culture of England' (pp. 114–15).

The arrival of these sisters coincided with a further significant factor: the development of a system of Catholic schools, for which the sisters were frequently given responsibility. The stable structure offered by the schools at last made possible across the population the creation of ordered catechetical processes. This, given the climate of continentalization in devotional and liturgical practice, would have provided fertile ground for the spread of the ritualized first communion process. That spread would have been assisted as the century progressed by the publication of catechetical material, both translations of continental works and home-grown texts. In terms of content these works continued to draw on themes that had been well established over the preceding centuries. The celebration of first communion marched forward, then, at the very heart of the emerging structures of Catholic life that followed the restoration of the hierarchy in 1850. By 1910, and the publication of the decree *Quam Singulari*, the ritual was well established.

What did English Catholics believe they were doing in celebrating this ritual? The next chapter will seek to answer this question through an analysis of the texts published for use by English Catholics in the period between the Protestant Reformation and the promulgation of *Quam Singulari*.

CHAPTER 2

The Eucharist in English Published Texts (1568–1910)

There is no direct evidence for how English Catholics admitted children to the eucharist between the late sixteenth and mid-nineteenth centuries, but we do know what they believed about the sacrament. Or, to be more precise, we know what the Church expected them to believe! This is because from the Reformation onwards, the English Catholic community produced a series of doctrinal and catechetical texts that, alongside other matters, contained discourses concerning the eucharist. By the late eighteenth century, these general texts were joined by catechetical material that directly related to the preparation of children for first communion. The later nineteenth century witnessed a flowering of instructional texts designed to prepare children for the event. These texts laid the foundations for the intellectual content of the faith of generations of English Catholics – not least by helping to form their knowledge, expectations and anxieties around the eucharist.

None of these early catechetical works is referred to in the material in use for first communion preparation today. There is no sense of today's practice as having any continuity with this period of Catholic life and experience. Yet it was during this period of history – not in the patristic period that is today's primary period of theological inspiration with regard to first communion – that the ritual of first communion arose. It is these texts, and not the ancient Church Orders, that bear witness to the presence in England of exactly those theological and pastoral concerns that fed into the radical reform in 1910 from which today's discipline emerged. If we are to understand today's discipline, therefore, it is essential that we access this hitherto submerged body of information – and in particular that we uncover the discourses that were at play around first communion across the centuries that led up to the reform of 1910.

The texts considered here were selected according to three broad criteria. All English Catholic texts published before 1800 have been formally catalogued (Allison and Rogers, 1994; Clancy, 1996; Blom et al., 1996). I consulted those catalogues and examined all the relevant texts available in the British Library collection. I paid particular attention to texts that were cross-referenced by others from the period. Then, for the period 1800 to 1910 I considered all texts in the British Library dedicated to first communion that were published in England. Finally, I looked at a range of later nineteenth-century broader catechetical texts that also contained direct instructions for first communion preparation; once again, the British Library catalogue was my primary point of reference.

When these texts are examined, a number of discourses emerge consistently across the three-hundred-year period during which the texts were written. Three such discourses stand out in particular, and all three introduce a note of anxiety concerning any reception of communion. The first is that whilst the reception of holy communion ought to be a supreme act of worship, it can also become the occasion of an act of sacrilege. The second discourse expands upon the first by insisting that a sacrilegious communion is remarkably easy to commit; indeed, at times the literature appears to presume that a sacrilegious communion was more likely to take place than a pious one. Why that should be is partly explained by the third discourse – that communion and sexual impurity stand in particular antithesis. A fourth discourse that builds upon the previous three comes into play with the appearance of the material directly related to first communion – that the manner in which the first communion was received could exercise a determining influence upon the life-course.

These discourses were not unique to England – a parallel has already been noted between the first-known English catechism for first communion and an earlier continental text, with regard to their discussion of the determining role played by the eucharist in the life course. Furthermore, there is evidence not only of direct translations into English of continental catechetical material, but indirectly the same material – particularly in the form of illustrative stories – emerges on both sides of the English Channel. For example, Gibson (1877) contains stories that are also found in Huguet (1902). These discourses fed directly into the expectations that fuelled the reform of 1910, and more indirectly into some of the popular discourses still at play today. They do stand, on the other hand, in marked contrast to the approach that the Catholic Church today attempts to foster.

Before considering these four discourses more fully, it is useful to provide a more detailed overview of the texts concerned in order to locate them in their historical context.

Early General Catechetical Texts

Catechetical texts for the use of English Catholics were published throughout the penal period. Initially these were printed and disseminated from outside England. Douai (frequently anglicized as Douay) in the Low Countries was the home of one of the major centres for the training of Catholic priests for the English mission; it was also a major centre of English Catholic intellectual activity. An interrelated sequence of catechisms was produced at Douai during the sixteenth and seventeenth centuries. This prepared the ground for what was to become in the nineteenth century the standard English catechism, forming the basis of all religious education in schools (Crichton, 1958 and 1981a; Pickering, 1980). The earliest of these was the *Catechisme, or a Christian Doctrine Necessarie for Chyldren and the Ignorant People* (Vaux, 1568). More influential was *An Abridgement of Christian Doctrin.* [*sic*] by the English secular priest Turberville (1607–78), first published at Douai in 1648. This became known as the Douai Catechism. In 1672 an anonymous abridgement of Turberville's work received ecclesiastical approval under the title of *An Abstract of the Douay Catechism*. These last two works were republished in England during the brief reign of James II (Turberville, 1685; *Abstract of the Douay Catechism*, 1697).

The same reign witnessed the printing in London of continental religious treatises (*Catechism for the Curats*, 1687; Lewis de Granada, 1688; Gobinet, 1689). At the same time, the works of a prolific English Catholic author were also published. This was John Gother (or Goter, Gootyer, Goodyer, 1654–1704), a secular priest who taught in the English College in Lisbon, and then ministered in England between 1682 and 1704 (Norman, 1972, pp. 306–309). Historically, his primary importance lies in the fact that he was responsible for the religious education of the young Challoner, who was to become the dominant Catholic voice in eighteenth-century England. However, Gother also wrote a number of instructions for various categories of people, some of which remained in print throughout the eighteenth century and which cast some light upon religious and catechetical practice in his time. The works considered here are his *Instructions for Youth* (1698), *Instructions for Confession and Communion* (1700) and *Instructions for Children* (1704).

A further exemplar of the catechetical genre is James Carnegy, *Instructions and Prayers for Children* (1725). The only extant copy is held by the British Library. The motives for the production of the book are telling. Carnegy says he wrote it after observing the poor state of religious instruction of country children, which he concluded was because of their being scattered from each other and because of the small number of priests to educate them. This work was produced, then, to assist parents in educating their children. Curiously, the book contains a full translation of the Mass into English; yet the publication of vernacular translations of the Mass had been prohibited under threat of excommunication by Pope Alexander VII in 1661. This prohibition technically remained in force until 1897 (Jungmann, 1959, pp. 108, 121–2; Cabié, 1986, pp. 180–81).

In the mid-eighteenth century we also begin to witness the publication of catechetical texts written by the Apostolic Vicars – missionary bishops appointed by Rome to have charge of the ecclesiastical districts that had been established under James II. The first of those represented here is John Joseph Hornihold (1706–78) who was Apostolic Vicar of the Midlands district from 1756 until his death. The earliest known version of his *The Sacraments Explained in Twenty Discourses* dates from 1741 (Blom et al., 1996, no. 1471); the version I consulted was an 1814 reprint held at the British Library.

The other eighteenth-century Apostolic Vicar who was active in the field of catechetical publishing was Richard Challoner (1681–1781), whom we have already met. He was Bishop of the London district from 1741–81, and had the greatest influence in moulding English Catholicism during the second half of the eighteenth century (Burton, 1909; Duffy, 1981). Three of his works have been consulted: *The Catholick Christian Instructed ...* (1737), *An Abridgment of Christian Doctrine ...* (1759a) and *The Garden of the Soul*. The earliest known imprint of this last book dates from 1740 (Blom et al., 1996); the copy I consulted dates from 1759. This book enjoyed enormous popularity within the English Catholic community, continuing in print until the twentieth century. For the century after its initial publication it was effectively the prayer-book of most English Catholics, and the sober liturgical and devotional life it articulates stands in marked contrast with the later exuberance of continental-inspired worship. In addition to prayers and devotions, *The Garden of the Soul* also contains a body of instructional material, recommending as additional reading the above-mentioned Lewis de Granada (1688), Gobinet (1689) and Gother (1700). Whilst it makes no reference whatsoever to the first communion of children, in both its prayers and catechesis it casts light upon contemporary eucharistic practices, and contains discourses that continued into the later first communion catechisms.

Later Texts that Directly bear upon First Communion

With the closing decades of the eighteenth century comes the first exemplar of a new genre, a catechism specifically for use by children preparing for first communion. The diffusion of this genre can be tracked across the nineteenth century in a number of publications dedicated to the first communion process. The three earliest of these specialist texts to be considered here have already been alluded to in the previous chapter. They are the 1781 *Catechism for First Communicants* and the two texts associated with the early Rosminians, that is, *First Communion: A Series of Letters to the Young* (1848) and *A Catechism for First Communion* (1850). I have also considered five texts dating from the second half of the nineteenth century that were specifically produced as resources for the preparation of children for first communion. The earliest of this set is the anonymous, *Instructions for First Communion* (1860). This book offers the greatest details of all the texts on ancillary rituals after the French model for the first communion day – that is, the renewal of baptismal promises (pp. 69–72) and the act of consecration to the Virgin Mary (pp. 72–4). Considerably less French influence is found in Richards' *A Catechism of First Communion* (1883), with no mention made to either the renewal of baptismal promises, nor of a consecration to the Virgin Mary. The restrained note is also to be found in the translation of de Ségur's *To Children. Practical Counsels for Holy Communion* ... (1887).

A rather more scriptural approach to the preparation of first communion can be found in the latest two texts considered here: Gibson's *Instructions on First Communion* (1892) and Mary Loyola's *First Communion* (1896). The second of these is particularly useful because the author, Mother Mary Loyola (surnamed Giles: 1845–1930), produced material for first communion both before and after *Quam Singulari,* and thus highlights the radical change in pedagogy that the reform required. She was a sister of the Bar Convent in York who wrote extensively on sacramental preparation and on eucharistic devotion. Her texts were edited and in this case prefaced by Herbert Thurston S.J. (1856–1939). Thurston retained his good standing with the ecclesial authorities throughout the anti-Modernist crisis, whilst remaining a correspondent and friend of the excommunicated George Tyrrell (cf. Crehan, 1952; Leonard, 1982; Barmann, 1972).

None of the texts so far mentioned regard the age at which children received first communion as being in any way an issue. However, in early 1910, the Anglo-Spanish Jesuit Francis M. de Zulueta (1853–1937), who was uncle to Pius X's Secretary of State, Rafael Merry del Val y de Zulueta, published *First Communion of Children and its Conditions*, a translation of *La Communion des Enfants* by the Belgian Mazure. With this book the debates raging at that time around the age of reason can be seen to penetrate into the genre of popular Catholic literature. Mazure argued that delaying the reception of first communion to the then normative age was a relic of Jansenism; instead, he proposed the admission of younger children to the eucharist in as informal a manner as possible. He became a vigorous promoter of the Vatican's reform programme, including *Quam Singulari* (de Zulueta, 1911, 1920).

General Catechetical Works, 1800–1911

Finally, a number of general catechetical texts from this later period also expand on discourses that relate to the expectations around first communion. These are Jones (1822), Lingard (1840), Gibson (1877, 1879) and Cafferata (1910, 1911a). With the single exception of Lingard (1840), all of these texts took the form of commentaries upon the catechisms used among English Catholics, and particularly upon the 'Penny Catechism', which was the primary tool for educating English Catholic children in their faith from 1859 until the eve of the Second Vatican Council. For the history of this catechism, and its relationship to Vaux (1568), Turberville (1648) and *An Abstract of the Douay Catechism* (1672), see Crichton (1958, 1981a and b).

Discourses

Having identified the texts, we can now consider the four major discourses that emerge from them. Finally, we can consider what further information can be gleaned from these texts about the manner in which first communion may have been celebrated in England during the nineteenth and early twentieth centuries.

The 'Sacrilegious' Communion

The sacrilegious (or 'bad') communion is defined as one 'knowingly and deliberately made in mortal sin' (Richards, 1883, p. 8). This is a long-standing discourse, well attested in the general catechetical materials, both in England and in France (Robert, 1987, pp 87–8). Indeed the section of *Catechism for the Curats* treating the eucharist opens by warning that:

> ... there is no greater Punishment to be fear'd from God for any sin whatsoever, than if this thing which is full of all sanctity, or rather which contains the Author and Fountain of Sanctity, be not holily and religiously us'd by the Faithful. [p. 193]

Gobinet (1689) compares the sense of horror that an unworthy communion ought to evoke to the natural human outrage towards parricide (p. 316). He discusses the eucharist in terms of its vulnerability – it is treated 'injuriously' when received into 'a profane place'. As chief illustration of this concept he resorts to the figure of Judas who at the Last Supper received his first (and, presumably, only) communion, having set into motion the betrayal of Christ:

> The sin of an unworthy Communion is the sin of Judas. It was he who first committed it, and those who fall into it imitate his Example and become his Disciples. They receive

him, as did he, in a Criminall ... and guilty Soul: They betray him not indeed to the Jews, but which is worse to the devil, who inhabits in them. [p. 319]

A parallel is thus drawn between the vulnerable Christ of the passion story and the eucharistic body of Christ. If anything, however, the catechetical texts exhibit a greater horror at sin against the latter, as the eucharistic Christ is not betrayed to 'the Jews', but to the devil who dwells within the sinner (Hornihold, 1814, p. 113). The same discourses of the vulnerability of the eucharist and the Judas-sin emerge later in the material prepared especially for the first communion of children. To receive communion whilst withholding from one's confessor a mortal sin constitutes a 'violation' of the eucharist and is 'one of the greatest crimes of which a Christian can render himself guilty' (de Ségur, 1887, p. 34). So we find:

> The great day arrives, and behold him, more audacious than Judas ... he rises and advances coldly to consummate his crime; a hideous troop of infernal spirits wait upon him, ready to exercise their fury on the Lamb of God ... Nothing stops, nothing moves him. Already this hypocrite is on his knees at the foot of the altar: the priest brings his Saviour to him. It is done. Like Judas, he touches with impure mouth the adorable body of the Son of God; he has consummated his crime. [*First Communion: A Series of Letters to the Young*, 1848, pp. 52–3]

Other examples of the Judas parallel can be found in de Ségur (1887, p. 34); Gibson (1892, p. 76); Mary Loyola (1896, p. 405). A different New Testament parallel is drawn by Jones (1822), who likens the sacrilegious communicant to the 'Jewish priests and pagan soldiers' at the crucifixion (vol. iii, p. 170). Not surprisingly, then, the confession of sin to a priest emerges from these texts as standing in a special relationship to the eucharist. For Turberville (1685) such confession is the necessary disposition of anyone who is to receive communion (p. 127). This notion of confession as preparation for communion recurs throughout the literature. Indeed it is still part of the official discourse of the Catholic Church that anyone conscious of having committed grave sin may not receive the eucharist until confession has been made (*The Code of Canon Law in English Translation* 1983, § 916; hereafter CIC; *Catechism of the Catholic Church* 1994, § 1415; hereafter CCC).

The Ease of Making a 'Bad' Communion

Anxiety for the vulnerability of the eucharist was reinforced by a sense that it was remarkably easy to fall into the type of 'mortal' sin that would render the reception of communion sacrilegious. Thus Gobinet (1689):

> And if by misfortune it have so happen'd, that you are already fall'n therein for want of due foresight of the fall (which easily happens not only to young people, but to many others, by reason they are not sensible of the evil before it fall upon them) in this case, *Theotime*, take care to confess your self forthwith. [p. 394]

Moreover, it is not just active failings that constitute mortal sins – 'ignorance of the principal mysteries of faith, the Apostles' Creed, the Sacraments or the commandments ordinarily speaking are mortal sins' (p. 231). For the author of *An Abstract of the*

Douay Catechism (1697), the risk of a sacrilegious communion is compounded by the frequency of inadequate confessions made after such mortal sins:

> It often happens, either for want of instruction, of due sentiments of piety, or thrô negligence in things that concern Salvation, that persons, especially in their youth, make bad and sacrilegious Confessions. Because either they do not sufficiently examine their consciences; or out of shame or some such motive conceal something necessary to be confess'd; or have not a true sorrow for their sins; or want a real and firm purpose of mending their lives. [pp. 191–2]

Given this perceived ease with which a mortal sin could be committed, the practice arose of individuals making a 'General Confession' from time to time – that is, reviewing their life and confessing all their sins, irrespective of whether they had been confessed in the past. When the process for first communion emerged into print, such a general confession of sins stood at its heart. This would have ensured as far as possible that a non-sacrilegious communion was guaranteed. The children would normally have begun to confess their sins around the age of seven (Turner, 2000, 9, 10), but this General Confession was intended to take them back through their entire life. *Catechism* (1781) states that this General Confession should be preceded by eight days of preparation during which the children should recall all the sins of their past life. During this period they are to

> ... reflect seriously that by Sin we affront the Majesty of God, who is our most tender Father and liberal Benefactor; secondly, that we act over again the tragical scenes of Christ's Passion, and crucify him a second time; thirdly, that we give up our Right and Title to the Kingdom of Heaven, which was given us in Baptism; fourthly, that we make ourselves the most wretched Slaves of the Devil, and bind ourselves over to the eternal Torments of Hell. [p. 8]

Given the potential trauma of this self-examination, it is not surprising that the author should suggest that the General Confession should be made at least a month before communion, 'that their Thoughts may be more composed for the more immediate Preparation for approaching the holy Table' (ibid.).

The 1860 *Instructions*, on the other hand, suggest that the General Confession should be carried out over the four weeks immediately preceding first communion. During each week the child should confess any sins committed against a particular set of commandments – the first three during week one, and so on (p. 20). De Ségur (1887) does not offer the same detailed process, but nevertheless insists that 'hatred of sin is the first condition for a good preparation for Holy Communion' (p. 13). There appears to be some softening as the century progresses; for Gibson (1892) a General Confession is 'usual' before first communion (p. 81), and instead of the four-week process of 1860, he simply suggests a private examination of conscience in church immediately before a single-occasion confession (p. 82).

That children might present themselves for communion in a state of mortal sin was a source of anxiety throughout the nineteenth century. The ease with which this could be done was compounded by the laws regarding fasting. Until 1957 Catholics were bound to maintain an absolute fast of food or drink from midnight to whenever they received communion (Jungmann, 1959, p. 502). To break this fast and still receive communion constituted a mortal sin – and thus rendered the communion sacrilegious. The potential for disaster posed by this is brought out by the story in Mary Loyola (1896) of a girl who, whilst processing into church to receive her first communion, absent-mindedly ate a chocolate that she found on the way:

> She could not bear the thought of what everyone would think and say. She would go to Communion as though nothing had happened, and she would confess her sin afterwards. All through the Mass her angel tried to frighten her by the thought of the sacrilege she was going to commit, but she would not listen because – 'What would people say?' At the *Domine non sum dignus* she went up to the rails with the rest, went up in her white dress, her white veil, and her wreath ... her soul dead in that whited sepulchre, and so she received her God and made her First Communion in mortal sin. [pp. 414–15]

It was possible, therefore, to undertake the most rigorous possible preparation for first communion, and still to fall at the last fence. The event was surrounded by anxiety: so much depended upon it – even the child's future happiness and immortal destiny – yet it could be spoiled so easily.

The Eucharist and Sexual Activity

Whilst even relatively minor peccadilloes had the potential force of mortal sin, one area of life emerges from the texts as the dominant source of anxiety around contamination of the eucharist, namely improper sexual activity. Lewis de Granada (1688) in discussing the 'purity of conscience' necessary to communicating well, identifies the two most 'dangerous' mortal sins from which a communicant must be purified as hatred and impurity. His argument is that the 'holy flesh' of Christ should not be received into a human body rendered impure by sexual sin. This anxiety extends beyond wilful actions:

> The saints have believ'd, a nocturnal illusion, caused by the Devil in a Dream, was a sufficient cause to abstain ... St. Bernard counsels in this case, even not to serve at the holy Mass, so much does this divine mystery require ... And if in the old Law one dishonest Dream caus'd him, to whom this dream happned, to be excluded during a whole day from the Tents and company of GOD's people, with what more reason ought it to separate us from so strict a communication with GOD himself? [pp. 183–4]

This is more demanding than the *Catechism for the Curats* (1687), which merely demands sexual abstinence within marriage for some days before reception of communion (p. 227).

The 1860 *Instructions* regard sins against purity as 'the most terrible and most sinful habits, the most criminal, and the most opposed to the sanctity and reception of Holy Communion' (p. 56). The same discourse is found in the *Doctrine Explanations* (1899): 'Of all sins, the dreadful sin of impurity would keep a soul furthest from God and would make it least fit to be his resting place' (p. 41). Not surprisingly, therefore, the 1860 *Instructions* regard the correction of juvenile impurity as essential if a sacrilegious first communion is to be avoided (p. 56). Children are, therefore, directed to 'destroy and tear up or burn your bad books ... destroy your immodest statues, paintings and pictures; otherwise you will not obtain pardon from God' (p. 38). A similar anxiety over the tendency for young people to be overwhelmed by their 'growing passions' emerges in de Ségur (1887, pp. 37–8). However, we note here a shift in emphasis that was to become a key note in *Quam Singulari*. De Ségur was convinced that without frequent and regular communion, it would be impossible for the majority of children to remain pure. The eucharist, he argued, could guard against this because it united the flesh of the children with the 'incomparably pure' flesh of Christ (p. 37).

By the late nineteenth century, this emphasis upon the preservative qualities of the eucharist was being used to justify calls for a reduction in the age at which first communion was administered. It was argued that by the age of twelve the passions of children would already have been inflamed, habits would have been formed, and so the efficacy of the eucharist to preserve against impurity would have been compromised. This discourse emerged in the course of a diocesan controversy in France into which the Roman authorities were drawn. Mazure (1910) argued the case for the lower age. The author cites a curate's statement, dated December 1908, that traces the career path from childhood innocence into impurity:

> Up to the age of eight or nine a child has been spotless through ignorance of evil. But after this period it will some day or other almost certainly come across a bad companion. Then follow curious revelations, disturbing in themselves, and doubly dangerous for the manner in which they are made: then immodest jokes, corrupt suggestions, and presently shameful conduct. How can you expect the child to resist? It is all so new, and so seductive. Curiosity, sensuality, vanity – all these conspire to drag it along. The child will then fall continually until the period of its First Communion. And do you imagine that the impressions of that solemn day will suffice for the complete uprooting of habits indulged in, perhaps, for years? Generally it will not. The child will go to Confession once a month for the regulation Communion. Between these Communions it will fall into sin; this monthly approach to the sacraments will gradually become an irksome task, and in a few years, when at last emancipated from the control of parents and of parish priest, he will drop his monthly Communion, and go to swell the ranks of those Christians who spend the greater portion of their lives out of the grace of God. [Mazure, 1910, pp. 23–4; cf. also Hedley, 1912, p. 10]

The issue is expressed most clearly by de Zulueta (1911):

> There is no use in disguising the truth. If a child lose the grace of God, this will almost invariably be through its weakly yielding to sensual impulse. Practically speaking, loss of holy purity is the only serious danger to the baptismal innocence of young children. No other form of mortal sin is at all likely to enter into the child's life. [p. 13]

The broad range of potential mortal sins found in the early texts is thus reduced to a single focus upon sexual fallibility. Both the prize that early twentieth-century commentators such as de Zulueta imagined could be gained by anticipating first communion before the onset of sexual curiosity, and the cost of failing to do so, are clarified when a final discourse is taken into account.

First Communion as a Life-Defining Moment

In many of the texts, the eucharist has a strange duality: whilst it generally is life-giving, it can in certain circumstances be death-imparting. Thus, Lewis de Granada (1688):

> No man ought to flatter himself on this occasion, or vainly think himself secure, because of the Vertue of this Sacrament, which is the Life of Souls. 'Tis true that it gives life, but 'tis no less true, that it gives also Death to those who prophane it by approaching it unprepar'd. [p. 191]

In other words, the potential consequence of the 'sacrilegious' communion went far beyond having a bad conscience. The 'bad' communion

> ... heaps upon the head of the unworthy receiver, dreadful and almost irreparable ruins, changing the fountain of life into the cause of death; and that, which of itself, and by its first institution, was a pledge of salvation, a Sacrament of Love and Mercy, into a Sentence of Condemnation or Everlasting death. [Gobinet, 1689, p. 281; cf. also Vaux, 1568, p. 90]

In *Letters* (1848) this duality is explained in theological terms: any act of divine grace necessarily has an effect on the recipient, which can be positive or negative, depending upon the disposition of the one who receives – 'it necessarily renders us better or worse ... enlightens or makes us blinder, softens or makes us more obdurate' (p. 21).

The sacrilegious communion is regarded as so grave a fault that once it has been committed, real return is almost impossible:

> ... alas! How seldom is it that we find the unworthy communicant returning to God by a sincere repentance! On the contrary, he usually comes every day more hardened in guilt, and going from sin to sin, from sacrilege to sacrilege, sinks continually deeper into the abyss. At length death comes, and as he has lived, so does he die, with his lips sealed by a guilty shame, his heart still hardened against the grace of God, a prey to anguish, terror and despair. [Gibson, 1892, p. 77; cf. also Gibson, 1877]

Indeed, physical sickness and death itself may come as a direct punishment from God upon the sacrilegious communicant (Richards 1883, p. 8). Therefore, a bad communion could set in train a downward moral process that could have life-threatening consequences with eternal overtones. It was, therefore, understood as a life-defining moment. Thus, the 1781 *Catechism* opens with the declaration that first communion is the most important task that children have on their hands (*Catechism*, 1781, p. 1).

This discourse continues to be developed in the nineteenth-century English publications. Throughout the period, the attitude that the individual has towards his or her first communion, the seriousness of the approach made towards its preparation and the manner in which it is performed, are described as having an enduring effect. Thus the first communion is 'the greatest, the holiest and the most important action of our whole lives' (*A Catechism for First Communion*, 1850, p. 4), and 'its effect commonly last through life' (Richards, 1883, p. 9). The capacity for first communion to have this effect is explained in terms of human development: the age at which first communion was celebrated – between ten and twelve years (*A Catechism for First Communion*, 1850, p. 6; de Ségur, 1887, p. 42; Richards, 1883, p. 4) – was regarded as a period during which habits were established and life-long patterns of behaviour determined:

> Fortunate children! You are at the happy age in which you may contract habits which will remain for the rest of your lives: absolute masters of your own destiny, you can, if you please, secure your own present and future happiness. [*Letters*, 1848, p. 20]

First communion 'impresses upon youth its seal and direction' (ibid.). The event, therefore, is 'decisive' – it fixes for life the interior dispositions that each participant brings to it. Thus, for the one who 'makes it well', the forces of habit established at that time will always exercise a controlling influence, and act as a restraint in later life (cf. also Gibson, 1892, p. 3).

Conversely, first communion can set the seal on bad habits and fix them for life. This concept is particularly developed by the author of *Letters* (1848). Following on from his comments about the positive and negative effects of any encounter with divine grace, he observes that as the eucharist is 'the greatest of all graces' (p. 21), then its initial reception at the most impressionable age is going to exercise the most profound influence possible. The first communion sets the seal on a person's life and stands as an anticipation of the Last Judgement. Quoting an unnamed 'celebrated preacher', he writes:

> On this day ... children decide their eternity; they go together to the same table and partake of the same banquet; but if their dispositions are not alike, they return from it separated by an infinite distance. Whilst some have received life, others have received death; whilst these are gathered on the right, those are on the left ... On the day of judgement the Son of Man will only manifest, in the presence of the assembled nations, that terrible separation which was commenced at the sacred table on the day of First Communion. The last sentence which He will pronounce, from the height of His dread tribunal, will only be a confirmation of that which He pronounced in the depths of the sanctuary. [pp. 21–2]

1 Corinthians 11:29 is cited as justification of this linkage of first communion and final judgement: 'he that eateth and drinketh unworthily, eateth and drinketh judgement to himself'.(Douay Bible translation). Thus, the children are warned that should they receive first communion 'unworthily', they bring down judgement upon themselves. They are made to understand that they would, indeed, receive the Body of Christ, but it would only be 'to their greater condemnation' (Richards 1883, p. 8). Such use of 1 Corinthians 11:29 runs throughout the catechetical corpus: see Challoner (1759a, p. 18); Hornihold (1814, p. 111); Lingard (1840, p. 112); Gibson (1877, pp. 3, 85); Cafferata (1910, p. 122).

The Sacred and the Profane?

The discourses reveal a high degree of anxiety on the part of the Catholic community with regard to its adolescent members at first communion before 1910. It was about to entrust to them its most sacred possession at exactly the time when the stirrings of their sexuality were most likely to render their reception of the sacrament improper. At the same time the power of the eucharist to establish a positive life course and to serve as 'antidote' to sin was desirable. This placed the Church on the horns of a dilemma. It was right and essential that its members should communicate; yet the encounter between the communicant and Christ present in the eucharist was fraught with a double peril. On the one hand it exposed the Deity to the risk of sacrilege that paralleled – and even intensified – the historic betrayal by Judas. On the other, it drew the first communicant in a ritual encounter with the divine that, if unsuccessfully performed, might determine a negative life-course and an almost inescapable sentence of eternal damnation.

The sharp polarity seen in the catechetical texts between the sacred eucharist and the sinful condition of its recipients invites comparison with the insistence of Emil Durkheim upon the absolute polarity between the sacred and the profane (Durkheim, 2001). Mortal sin (especially sexual), lack of physical preparation through observance of the fasting regulations, even an inadequate understanding of the meaning of the ritual, could all invite contagion of the sacred by the profane. Consequently the ritual of first communion, which in Durkheimian terms would be a 'positive rite' (Durkheim, 2001, pp. 221ff.), would be diligently prepared for by the 'negative' rituals that ensured a safe encounter – chief among them the confession of sin and the abstinence from food and drink before communion.

Durkheim's essential dichotomy between the sacred and the profane has been repeatedly challenged (for example, Evans-Pritchard, 1965; Stanner, 1967; Lukes, 1973; Douglas, 1975 and 2001). The mapping onto the first communion texts of a hypothesis built upon a debateable Durkheimian reading is certainly insecure. Moreover, as consideration of the French celebration established, the ritual itself was a mixture of 'sacred' and 'profane' elements that from an anthropological perspective cannot be easily separated. Whilst the Church consistently attempted to filter out 'secular' elements, the event had a broader focus for its participants than merely admission to the eucharist. If Durkheim's dichotomy were to be applied to first communion, only part of the event could be examined, and the totality of the experience of its participants would need to be discounted.

Durkheim's thesis thus fails to account for the event in its entirety. It none the less helps to pull into sharper focus the contrast between sin and eucharist that the catechetical texts (and, indeed, the current formal teaching of the Church) insist upon. It also offers a language of negative ritual and of contagion with which to describe the element of confession that preceded communion. Within this perspective, the dilemma faced by the Catholic community at the end of the nineteenth century is placed in stark relief. There were considered to be three most likely causes of contagion for communion: fast-breaking, sexual sin and inadequate understanding. The first was not at that time the cause of serious debate, but the second and third were in tension with each other. The risk of sexual sin could be overcome by reducing the age of reception to pre-puberty, thereby introducing the children to the eucharist at an age when innocence could be presumed. Yet, to do so would accentuate the risk that first communicants might receive with inadequate understanding, and thus break the boundaries between the sacred and profane by failing, in New Testament terms, to 'discern the body and blood of Christ' (1 Corinthians 11:27–9). As will be examined in the next chapter, the reform of 1910 was an attempt to overcome these tensions. It reinterpreted the age of reason in such a manner as to permit the reduction in age that guaranteed innocence. The positive force of the eucharist for life-course determination was thus harnessed whilst the distinction between the realms of sacred and profane was respected.

The Ritual of First Communion

The discourses found in the English texts, therefore, resonate with the life-course-related concerns that surfaced in the French ritual. We may now ask whether the texts also point to the liturgical celebration of the event along French lines.

Dress

From the texts published in English it is impossible to determine with certainty what the dress was for first communions before 1910. The author of the *Letters* (1848) comments with concern on the sight of first communicants 'loaded with worldly finery which, to say the least, exhibits the most foolish vanity' (p. 78). Mazure (1910) similarly inveighs against parents who vie with their neighbours 'in richness of display' (p. 45). However, both of these may be reflecting continental practice. Although Mary Loyola gives a description of first communicants dressed in white, with veils and wreaths, it is in the context of a celebration at a French convent (1896, pp. 414–15). Gibson also mentions the veil and wreath in a salutary tale of a girl who kept these items and would deck herself in them in private before her monthly communions; the origin of this story is not specified (1892, pp. 6–7). All that these texts can establish with certainty is that there would have been knowledge, at least, in England of the tradition of first communion dress from the mid-nineteenth century onwards, and a recognition that it may have been problematic. It is only with the accounts of the 1911 rituals that solid evidence of the use of similar dress in England becomes available. However, those accounts witness to use so widespread, and so clearly representing established practices, that the custom must have been introduced earlier.

The Mass of First Communion

The publications make very little reference to the ritual followed in the Mass of first communion itself. The liturgy of the eucharist was closely guarded by a system of rubrics that effectively rendered it immutable. I have found no evidence in the texts of the 'very short but emotional exhortation' given to the children before communion attested to in France[1] – though these certainly did take place later in the 1911 celebrations. Nor is there evidence, from these texts or from the accounts of the 1911 celebrations, of the pattern found in the Boulogne and Bayeux rituals of the children coming forward with lighted candles at the offertory, which in Bayeux were held till the end of Mass.[2] For the main part, then, congregational participation in the first communion Mass appears to have been entirely passive and silent. Any expression of personal devotion or adherence on the part of the children had necessarily to take place outside the Mass. Hence the importance of the ancillary rituals carried out later in the day, which offered greater possibilities for emotive expression and for the spotlight to fall on the children themselves.

The Renewal of Baptismal Promises

The ritual of the renewal of baptismal promises at first communion is found in the *Catechism for First Communicants* (1781). They are renewed because:

> Not having the use of Reason, when we received that Sacrament, we are certainly obliged, as soon as we begin to know ourselves, and understand what we are doing, to ratify what the Church did for us, when we were incapable of answering for ourselves. [p. 9]

This renewal is thus the ratification of the promises made at baptism by the now rational person. However, the act is not restricted to first communion:

> It is good to renew them often and especially, *first*, when we receive the Sacrament of Confirmation; *secondly*, when we are to make our First Communion; *thirdly* on the Eves of *Easter* and *Whitsuntide*, these being Days appointed by the Church for the solemn Administration of Baptism; *fourthly*, on the Anniversary Day of our Baptism; *fifthly*, at the Article of Death. [ibid.]

The 1781 *Catechism* does not offer details of the ritual of renewal, nor how it might have fitted into a first communion ritual sequence, as in France. So there is no way of knowing whether this is a French influence, or represents an independent English practice of the renewal of baptismal promises at significant events.

A more certain continental influence can be found in the two texts associated with the Italian missionary priests Gentili and Pagani, whose influence will be considered more fully below: *Letters* (1848) and *A Catechism for First Communion* (1850). Both make passing references to the renewal of promises. The first text twice refers to it as an evening ritual celebrated during Vespers at the font (pp. 196 and 200). The 1850 work specifies neither the time nor the location, but returns to the *Catechism* (1781) discourse of conversion:

---

1   Beuvelet, Matthieu (1668) *Reglements et matiers des chatechisms qui se font en la paroisse de St.-Nicolas-du-Chardonnet*, Paris: Gabriel Targa. Cited in Turner (2000, 10, 7).

2   *Rituel du Diocèse de Boulogne* (1750), Boulogne, and *Rituale Bajocense* (1774), Paris. Both cited in Turner (2000, 10, 7).

It is very proper to renew them at this time, and humbly to ask pardon of Jesus Christ for our want of fidelity in fulfilling them, and to promise Him again our love, and our inviolable and eternal fidelity. [p. 22]

The fullest discourse is contained in the 1860 *Instructions*, which also includes a ritual and a text for the renewal of promises. The context is again one of conversion: the ritual seals the confessional process that has led up to first communion. Having repented of all previous failings, the children now mark out their future life-course:

Alas! How many times, perhaps, since the years of discretion, have you, guilty children, abandoned Jesus Christ, and transgressed His divine commandments by yielding to sin, rendering yourselves again slaves of the devil, in following his pomps and his evil maxims! But you have confessed and shed abundant tears for all these wanderings of your childhood: God in His mercy has forgiven you; my dear children, you must now evince your gratitude, and consecrate yourselves to Him for ever, by renewing your baptismal vows. [p. 69]

The ritual itself gives a quasi-legal tone to this consecration:

Go, then, yourselves, my dear children, to this sacred font, and there, standing before the crucifix, in the presence of your holy Angel Guardian, placing your right hand on the Gospel, and holding a wax taper in your left, willingly and courageously pronounce, with a loud voice, the solemn contract which, on the day of your baptism, by interpretations of your sponsors, was passed between you and God. [pp. 69–70]

The renewal of promises echoes a formal oath, and the religious elements (crucifix, font and bible) combine with the discourse of an angelic witness to produce a sense of heightened drama. The same elements of gospel and angels also occur in the formula given for the act of renewal:

I firmly believe in God, and in Jesus Christ, his only Son.
I believe all the truths that He has revealed in his holy Gospel, and that the Catholic
       Church proposes to our belief.
I renew before God and His angels and saints all these engagements of my baptism.
I am resolved to observe all my life the commandments of God and of His holy Church.
I renounce Satan and all his works.
I attach and devote myself to Jesus Christ, at once, and for ever. Amen.
[p. 72]

Lest the event should be forgotten, the candle serves as a permanent witness across the life-course:

I advise you to preserve this candle during your life, as a remembrance of your holy 'First Communion'; light it sometimes for a few moments, and meditate – meditate, my dear children, on the significance of these words, 'my First Communion' … The day of your death, this taper will serve at your Viaticum, and will brighten your glory. [p. 71]

The other texts I studied do not mention the renewal of baptismal promises.

The Consecration to the Virgin Mary

The axis Mary–eucharist is found in earlier texts. Thus, Gobinet (1689) advises prayer to the Virgin Mary before and after the reception of communion (pp. 382–6). The prayer before communion introduces a note of anxiety:

> It concerns thee that he be received with all the respect and honour he deserves, and that he not be unworthily treated by those upon whom he bestows himself with so much love … Beg, and by thy powerful intercession obtain of him these two dispositions for me, these two important virtues; which assured him unto thee, and render'd thee deservedly his worthy mother, I mean Purity and Humility That he may find nothing in me, which may taste of Impurity or Pride. [pp. 383–4]

Mary thus begins to emerge as the bulwark against the sacrilegious communion, and the guarantor of an appropriate sacred/profane distinction. This theme is further developed in the two texts from the mid-century which give details of the consecration of the first communicants to the Virgin Mary (*Letters*, 1848, p. 196 and *Instructions*, 1860, pp. 72–4). In both, consecration follows on directly from the renewal of baptismal promises: the children process from the font to the altar of Mary (*Letters*, 1848, p. 196; *Instructions*, 1860, p. 72). If the renewal of baptismal promises represents a definitive moment of commitment, this ritual underlines the fragility of that commitment and the need for both it, and the eucharist that the child has received, to be protected. Thus, *Letters* 1848:

> Ah, how can we possibly forget on this day her to whom we owe our Saviour? It is but just to place under the protection of the Queen of Heaven both your resolutions and the precious treasure you carry in your heart [p. 72]

This theme of placing the received eucharist under Mary's protection also emerges in the formula for dedication proposed in the *Instructions* (1860):

> Holy Virgin Mary, Mother of God, in virtue of the last words of Jesus on the cross, I come to consecrate my childhood, my youth, and my life to you: 'Behold thy Mother! Behold thy son!' … I place under your holy protection the 'First Communion' that I have had the happiness to make this morning. Do not permit, O Mary, that I ever abandon the God of bounty, who has vouchsafed to descend this day into my heart for the first time; obtain for me grace that I may remain faithful to the hour of my death. [p. 72]

Thus, there is concern for the eucharist itself that once having been received it was in some way vulnerable, needing the protection of Mary.

Although the later nineteenth-century texts do not make specific mention of either the baptismal renewal or the dedication to Mary, the accounts of several of the 1911 first communions include clear reference to them, so the practice evidently took root, in some places at least. The latest occurrence I have identified was in 1942 among the pupils at the Notre Dame Preparatory School, Wigan (personal conversation).

Conclusion: Personal Crisis and Conversion

The pre-1910 ritual complex of first communion was designed to provoke in the twelve-year-old participants a profound personal crisis on a moral level, and to lead to a commitment to personal adherence to Christ within the Catholic Church. The process of preparation was above all penitential in character, emphasizing the need for repentance from previous sins, and focusing around the 'good' confession whose desired outcome was conversion. The rituals of the first communion day itself sought to set the seal on this conversion. The renewal of baptismal promises solemnly proclaimed the path of life now chosen, and the consecration to Mary had the aim of ensuring that this commitment endured through life. Underpinning all this was the discourse that this event set the seal on an individual's future life-course – indeed, establishing an eternal destiny.

This ritual, therefore, had a powerful initiatory character. Through the ordeal of the confessional and ritual process, the individual emerged with a strong Catholic identity fixed for life. Moreover, the underlying concern over the sexual awakening of the participants suggests that it genuinely was a rite of puberty. Yet the discourse of Christian initiation does not occur in the texts; there is no sense that the reception of communion for the first time marks a stage in, or completes, the initiation of the child. There is a clear reference to baptism in the renewal of promises, but it appears that the purpose of this act is to underline the definitive path upon which the individual has now set him/herself. This contrasts markedly with the current Catholic discourse of the three sacraments of Christian initiation that will be considered in Chapter 5.

All of this makes clear the enormous change that took place in the wake of the decree *Quam Singulari*. Even though the rituals continued to be celebrated according to the previous pattern, the experience that they articulated was considerably different – it had to be, given the almost halving in the age of its participants. The contrast between the 'before' and 'after' has been heightened by the development within the Catholic Church of the concept of first communion as a 'sacrament of initiation'. The Catholic community has passed from a ritual that was initiatory in experience but lacked a formal discourse of initiation, to one where a discourse of initiation is married to a ritual that is not so experienced. The tensions arising from this became evident in the course of my fieldwork, and will be considered in due course. Before that, however, we must consider in greater detail the impact of the reform of 1910 – not least because the first communion celebrations that followed in its wake were widely reported. Those reports offer a detailed picture of the rituals that were used across England and Wales at that time.

CHAPTER 3

The Implementation of the Decree
Quam Singulari in England (1910–11)

Introduction

All the post-Tridentine texts and rituals discussed in the previous chapter presume the admission to the eucharist of children around the age of twelve years, in accordance with a received understanding of cognitive development based upon the age of reason discourse. As Mazure (1910) revealed, however, by the start of the twentieth century the consensus within the Catholic community with regard to the most appropriate age for reception of first communion had been lost. For some, an anxiety with regard to the capacity of children to grasp the complexities of Catholic eucharistic doctrine suggested a later age; for others, the twinned discourses of first communion as life-course-defining act and of the potential for sexual maturation to render first communion sacrilegious suggested an earlier age, before the onset of puberty. Rome entered definitively into the debate in 1910 with the publication (8 August) of the Decree *Quam Singulari* of the Sacred Congregation for the Discipline of the Sacraments.

This document established three principles that closed the post-Tridentine debate concerning the age of reason discourse and laid the foundations for current practice. First, the distinction between the two separate ages of discretion and of reason for the start of confession and communion was collapsed: the onset of rational thought was now judged to coincide with the capacity to distinguish between right and wrong. Second, what was required was only the most initial understanding of the eucharist, consonant with the beginning rather than the full development of reasoning powers:

> Neither for first confession nor for first communion is full and perfect knowledge of Christian doctrine requisite. But a child ought afterwards gradually to learn the entire Catechism according to his capacity. [norm II]

> The knowledge of his religion which is required in a child before he can make his first communion is such as will enable him to grasp according to his capacity those mysteries of faith which are necessary as means to salvation, and to distinguish between the Bread of the Eucharist and ordinary material bread, so that he may come to the Holy Eucharist with a devotion proportionate to his years. [norm III]

Third, this first use of reason was deemed to happen at the age of seven, 'more or less' (norm I). It was this reinterpretation of the age of reason discourse that permitted *Quam Singulari* to reduce the age of first communion and thereby isolate reception of the sacrament from the sacrilegious potential of sexual maturation. The decree brought to an end the previous practice, precipitated a pastoral, and more particularly, catechetical crisis, and initiated the discipline for the event that remains in force today. This chapter describes and analyses the process of the decree's implementation in England and Wales. Particular focus will be placed upon the first rituals of the reception of first communion from age seven as described in contemporary sources. The chapter concludes with the optimistic assessment of the implementation and its consequences in the Liverpool diocese on the part of the bishop at that time, Thomas Whiteside.

Formal Provision for Implementation in England and Wales

A little over two weeks after the promulgation of *Quam Singulari*, a full translation was published in the *Catholic Times*.[1] The accompanying editorial by James Hughes highlights perceived failings in the current practice:

> Hitherto, when children were kept waiting till eleven or twelve for First Communion, some in spite of every care left school without this necessary grace, and perhaps never received it till manhood or old age. And even those who received it had only a year or two to form the custom of going to Holy Communion. [p. 10]

Hughes regards the new decree as redressing this situation:

> But now it will be practically impossible for any child to be overlooked, and when children leave school they will from their seventh to their fourteenth year have in their days of childish innocence time to form the habit and become accustomed to the idea of frequent daily Communion. [ibid.]

The reduction in the age of first communion thus was intended to establish a discipline by which children were to be formed in the pattern of frequent communion. This was to be enforced, for example, through the frequent practice of children being seated with their classroom peers at Sunday Mass, under the controlling gaze of their teacher.

Hughes was in no doubt that this new discipline would produce lasting – even dramatic – positive effects within the Catholic community. Within the Church at large, however, this optimism was not universally shared, and thanks to the Catholic press, the Catholic community in Liverpool would have been aware of the criticism of the decree that was raised within two months of its promulgation.[2]

A formal policy for the implementation of the decree was not determined until the regular meeting of the bishops of England and Wales in November 1910. At their meeting on 3 November, they agreed to communicate the decree to the clergy and

---

1   *The Catholic Times*, London edition, no. 2,246, 26 August 1910, p. 10.

2   The decree was particularly criticized in France: cf. *Liverpool Catholic Herald*, St Helens edition, no. 774, 1 October 1910, p. 4; ibid. no. 776, 15 October 1910, p. 4; *The Tablet*, vol. 116, no. 3,674, 8 October 1910, p. 573. For an account of criticism in Italy cf. *The Liverpool Catholic Herald*, St Helens edition, no. 780, 12 November 1910, p. 4.

to draw their attention to the requirement that the decree should be publicly read each Easter.[3] They further agreed to refer to the Inspectors of Religious Instruction the question of any alterations in the syllabus of religious instruction that would be required by the change in practice. The Inspectors were to report to the archbishop ahead of the 1911 Low Week meeting of the bishops.

Two days after the bishops' meeting, the *Tablet* published a lengthy article, 'The Age of First Communion'.[4] As with all the *Tablet*'s articles its author remained anonymous. However, given that the Archdiocese of Westminster owned the paper[5] and Bourne took considerable interest in its editorial policy, it is quite possible that he had a role in commissioning the article. The full English text of *Quam Singulari* was published in the *Tablet* the following week.[6] Nine days later Bishop Thomas Whiteside enclosed a copy of the English text with a thematically unrelated Pastoral Letter addressed to the Diocese of Liverpool.[7] At the close of the letter he added a note to the clergy on first communion: they were to read the English text of the decree to their parishes on the coming third Sunday of Advent, and in succeeding years every Easter Sunday.[8] He further instructed the clergy to take steps at once to ensure that the provisions of the decree were carried out, giving immediate priority to those children who had already made their first confessions.

In contrast to events in France and Italy, there was no significant public objection to the reform in England and Wales. On 28 November 1910 Bourne assured the pope that there was no 'difficulty or prejudice to conquer' in England with regard to the implementation of *Quam Singulari*.[9] However, Bishop Amigo of Southwark acknowledged a potential difficulty in his Advent Pastoral Letter.[10] 'How many fathers and mothers', he wrote, 'will tell the priests and teachers that the children are not old enough to approach such a sacrament?' (p. 947). Amigo countered by arguing, along the lines of *Quam Singulari*, that the reception of communion during childhood innocence would act as an antidote against present and future temptation. However, he also warned parents of the increased potential for culpability that *Quam Singulari* laid upon the children and their parents. By setting the age of reason at seven, the decree had enforced upon that age group the demands of Easter duties set by the Fourth Lateran Council. Because failure to fulfil those duties itself constituted mortal sin, the extension to young children of the 'antidote to sin' had

---

3   See Bibliography, Section B.

4   *The Tablet*, vol. 116, no. 3,678, 5 November 1910, pp. 723–5.

5   *The Tablet*, founded in 1840, had originally been in lay ownership. It was purchased in 1868 by Herbert Vaughan (1832–1903), who became Bishop of Salford in 1872. In 1892, Vaughan was translated to Westminster, becoming a cardinal in 1893. Under the terms of his will, the journal passed to the Archdiocese of Westminster, which sold it upon Bourne's death in 1935. Cf. Crichton, Winstone and Ainslie, 1979, p. 31.

6   *The Tablet*, vol. 116, no. 3,679, 12 November 1910, pp. 782–4.

7   Whiteside CLIX. Formal documents written by Whiteside are numbered in the archives from the onset of his episcopate. Full details are given in the Bibliography, Section B, together with an explanation of the page-referencing convention used in this book.

8   Ibid., p. 12.

9   *The Tablet*, vol. 116, no. 3,683, 10 December 1910, p. 940.

10   *The Tablet*, Supplement to vol. 116, no. 3,683, 10 December 1910, pp. 947, 963.

the extraordinary corollary of exposing them at an earlier age to potential culpability. Furthermore, such culpability extended to the children's parents, who were thus required to submit to a double discipline: to agree to the first communion of their children at a younger age and then, under pain of themselves committing mortal sin, to ensure that the children then observed the minimum requirements for eucharistic participation.

First Signs of Implementation: Advent-Christmas 1910

The first instance recorded in the Catholic press of first communion at the new age was during Advent 1910. Eight children received communion at the Premonstratensian priory at Storrington in Sussex on 11 December.[11] Usefully, it is possible to establish with precision the ages of two of the participants, whose father was identified in the newspaper reports: Hilaire Belloc's daughters Eleanor and Elizabeth, then eleven and ten years old.[12] The younger girl at least would not have received first communion at this age under the former dispensation, and the event therefore prefigures the first communions of 1911 that drew in all children aged between seven and twelve. At Storrington a highly complex ritual was followed. At the beginning of Mass the children processed into church, preceded by crucifer and acolytes. When they arrived at the sanctuary the *Veni Creator* was sung. A full sung High Mass was celebrated, but at the moment of communion the Prior addressed 'a few simple moving words' to the children. A cluster of rituals occurred later in the day. Compline (Night Prayer) was sung, and the first communicants processed to the font where they renewed their baptismal vows. Returning to the sanctuary, they then consecrated themselves to the Virgin Mary. Solemn Benediction brought the celebration to a conclusion. There is a remarkable similarity between this ritual complex and the eighteenth-century French first communions noted earlier. Many of the features were also to be encountered during the mass first communions of early 1911.

There is also evidence that at least one parish, English Martyrs at Sparkhill in the Birmingham diocese, admitted small children to communion on Christmas Day 1910. After the early morning Mass of first communion, the children took breakfast, and returned to church for a further Mass of Thanksgiving at 11.00 am. During the afternoon Benediction service they were consecrated to the Virgin Mary. Then, on 29 December, the feast of St Thomas of Canterbury, they were entertained to a tea-party.[13]

---

11   *The Tablet*, Supplement to vol. 116, no 3,685, 24 December 1910, p. 1042. Each particular celebration of first communion was reported in a single edition of the various newspapers. To avoid excessive footnoting I give the reference to the reporting edition on the first occasion only of discussing a particular celebration. To assist the reader in tracking the various celebrations, an index of locations and references is given as an Appendix.

12   Eleanor Belloc was born in July 1899, Elisabeth in November 1900 (Speiaght, 1957, pp. 86, 95).

13   *The Tablet*, Supplement to vol. 116, no. 3,686, 31 December 1910, p. 1082.

Educational and Catechetical Texts

Implicit in the comment of Whiteside cited above is a sense of the scale of the challenge that the reform posed for educational and catechetical practice. Those responsible for religious education had very little time to adapt themselves to the significantly different task of preparing much younger children. Moreover, the task for the academic year 1910–11 was enormous. The reform was not phased in gradually; rather, in the space of a single year, every child aged between seven and twelve was to prepare for and to receive first holy communion.

The Bishops' Lenten Pastoral Letters (1911)

During Lent 1911 several of the bishops of England and Wales devoted all or part of their Lenten pastoral letters to the theme of *Quam Singulari* and its implementation.[14] The letters of Bourne in Westminster and Whiteside in Liverpool are particularly useful because they evidence the authors' interpretation of the educational instructions in the decree.[15] Whiteside stressed that only the 'slightest' preparatory instruction was absolutely required, and promised future regulations that would direct the gradual supplementing of the initial instruction.[16] In addressing the requirement of *Quam Singulari* that the child should grasp 'according to his capacity the Mysteries of the Faith that are necessary as means to salvation' (norm II) Whiteside explained that this meant 'there is one God, in three Persons, the Father, the Son and the Holy Ghost, Who rewards the good and punishes the wicked, and that God the Son became man and died on the cross for our salvation.'[17]

Bourne offered the same basic framework, though with some slight elaboration:

> The child must know that there is only one God and that God loves us, and will reward the good and punish the wicked; that the Father, the Son and the Holy Spirit are equally God, though there is only one God; that God the Son became man and died to save us from sin and hell.[18]

---

14 Not all the Lenten Pastorals for 1911 treated the subject of first communion. The Bishop of Birmingham wrote on the liturgy as 'the fountain of devotion', and the Bishop of Portsmouth chose to focus upon Lenten penance. Cf. *The Catholic Times*, New Series no. 2,274, 10 March 1911, p. 10.

15 Bourne, *The Tablet*, Supplement to vol. 117, no. 3,696, 11 March 1911, pp. 393–4; Whiteside CLXIII, p. 5. The Lenten Pastoral of Louis Charles Casartelli (1852–1925), Bishop of Salford from 1903, focused on the devotional rather than educational requirements of the reform: *The Tablet*, Supplement to vol. 117, no. 3,698, 25 March 1911, p. 474, and *The Catholic Times*, Manchester edition no. 2,282, 5 May 1911, p. 5.

16 Whiteside, loc. cit. The 1910–1911 cohort included all children aged between the new age of seven and the previous one of twelve; in recognition of this, Whiteside stated that the older children were still to receive a fuller instruction.

17 Whiteside, loc. cit.

18 *The Tablet,* Supplement to vol. 117, no. 3,696, 11 March 1911, p. 393.

In discussing the second doctrinal requirement of *Quam Singulari*, namely that the child should be able to 'distinguish between the bread of the eucharist and ordinary material bread' (norm III), the less elaborate explanation is again offered by Whiteside: 'The only special knowledge of the Blessed Eucharist required for the first Communion is, that what is received is not common or ordinary bread, but a special food given by God for the good of our souls.'[19]

Bourne again offers further detail: 'The child must know further that the Blessed Sacrament is not common bread, but a holy gift bringing Jesus, the Son of God made man, into our souls.'[20] However, whilst Whiteside simply stated that all this knowledge will be 'supplemented as the child grows older',[21] Bourne attempted to justify the change in educational terms:

> Later, as the child grows older, fuller and more detailed information will be given in Christian doctrine, and especially regarding the Blessed Sacrament. Thus its Eucharistic knowledge will grow with its intelligence, and instead of being imparted – sometimes with, perhaps, too great insistence and intensity – at a later age, as was formerly the case, it will develop with the child and become, in a much fuller and more real sense, an essential part in its spiritual and mental preparation.[22]

The Graduated Syllabus of 1911

An attempt to map out this developmental approach is found in the course of gradual instruction for first communion approved for publication and use at the bishops' Low Week Meeting in 1911. This course was incorporated in all subsequent diocesan syllabuses for religious education (cf. Archdiocese of Liverpool, 1915, pp. 10–12). First communion was administered during Standard One (corresponding to today's Year Two – ages six to seven.) However, the course spanned six years from Infants (two years) through to Standard Four, and thus sought to fulfil *Quam Singulari*'s directives. Beginning with instructions on sin, conscience and sorrow in the first class of the infant school, the course set out to answer the requirement that first communicants should have a basic understanding of the mystery of salvation. The next aspects covered were the real presence and behaviour in church. During Standard One, attention was given to both 'Proximate Instruction' and 'Proximate Preparation' (Archdiocese of Liverpool, 1915, p. 11). The former included lessons on the Last Supper, the Consecration, the Real Presence and the eucharist as 'food of the soul' (ibid.). The latter dealt with the practical issues such as the requirement that communicants fast from midnight and how to receive communion. Considerable depth of doctrinal and theological instruction was reserved for Standards Two, Three and Four, that is, after the children had received their first communion (pp. 11–12).

---

19   Whiteside, loc. cit.
20   Bourne, loc. cit.
21   Whiteside, loc. cit.
22   Bourne, loc. cit.

Catechetical Works

The reduction of the age at which first communion was celebrated presented those responsible for preparing children for the celebration with the need to handle a significantly younger age group. The difficulties this created, and some of the solutions adopted, may be seen in a number of texts produced in 1911 in the wake of the decree. Significantly, Mary Loyola published a resource for teachers (Mary Loyola, 1911).[23] As this is the fullest and most closely argued of the 1911 texts studied, I will use it as the base text for this discussion.

The educational difficulties were starkly presented in the preface by Mary Loyola's editor Fr Thurston:

> For teachers, at least, if not for priests, the new legislation can hardly fail to add to their burdens and responsibilities … We cannot doubt that all the practical bearings of the case were fully weighed by the Holy Father and his advisors before the decree was promulgated. But it is not difficult to understand that many a teacher may be oppressed by a sense of dismay as she thinks of the difficulty of communicating to her little charges even such a simple desire of the Sacrament and such small measure of comprehension of its nature as the Holy Father requires by way of preparation. [pp. viii–ix]

Mary Loyola's response was framed within a continuing insistence on the life-course-determination discourse. She thus retained the earlier conviction that first communion was 'the most important religious event', the 'great epoch' in a child's life (p. 84). However, she now linked this discourse to her understanding of personal and educational development: the reduction in the age had placed the event at precisely the time at which a child's 'conscience is trained, its will braced, its principle of action formed' (ibid.). This is in contrast with the previous age, which stood on the threshold of what Mary Loyola described as the 'critical years from thirteen to sixteen, known to those of wide experience as the "criminal stages of a child's life"' (p. 172). The reform instituted by *Quam Singulari* now presented an unique opportunity to imprint a pattern of religious observance that would carry children through the 'battle with self' that lay ahead during those later critical years:

> Now is our chance with the children. Never again will we have a right to claim them so entirely for a course of instruction. Never again will their hearts be so fresh, so teachable, so eager. Oh, let us do all we can for them *now*. [p. 86; original emphasis]

As *Quam Singulari* had established a common age for admission to the eucharist and the onset of culpability, the event was now closely linked to a child's first confession, to which the first part of the book is dedicated. In contrast with the lengthy treatment given to the subject of sin and the examination of conscience in her earlier work, Mary Loyola now warned against 'the tendency to give an undue proportion of time to examination of conscience', suggesting that five minutes preparing for confession was adequate: 'What can we expect from poor little creatures whom we send into the confessional thoroughly tired out?' (p. 13). None the less, she insisted that teachers

---

23   Note, however, that the 1903 edition of her 1896 work was reissued without changes in 1911.

should do all they could to 'inspire the children with a fear and hatred of sin', and suggested that a graphic presentation of the sufferings of Christ as punishment for human sin should be used to instil a 'hatred and horror' for mortal sin (p. 21). However, unlike earlier first communion texts, there is no longer a sharp focus upon sexual sins. An anxiety remains around sins of the flesh, but that concern is now to prevent the teachers themselves introducing the concept to the children: 'Pass quickly over the sixth commandment,[24] taking care in what you say, and in the examination of conscience you may put into their hands do not bring anything before their minds suggestive of evil' (p. 17).

A similar discretion with regard to sexual sin is to be found in a first communion catechism published in 1911 by another established catechetical author. Henry Taylor Cafferata had earlier produced an explanation of the catechism for adult converts to Catholicism, and in 1911, he published two books for children, an explanation of the catechism (1911a) and a book for first communion (1911b). Whereas Mary Loyola's book was written for teachers, Cafferata addresses the child directly, and seeks to employ an appropriate vocabulary for 'child minds' (p. viii). Thus the issue of sin is framed in terms of 'naughtiness' – with the child told that it is urged on to sin by the 'naughty devil' (p. 9). Sexual sins find no mention, and instead Cafferata invites his readers to repent of stealing cakes and jam and of telling stories (p. 14). The concept of 'big sins' replaces the language of 'mortal sins', but the consequences remain grave: 'I must never go to Holy Communion with any very big sins on my soul. Dear Jesus would not love me and perhaps He would be very angry with me' (p. 15). Angry enough, perhaps, to bring the sinner to the point of death: 'Sometimes [God] lets people nearly die to make them see how wicked they have been, and when they are sorry for their sins and promise Him not to do any more, He lets Extreme Unction make them better' (p. 20). The vocabulary may have been simplified and the sixth commandment glossed over, but the concerns about sin and the desire to instil anxiety over it continued.

Beneath its simplified language, Cafferata's text is doctrinally dense.[25] By contrast, Mary Loyola insisted that only the very minimum of knowledge was required, stressing that its primary content should be a familiarization with the story of Jesus, and particularly of his infancy: 'Put before them now in very simple language the child life of Him who – a child like themselves – is coming to help them to be like Him' (p. 85). This focus upon the child Jesus spills over into the prayers that she suggests be said quietly by the children during the first communion Mass.[26] The teachers were to tell the children that after they have received communion they should think that Mary had laid the infant Jesus in their arms. Returning to their

---

24 Catholic numbering – 'Thou shalt not commit adultery'.

25 The range of material included is indicated by the chapter headings: God and the Soul, The Incarnation, Prayer, The Commandments, The Commandments of the Church and the Seven Sacraments.

26 Mary Loyola does not acknowledge the authorship of the texts she offers. The same complex of Christmas-themed verses was published in the following year in *Communion Verses for Little Children by a Sister of Notre Dame* 1912 (republished, still anonymously, 1959). The archivist of the Sisters of Notre Dame de Namur identified the author to me as Sr Cuthbert of St Joseph (born Rose Meeres, 1879–1962).

places, the children were to imagine themselves carrying this baby, whispering to him:

> Baby Jesus, wilt Thou lie
>> In my arms a little while?
> I will hold Thee tenderly,
>> Look at Thee, and Thou wilt smile. [p. 132]

Upon returning to their places, the children were to imagine themselves in the cave at Bethlehem, holding the child Jesus, and were to be taught to speak to him as though to a baby:

> O Babe Divine, O Babe Divine,
>> Just for a moment Thou art mine,
> And I can press thee to my heart,
>> All great and holy as Thou art.
>
> My Brother sweet, my Brother sweet,
>> I kiss thy tender little feet,
> And lay my face against thy Cheek
>> And am too happy quite to speak. [pp. 132–3]

Mary Loyola is thus mapping the child's reception of the eucharist onto the Christmas story. This permits her to weave in the discourse of Mary as protector of the eucharistic Christ – now presented as the mother of the infant Jesus. The Mary/infant–eucharistic–Jesus axis is found in a series of prayers for the new cohort of first communicants published in France in 1910 and in English translation the following year (de Gibergues, 1911). Before communion the children were to pray that Jesus would rest in their hearts as he did in Mary's arms, and after they had received they were to pray to 'Dear Little Jesus', 'How I would love to see You and hold You in my arms, as our Blessed Lady did. I have not that happiness: but I have another which is greater, that of having you in my heart' (p. 11). A similar marriage of the Christmas story and the concept of the infant eucharistic Jesus is found in Nist (1914), an American text also published in London. The consecrated host is 'the living Infant Jesus', the tabernacle in which the hosts are reserved is compared to the stable at Bethlehem, and the sanctuary lamp that indicates in Catholic churches the presence of the reserved sacrament is the Christmas star (pp. 2–3).

The image of the infant eucharistic Jesus predates the 1910 reform. In her analysis of souvenir images of first communion, Rosenbaum (1987) offers reproductions of several such images from late nineteenth-century France, in which an infant Christ is depicted either within the tabernacle or administering the sacred host. However, none of the catechetical texts I studied which were published in England before *Quam Singulari* drew on this image, still less constructed a mode of ritual participation around it. There is evidence of the prevalence of the image of the infant eucharist Jesus as late as 1924, when the hymns cited by Mary Loyola were set for a first communion celebration in Clapham (*Hymns and Benediction [...]*, 1924). However, after its initial appearance in the texts immediately following *Quam Singulari*, the infant eucharistic Jesus discourse disappears from the catechetical resources available for use in England, either home-grown (Hull, 1937) or republications of American originals (Kelly, 1925; Bolton, 1931).

Communion of Young Children: Lent and Easter 1911

The *Catholic Times* and to a considerably lesser extent the *Tablet* carried reports of first communion celebrations between 4 March (Second Sunday in Lent) and 23 April (Low Sunday) 1911. These accounts provide a snapshot of the ritual of first communion in parishes across the country. In some, for example, St Peter's, Seel St Liverpool[27] and Westminster Cathedral,[28] the unusually large cohort of first communicants was broken into smaller groups who made their first communion over a number of Sundays. Elsewhere the children all received their first communion together. The largest single group reported was at SS Peter and Paul's, Bolton, where 'close upon six hundred children' made their first communion during the nine o'clock Mass on Maundy Thursday morning.[29] Whiteside summarized the impact of the younger first communicants to the Liverpool clergy in November 1911, 'From every side there is the same consoling story of the wonderful reverence of the little ones of six and seven in making their First Communion.'[30] For a Catholic community that was occasionally, at least in Liverpool, literally embattled, the events of Lent-Eastertide 1911 would have been one of the strongest possible visual statements of its hope for future survival. A sense of gratitude to Pius X emerges in the course of the press accounts in Liverpool, and at least one parish priest telegrammed his gratitude (and that of '400 little country school children') for the decree.[31]

The First Communion Mass

Compared to many modern first communion Masses, those of 1911 would have appeared surprisingly simple. For example, although the Mass described in Westminster Cathedral was celebrated by the auxiliary bishop, it was without singing. The dramatization of the moment of reception offered one of the few possibilities for adaptive ritual within the Mass itself; the liturgy generally conformed to the Roman Missal. Only five of the accounts offer details of arrangements for the actual reception of communion. In Westminster Cathedral communion was administered to the children at the altar rails in front of the High Altar, whilst adult communicants presented themselves at the Chapel of the Blessed Sacrament, to the left of the sanctuary. In St John the Evangelist in Norwich[32] the opposite arrangement was

27   *The Catholic Times*, Liverpool edition, New Series no. 2,274, 10 March 1911, p. 5.

28   *The Tablet*, Supplement to vol. 117, no. 3,698, 11 March 1911, p. 392.

29   *The Catholic Times*, Manchester edition, New Series no 2,280, 21 April 1911, p. 5.

30   *Synodus Diocesana Liverpolitana Duodevicesima. Anno 1911*, p. 8. Full bibliographical details for the Liverpool synods are given in the Bibliography, Section B.

31   The priest was Thomas Carr, parish priest in Formby, who also occupied the senior post of Vicar General in the diocese. *The Catholic Times*, Liverpool edition, New Series no. 2,279, 14 April 1911, p. 5.

32   *The Tablet*, Supplement to vol. 117, no. 3,697, 18 March 1911, p. 435.

adopted. The children, whose number is not stated, were seated within the transepts of the church. Temporary altar rails were placed across the entrance to the transept chapels, and the children received there. Meanwhile, all others received as usual at the main altar rails. These two procedures are adaptations of normal practice. In two other places a more elaborate ritual of reception was developed, which individuated the child to a far greater degree and heightened the experience. The simpler took place at the Servite Church on the Fulham Road, London. Here, two prie-dieus had been placed within the sanctuary, to which the children were led two at a time by their teachers to receive communion.[33] A more elaborate variant was found at the German Church in Whitechapel, London:

> 123 children made their First Communion last Sunday ... The scene as they approached the special prie-dieu within the sanctuary was most touching. They proceeded four at a time, and were reverently escorted by two little girls in white bearing lighted candles. Besides these there were several other very young girls in the sanctuary, similarly attired, holding white lilies in their hands.[34]

The fifth account highlights not so much a ritual action as an admonition. At the Franciscan Church in Peckham, immediately before the reception of communion, one of the priests (Fr Rudolph) reminded the children 'of the importance of the act they were about to perform'.[35]

However, whilst the rubrics governing the Mass itself offered relatively few possibilities for creative ritual adaptation, once the Mass had, strictly speaking, come to an end, rituals specific to the event and its participants could be introduced. Three such additional rituals are reported in the newspaper accounts. The simplest was at St Charles' Church in Aigburth, Liverpool, where at the conclusion of Mass the children and congregation joined in the singing of 'God Bless our Pope'.[36] After Mass in Peckham, a sermon on 'The Joys of a First Communion Day' was preached by a different priest (Fr Pacificus, who had given the children a week's retreat before the event), and the first communicants renewed their baptismal promises. The most complex series of morning rituals was in the parish in Bow Common, London. Here, as it was St Patrick's Day, the first communion Mass was also associated with the blessing and distribution of shamrock. After Mass the children ate breakfast in the convent. They then returned to the church and participated in a complex of rituals:

> ... the First Communicants will return to the Church to be enrolled in the scapulars and to receive each a rosary and a memorial card of First Communion. They will be consecrated to Our Lady and will take the total abstinence pledge against all intoxicating drink until they reach the age of twenty-one.[37]

---

33 *The Catholic Times*, London edition, New Series no. 2,277, 31 March 1911, p. 5.

34 *The Catholic Times*, London edition, New Series no. 2,281, 24 April 1911, p. 5.

35 *The Catholic Times*, London edition, New Series no. 2,277, 31 March 1911, p. 5.

36 *The Catholic Times*, Liverpool edition, New Series no. 2,275, 17 March 1911, p. 5.

37 *The Catholic Times*, London edition, New Series no. 2,274, 10 March 1911, p. 5. I have found no reference other than at Bow Common to first communicants taking the pledge against liquor.

Afternoon and Evening Services

If the strict observance of the rubrics of the Roman Missal proscribed major adaptation of the first communion Mass itself, far greater scope was offered by the non-eucharistic services that were commonly held throughout the year in the afternoon or evenings of Sundays and feast days. These were normally the locus for popular devotions such as the Rosary, Benediction and processions within the body of the church. They were also the occasion for the use of vernacular hymnody. The 1911 accounts testify to the possibility for including the first communicants in these ceremonies, in such a way that the first communion event was extended across the entire day.

Four afternoon services are described in detail. One of these differs markedly from the others in that it involved the bishop. I will first discuss the other three together as they have certain features in common. Each of this group incorporates the renewal of baptismal promises. This was combined with a sermon at Norwich, and also at West Battersea.[38] In two cases the service also included some form of dedication to Mary: in the Servite Church this was specifically to Mary as 'The Mother of Sorrows', whilst in Norwich one of the first communicants read in the name of all 'an Act of Consecration to the Holy Mother of God'.

The fourth case is St Joseph's Home at Patricroft, Manchester.[39] Sixty children received their first communion on the Sunday morning. Then in the afternoon the Bishop of Salford arrived to administer the sacrament of confirmation to ninety children and five adults. It is not impossible that the first communicants would have been included among the confirmation candidates: a parallel is found in the account of the Whitechapel event, which notes that of the 123 first communicants, 'nearly all had received confirmation at the hands of the Archbishop when he had made his visitation a short time ago.' Furthermore, in Our Lady of the Holy Souls in Kensall, all the 365 children who received their first communion on 2 April 1911 had been confirmed four days previously by the auxiliary Bishop of Westminster.[40]

Eight of the newspaper accounts speak about a service held in the evening of the first communion day. Each service took the form of a Blessed Sacrament procession within the church. No details of the ritual are given in three cases (St Peter's, Seel St Liverpool, St Casimir's, Manchester[41] and Holy Name, Manchester[42]). The account given for SS Peter and Paul, Bolton is useful on two counts. It clarifies that the procession was conducted 'round the aisles of the church', that is, indoors, and it mentions the dress of the first communicants, which will be discussed below. Mention is made of the sermon preached at the evening service in three other churches. At St Benedict's in Hindley, Lancashire 'Fr. Caffrey preached an appropriate sermon

---

38   *The Catholic Times*, London edition, New Series no. 2,277, 31 March 1911, p. 5.

39   *The Catholic Times*, Manchester edition, New Series no. 2,276, 24 March 1911, p. 5.

40   *The Catholic Times*, London edition, New Series no. 2,278, 7 April 1911, p. 5.

41   *The Catholic Times*, Manchester edition, New Series no. 2,274, 10 March 1911, p. 5.

42   *The Catholic Times*, Manchester edition, New Series no. 2,278, 7 April 1911, p. 5.

to the children and their parents.'[43] More detail is offered for Forest Gate, London. Here, in a church 'filled to its utmost capacity' the Franciscan Fr Egbert took as his text the words, 'Suffer little children to come unto me, and forbid them not, for of such is the Kingdom of Heaven.'[44] At Holy Cross, Liverpool, again before a large congregation, Fr Leech, Oblate of Mary Immaculate, preached on 'The Church and the Child'.[45] The evening service here also included solemn Benediction, at which Fr Leech was assisted by two other priests of his order who took the roles of deacon and sub-deacon. Finally, the description of the evening service at St George's Cathedral, Southwark suggests an event at which all significant bodies within the parish were at least represented:

> In the evening there was a procession of the Blessed Sacrament. Representatives of the various confraternities in connexion with the mission took part, and the men of the Blessed Sacrament Guild in large numbers were present in their distinctive robes of office. The children who had made their First Communion earlier in the day also took part in the procession.[46]

Involvement of Parish School and Convent

As we have seen from the Servite Church, the children's teachers sometimes played a significant role in the first communion ceremony. Several other accounts draw attention to this role. The Westminster Cathedral account speaks of the teachers 'shepherding' the children. At Holy Cross Liverpool, the Superior of the parish thanked the teachers for their 'interest in the matter of costuming the little ones'. The accounts for West Battersea and Forest Gate name the various teachers who had charge of the children for the morning Mass and the evening Blessed Sacrament Procession. Among those named is a religious sister. As has already been noted from the Bow Common account, the convent, too, could play its part in the first communion event. The strongest example of this is Streatham in South London. On Low Sunday twenty-four children made their first communion not in the church but in the convent chapel. They then remained at the convent for the rest of that day.[47]

The First Communion Breakfast

The newspaper accounts give the times for fourteen of the first communion Masses they report. All begin between 8.00 am and 9.30 am, with 9.00 the most common:

43 *The Catholic Times*, Liverpool edition, New Series no. 2,280, 21 April 1911, p. 5.
44 *The Catholic Times*, London edition, New Series no. 2,274, 10 March 1911, p. 5.
45 *The Catholic Times*, Liverpool edition, New Series no. 2,277, 31 March 1911, p. 5.
46 *The Tablet,* Supplement to vol. 117, no. 3,698, 11 March 1911, p. 395.
47 *The Catholic Times*, London edition, New Series no. 2,281, 28 April 1911, p. 5.

8.00   Storrington, Kensall
8.15   Loreto Convent, Manchester[48]
8.30   St Werburgh's Birkenhead;[49] St Mary's East Finchley[50]
9.00   St Peter's, Seel St Liverpool; Corpus Christi, Manchester;[51] Bow Common; the
         Servite Church on Fulham Rd; Our Lady's, Birkenhead;[52] Holy Cross Liverpool
9.15   West Battersea
9.30   St Charles', Aigburth Liverpool; Holy Name, Manchester; SS Peter and Paul,
         Clerkenwell[53]

This early start contrasts with today's first communion Masses, which are normally held in the late morning. There is, however, a logical explanation for the 1911 timing: the children, like all communicants, would have been required to fast from midnight. This explains not only the early start, but also why the accompanying celebratory meal was a shared breakfast. Thirteen of the newspaper accounts mention this breakfast. At seven locations, the parish priest acted as host – albeit usually in a schoolroom: St Peter's, Seel St Liverpool; St Charles, Aigburth, Liverpool; SS Peter and Paul, Clerkenwell; St Mary's, East Finchley; Our Lady's, Birkenhead; Custom House East, London,[54] and Our Lady of the Holy Souls, Kensall. The Westminster Cathedral account names Lady Edmund Taylor as the host for breakfast in the school rooms at Great Peter Street. The children at SS Peter and Paul in Bolton took their breakfast in the 'Assembly Hall'. At Corpus Christi, Manchester and West Battersea the school is given as the location for the breakfast. No location was reported for the Servite Church and Holy Name, Manchester. The children at the Servite Church not only received breakfast together, but were also provided with tea following the afternoon service.

Dress

Four of the accounts specifically mention the dress of the first communicants. One of these, at Holy Cross, Liverpool, refers to the teachers 'costuming' the children. The other three give some details as to what is worn. As this has become a major focus in our own time, it is worth stating them in full:

> *Peckham*: 'Both boys and girls looked very neat, the former wearing white silk sashes and the latter white dresses and veils.'

---

48   *The Catholic Times*, Manchester edition, New Series no. 2,275, 17 March 1911, p. 5.

49   *The Catholic Times*, Liverpool edition, New Series no. 2,279, 14 April 1911, p. 5.

50   *The Catholic Times*, London edition, New Series no. 2,280, 21 April 1911, p. 5.

51   *The Catholic Times*, Manchester edition, New Series no. 2,274, 10 March 1911, p. 5.

52   *The Catholic Times*, Liverpool edition, New Series no. 2,279, 14 April 1911, p. 5.

53   *The Catholic Times*, London edition, New Series no. 2,278, 7 April 1911, p. 5.

54   *The Catholic Times*, London edition, New Series no. 2,277, 31 March 1911, p. 5.

SS Peter and Paul, Bolton: 'On Sunday evening the first Communicants, the girls in white and the boys wearing red sashes, took part in an imposing procession of the Blessed Sacrament round the aisles of the church.'

Whitechapel, German Church: 'The boys were all in black suits, whilst the girls wore white with wreaths and veils.'

The more elaborate dress worn at the Whitechapel church raises the question whether a particular German custom is being followed here. However, the same wreaths and veils are encountered in the description of the confirmation service at St Joseph's Home, Patricoft.

Gifts and Souvenirs

Three of the accounts mention the children being presented with souvenirs of the day. At Custom House East and West Battersea this gift-giving appears to have been associated with the breakfast, whilst at the Servite Church it is connected to the afternoon tea party. The form the souvenir took is not specified for Custom House East, but for the other two more details are given: at West Battersea, 'a valuable souvenir of the day in the shape of a Prayer Book and certificate', at the Servite Church, 'a prayer-book and mounted picture as mementos, besides the certificate'. In Battersea the souvenirs were the gift of the Superior of the parish, Fr Macey, SC. At the Servite Church they were given through the 'kindness of parishioners and friends'.

Conclusions on the 1911 Celebrations

The newspaper reports present a complex picture of the first celebrations of first communion in England and Wales in accordance with *Quam Singulari*. In many places the event extended across the whole day through a possible combination of three further rituals: in the late morning, afternoon and evening. The most common elements in the two earlier additional rituals are the renewal of baptismal promises and an act of dedication to the Virgin Mary. All the evening celebrations have at their heart a procession within the church, which may be associated with a sermon and Benediction of the Blessed Sacrament. A further frequently recurring motif is the participation of the children in a breakfast-party immediately after the first communion Mass. All this poses the question: was all this new to 1911, or was an existing practice now being applied to the new situation? The only direct mention of continuity is found in the description of the event at St Alban's, Manchester, which speaks of the children being 'entertained in the customary manner' after the Mass.[55] It seems unlikely that the ritual complex could have sprung up spontaneously in so many different locations.

---

55 *The Catholic Times*, Manchester edition, New Series no. 2,276, 24 March 1911, p. 5.

Conclusion: Whiteside's Evaluation of the Implementation of *Quam Singulari* in Liverpool

It is useful at this stage to gauge a contemporary evaluation of the immediate impact of the implementation of the reform. In Liverpool the requirements of *Quam Singulari* were rapidly and, from Whiteside's viewpoint, successfully implemented. On 25 October 1911 he addressed the Liverpool diocesan synod, commending the willingness with which the clergy had carried out the decree:

> His Lordship remarked that one of the most striking events in the history of the Church in these times has been the re-organization of the Sacred Congregations which assist the Supreme Pontiff in his office of teaching and ruling the Church, and next the revision and codification of the laws of the Church. He was gratified at the loyal obedience shown by the clergy of the diocese to the laws already published; and in consequence they had the satisfaction of seeing before their eyes the consoling fruit of that obedience. The decrees about the Instruction of the Faithful, Frequent Communion, and the First Communion of children were instanced.[56]

Whiteside here draws a link, as both he and Bourne had already done in their 1911 Lenten Pastoral Letters, between the impact of two key liturgical changes introduced under Pius X: the invitation to frequent reception of communion (1905) and the reduction in the age of admission to the eucharist. By comparing the number of communicants declared in parish annual returns over a number of years he sought to assess the combined impact of these decrees in terms of a numerical measure of success:

> As a result of the first decree, the number of Communions has risen by leaps and bounds, from about 1,900,000 made annually four years ago, to over 4,000,000 made during the past year. In consequence of the second decree, in the year following its promulgation the Easter Communions in the Diocese rose from about 198,000 to about 221,000, an increase of 23,000 in one year, due in the main to the number of little children who for the first time fulfilled the Easter precepts. Not only do the children approach the Holy Table in large numbers, but from all sides there comes the same gratifying account of their wonderful faith, and of the recollection almost beyond their years with which the little ones receive Our Lord. The silent work that is now going on in the souls of all, both young and old, through early and frequent Communion is a great consolation to pastors of souls, and inspires great hopes for the future.[57]

In a footnote, Whiteside lists the year-on-year increases of communions received across the diocese for the years 1907–12. According to his calculations, the number of communions rose from 1,955,012 in 1907 to 4,353,997 in 1912. 1911 had the peak increase of 691,440, with the increase falling back to 286,714 in 1912.

In a 1914 Pastoral Letter, Whiteside declared his belief that an overall increase was largely due to the admission of the younger children to communion:

---

56 *Synodus Diocesana Liverpolitana Duodevicesima. Anno 1911*, p. 6.
57 Whiteside CLXXV, pp. 1–2.

… we cannot resist the conclusion that what in all missions mainly decides the number of Communions made, is the regular frequent reception of Holy Communion by the school children. The fact is now admitted that, whilst a certain number of those whose school days are over, varying according to circumstances, can be, and are being, induced to take up the practice of frequent Communion, these, after all, form only a small minority. Manual work, both among men and women, or domestic duties, prevent the large majority of them from receiving Holy Communion more than once a week. An increasing number of these are making the Sunday Communion the ideal to which they aspire. But whilst this is true, it is nevertheless equally true that with the exception of a small number of the scholars, the school children of the Diocese, numbering some 50,000 who have made their first Communion, are still in the matter of frequent Communion a vast field white for the harvest.[58]

To contemporaries, then, it must have appeared that the hopes expressed by Hughes in his 1910 editorial were being fulfilled. However, the late twentieth-century comment paired with Hughes at the head of the Introduction invites the question whether such hopes have proved in the long term to be delusory. A response to that question cannot be framed in terms of the first communion ritual considered in isolation; *Quam Singulari* was just one element within a reform project carried out in the Catholic Church during the first decade of the twentieth century. We must now set the reform of first communion in its broader context, within which the question of the success or otherwise of *Quam Singulari* can then be reframed. Chapter 4, therefore, identifies the core elements of the reform, explores the role of *Quam Singulari* within the reform, and asks whether what has failed is not so much the first communion ritual but the attempt of the reform package as a whole to reinforce the Catholic community.

---

58 Whiteside CLXXVII, p. 5.

The Shifting Social and Religious Context for the Celebration of First Communion across the Twentieth Century

Introduction

In order to understand the various expectations and anxieties that feed into today's conflict around first communion it is essential to place the reform and implementation of *Quam Singulari* into its broader context. The 1910 reform of first communion was not an isolated piece of Church legislation. Rather, it formed part of a concerted Vatican-driven reform process that sought to define and regulate acceptable parameters of intellectual expression, personal relationships and ritual practice within the Catholic Church. This programme to mould clergy and laity alike into fixed patterns of life and thought solidified the construct of the Church at local level. In Liverpool the effect was the reinforcement of the parish along the lines described by Hornsby-Smith (1989, p. 26) as a 'fortress' – by which he means an all-embracing organization within which all the religious, educational and social life of its members could be carried out in the midst of a generally hostile external world. The same fortress-like structure that defended the Catholic community from external attack also served to observe, contain and control those within, as the reform effectively sought to limit personal freedom by defining what was 'acceptable' in the fields of intellectual assent, personal relationships and religious practice. The norms that this reform package established for personal praxis and for the parameters of Catholic identity continue to influence the expectations of many within the Church today, and feed into the current conflict over first communion.

At the same time, the expectations around first communion today are not simply the result of developments internal to the Catholic community. This is especially the case of Liverpool, in which the long term socio-economic factors also played a significant role in moulding the Catholic community and helped to develop a distinctive Catholic identity in the city. These factors also need to be taken into consideration if the issues currently at play around first communion in the city are to be fully understood. Therefore, after discussing the ecclesial reforms, this chapter will go on to examine the socio-ethnic environment within which the reform was implemented in Liverpool. What emerges from this discussion is a close interplay between the ecclesial reforms and the social realities within which Catholics lived their lives. The concerted attempt at the start of the twentieth century on the part of Church authorities to mould the lives of Catholics could be effective only so far as they engaged with the reality of people's life experiences within their social environment. The more the outer world was experienced as hostile, the more willing would people be to collaborate with the entire project. I shall argue that in the particular case of the city of Liverpool, the Catholic community had good reason to regard the world outside its parishes as hostile. Therefore, ecclesial hegemony over the intellectual, socio-relational and devotional life of its members was not simply imposed from above; it was achieved because many of the members themselves in effect collaborated in processes that considerably limited their freedom. Those who conspicuously failed to collaborate, most notably through disregard of the strict regulation of marriage, found that they had effectively excommunicated themselves. Around the time of *Quam Singulari* such people formed a not insubstantial group of alienated Catholics in the diocese of Liverpool.

Within this socio-historic perspective we can also glimpse the warning signs of the future decay of the construct of the Catholic community presumed within *Quam Singulari*. During the course of the twentieth century the social, economic and geographic divisions between Catholics and non-Catholics within the city were gradually broken down, the practices and regulations that bounded the Catholic community and rendered it distinct came to be regarded by the majority of Catholics as of diminishing relevance. Yet, despite these drastic changes in the Catholic community, the descendents of the first generation to be affected by *Quam Singulari* none the less continue to request the first communion of their children.

The Programme of Ecclesiastical Reform

Giuseppe Melchiore Sarto (1835–1914) became pope in 1903, taking the name of Pius X. This controversial pope has excited a broad spectrum of opinion within Catholicism – as evidenced in the biographies written about him. These range from the hagiographical (Bazin, 1928; Burton, 1950; Giordani, 1952; Dal-Gal, 1954) to the hostile (Falconi, 1967). More recent discussions of his pontificate take a more nuanced approach, whilst offering a generally negative critique. (Aubert, 1981; Launay, 1997; Chadwick, 1998; Chiron, 1999). From the onset of his pontificate he pursued a systematic programme of reform; he defined this in his first encyclical letter to the bishops of the Church as aiming to 'restore all things in Christ' (*E Supremi*, 30, 4 October 1903).[1] During the pontificate a series of regulations were set in place to fulfil his aims regarding the renewal of worship, discipline of the clergy, and marriage. The liturgical renewal was wide-ranging, touching on church music, the daily office and, most importantly, the promotion of frequent – even daily – communion. From a liturgical viewpoint, the reduction in the age at which communicating began was and remains most closely associated with the question of frequent communion (Chadwick, 1998). Indeed, contemporary commentators understood the early start of communicating as a means of establishing children in the new discipline of regular communication (cf. Hughes' editorial in the *Catholic Times*,[2] Whiteside's Lenten Pastoral,[3] and de Zulueta, 1920). However, whilst not negating the liturgical

---

1   AAS 36, 1903, pp. 129–39.
2   *The Catholic Times*, no. 2,246, 26 August 1910, London edition, p. 10.
3   *The Tablet*, vol. 111, no. 3,340, 14 March 1908, pp. 422–3.

association, I wish to view the implementation of *Quam Singulari* in Liverpool in the light of the other reforms that established the first patterns of intellectual and clerical discipline, and the parameters for and expectations of family life. These characterize the ecclesial structure that *Quam Singulari* simultaneously crowned and projected into the future. These two areas, therefore, will be considered in turn, with detailed consideration given to the manner of their implementation in Liverpool.

Intellectual and Clerical Discipline: Anti-Modernism

Pius X singled out the issue of clergy formation and discipline as of particular importance if the renewal programme was to succeed (*E Supremi*, 11). Behind this lay his concern at recent theological developments within the Catholic arena that were to be gathered under the title of Modernism. This word was a blanket term for various intellectual attempts to apply modern analytical approaches to Catholic teaching on such matters as scripture and dogma. Leading figures included the priests Alfred Loisy (1857–1940) in France and George Tyrrell (1861–1909) in England, both of whom were excommunicated in the wake of Pius X's reforms. A leading layman active in England, who avoided excommunication, was Baron Friedrich von Hügel (Ranchetti, 1969; Reardon, 1970; Barmann, 1972; Leonard, 1982; Sagovsky, 1990). Pius believed that he recognized in the work of these authors an distinct school of thought, whose primary characteristics he detailed in his encyclical letter *Pascendi Dominici Gregis* (8 September 1907).[4] To regard this group of very disparate intellectuals as forming in any way a school was stretching the point, as there was never any attempt by Modernist authors to present their work in a systematic synthetic manner. The pope thus left himself open to the accusation that he had created a fantastic caricature of something that did not exist – indeed, that he had 'invented' Modernism (Falconi, 1967, p. 58). Be that as it may, Pius described Modernism as he understood it as 'the synthesis of all heresies', aiming at 'the destruction not of the Catholic Religion alone, but of all religion' (*Pascendi*, 39). My concern here is not to enter into the theological issues around Modernism, but merely to indicate the Vatican's response to this perceived threat, and to consider how the directives were implemented in Liverpool.

Pius X's response is mapped through three Vatican documents. The first of these was the decree of the Holy Office *Lamentabili Sane* (3 July 1907).[5] This decree took the form of a Syllabus of sixty-five propositions that were condemned and proscribed. The name 'Modernism' was not used within the document, but its perceived tenets are clearly the document's target (cf. Aubert, 1981). A more detailed treatment of the same theme occurred a year later with the already mentioned encyclical letter *Pascendi*. Finally, on 1 September 1910 the formal instruction (or *motu proprio*) *Sacrorum Antistitum* was issued.[6] The cumulative effect of these documents was

---

4   ASS 40 (1907), pp. 596ff. English Translation from <http://www.vatican.va/holy_father/pius_x/encyclicals/documents/hf_p-x_enc_19070908_pascendi-dominici-gregis_en.html>.

5   ASS 40 (1907), pp. 470ff.

6   AAS 2 (1910), pp. 655–670.

three-fold: the institution of an integrated system of observation by which the belief system of every present and prospective member of the clergy could be observed, the establishment of a system of censorship that would uncover intellectual dissent and prevent the further propagation of views held to be erroneous, and the imposition of a formal oath which simultaneously bound the individual to the belief system of the central organization and smoked out dissenters.

Observation

The final paragraphs of *Pascendi Dominici Gregis* lay down a series of disciplinary measures through which Pius X intended to drive out Modernism from the Church by establishing a supervisory regime over the clergy and the Catholic press. Those responsible for Catholic education, whether in the university or in the seminary, were placed under particular scrutiny, and any teachers who were thought to be even secretly sympathetic towards Modernism were to be removed from their posts (§48). This discipline was to be reinforced by insisting that all teaching of priests and clerics, as far as possible, should take place within Catholic Institutes rather than civil universities (§49). Within the Catholic sector, scholastic philosophy was to form the foundation of all theology (§45). Indeed, criticism of scholasticism was to be regarded as covert Modernism, leading to exclusion from teaching posts (§48). A further aspect of observation was to ensure that the clergy gathered in large numbers only on rare occasions, and then subject to strict control (§54). Thus, the opportunity for developing and disseminating non-acceptable views was curtailed, and any priests who sought to do so would become more easily visible.

    Pascendi also established the means by which discipline was to be enforced at diocesan level through a comprehensive system of observation. In each diocese a Council of Vigilance, made up of carefully selected priests, was to meet in secret in the presence of the bishop every two months. They were to 'watch most carefully for every trace and sign of Modernism both in publications and in teaching, and, to preserve from it the clergy and young, they shall take all prudent, prompt and efficacious measures' (§55). These Councils of Vigilance were also to have regard to the Church's social institutions, lest they harbour any trace of Modernism.

Censorship

In addition to the Council for Vigilance, each bishop was to appoint censors in his diocese for the revision of works intended for publication. The name of the censor was always to be withheld from the author until a favourable opinion had been given and the bishop had granted his 'Imprimatur' (§52). If, on the other hand, the judgement were unfavourable, the author would be advised of the decision but would never learn the identity of his or her censor. Through use of this system, bishops were instructed to 'do everything in your power to drive out from your Diocese, even by solemn interdict, any pernicious books that may be in circulation there' (§51). They were even to keep watch on each other – the fact that a book had received an imprimatur in one diocese did not automatically exempt it from the scrutiny of the censor in another diocese. Furthermore, the bishops were warned that the pope was laying on them a serious charge: 'Let no Bishop think that he fulfils this duty by denouncing to Us one or two books, while a great many others of the same kind are being published and circulated' (§51). Thus the bishops themselves were subject to observation; they were required to submit an initial report on their implementation of the letter by September 1910, and thence every third year to provide a progress report (§56).

The Anti-Modernist Oath

The 1910 formal instruction *Sacrorum Antistitum* aimed to root out once and for all any clandestine Modernist societies within the Church. All clergy about to be ordained into the major orders, priests hearing confessions or preaching, parish priests upon taking possession of their parish, canons, diocesan and Vatican officials, and superiors of religious congregations were required to make a formal declaration of faith. This declaration specifically required an adherence to the Papacy's anti-modernist line:

> I also submit myself with due respect and I adhere wholeheartedly to all condemnations, declarations, and prescripts contained in the encyclical *Pascendi* and in the decree *Lamentabili*, particularly those referring to the so-called history of dogma' [AAS 2, 1910, pp. 669ff; English translation from Neuner and Dupuis, 1978, pp. 51–4].

It is with the oath that the disciplinary reforms impacted most directly upon the lives of ordinary parish clergy and demanded of each of them a solemn declaration of complete submission of intellect and will. Taken as a whole, subsequent evaluations of the anti-Modernist reform range from the enthusiastic claim of Dal-Gal (1954) that its publication on 8 September 'was a memorable day for Christendom, and equal in importance to September 9th, 325, the day on which the Council of Nicea dealt the death blow to Arianism' (p. 155) to the lament by Falconi (1967) that in effectively re-establishing the Inquisition, the Church under Pius X was 'devouring its own children' (p. 35). A more moderated analysis is offered by Aubert (1981), Launay (1997) and Chadwick (1998), all of whom outline its negative effect upon Catholic learning (particularly biblical scholarship) and the widening gap between the Church and modern culture. What is certain is that the Vatican's moves against Modernism induced an atmosphere of suspicion and of fear across the Catholic world, negotiated by the overwhelming majority of clerics through radical conformism. *Quam Singulari* was launched in this context: Whiteside's letters directing his clergy to implement the decree and to submit to the anti-Modernist oath were separated by only two weeks.[7] The admission of small children to the eucharist, therefore, was carried out in an atmosphere of heightened clerical discipline. Hence Whiteside's later approving comments on the 'loyal obedience' shown by the Liverpool clergy to the published laws of the Church.[8]

---

7   The letter relating to first communion is the earlier. Cf. Whiteside CLIX.

8   *Synodus Dioecesana Liverpolitana Duodevicesima. Anno 1911*; *Synodus Diocesana Liverpolitana Undevicesima. Anno 1914*.

Lay Discipline: Regulation of Marriage

Whilst the anti-Modernist reforms had a direct impact on the clergy rather than on the laity, the piece of Pian legislation that impacted most immediately on the daily lives of the laity was the 1907 decree *Ne Temere* (DS 3468–74). It was also the issue that provoked the greatest volume of correspondence in the Catholic press.

The promulgation of *Ne Temere* was an early implementation of one element of a far larger project, the codification of Canon Law. This project, completed in 1918, imposed for the first time a unified body of law throughout the Church and carried sweeping changes in its wake by regularizing anomalous situations in various geographical territories. In England, the two major changes were the formal creation of parishes and the reform of Catholic marriage law – both of which strengthened the structure of the local parish as an effective base for local ecclesial power. The extension of Canon Law down to the level of parish reform clarified and strengthened the canonical powers of the parish priest, not least by giving him right of tenure. The marriage reform tightened the Church's control over the family lives of its lay members and reinforced the boundaries of the Catholic community by defining them within the domestic setting. The desired fruit of this was a strengthening of the Church's control over the religious affiliation and formation of succeeding generations.

Ne Temere

Ne Temere revisited a long-running ecclesial concern to prevent clandestine marriages, by rendering as visible as possible any celebration of marriage and the true circumstances of those who presented themselves for it.[9] A key feature of the new legislation was the requirement of a carefully regulated transfer between parishes of information on the spouses both before and after a wedding; specifically, between the parishes of baptism and marriage. The exchange of such information permitted the cross-referencing of personal details within the registers of different parishes and rendered an individual's life-course more easily visible to the Church. An insistence that marriage should normally take place before the parish priest of the bride served as a further guard against any deceit: the bride was to be married where she and her family were known and before the clergy who were familiar with them.

The implementation of *Ne Temere* had a particularly marked impact in England, as until its promulgation the Catholic Church there had enjoyed only limited power to regulate the marriages of its members. The Council of Trent had sought absolute control over all marriages involving Catholics in its decree *Tametsi* (1563) (Schroeder, 1941, pp. 183–90; Sheehey et al., 1983, p. 622). However, that Tridentine decree was only formally promulgated in territories that had a Catholic government – effectively a recognition that in non-Catholic countries the minority Catholic community was not *de facto* in complete control of the regulation of marriage. Consequently, no

---

9   Cf. Lateran IV, Canon 51 (DS 817); Council of Trent, decree *Tametsi* (DS 1813. English translation in Schroeder, 1941).

such promulgation took place in England and Wales, nor in Scotland (Harty, 1908, p. 383). Therefore throughout Great Britain Catholics had continued to validly contract marriage without the involvement of a priest or any other member of the Catholic community. Indeed, between 1753 and 1836, English Catholics were required by civil law to be married in a parish church before a minister of the Church of England (Burton, 1909, vol. i, pp. 325–45; Leys, 1961, pp. 26–8). Even after the English 1836 Marriage Act removed this requirement, the continuing non-promulgation of the Tridentine Law there meant that the Church still recognized as valid, though illicit, any marriages made by Catholics outside the Catholic Church.

The enactment of *Ne Temere* in Easter 1908 brought about a radical reinforcement of the power of the Catholic Church in Britain over its members. This power extended beyond the parties in a marriage: it also offered an opening into the next generation. The significance of the power to control marriage lies not simply in the power it extends over the direct participants. Put simply, the constant expectation within the Catholic community is that Catholics beget other Catholics. Especially since 1850, that community in England has tended to suppose that it reproduces itself biologically across the generations rather than through evangelistic outreach. However, if two Catholics married outside the formal structure of the Church, there would be no guarantee that their children would be Catholics themselves. The Catholicism of the next generation was likely to be even more compromised in those cases where a Catholic married a non-Catholic – particularly as there appears to have been a general custom of boys following the religious affiliation of the father and girls of the mother (Ward, 1915, vol. i, p. 193). After the promulgation of *Ne Temere* all of that was expected to end. Thereafter, only those children of Catholics born of recognized unions would be recognized as legitimate by the Church. Moreover, as only mixed marriages carried out before the Catholic priest would be considered valid by the community, then the Church believed that it would be in a far stronger position to insist that all children born of a Catholic should themselves become Catholic.

Yet the question as to the effectiveness of this reform must be asked. Data collated in the household of the Bishop of Liverpool for the years 1903–1912 demonstrate that approximately one Catholic in five contracted a mixed marriage during that period The overwhelming majority of these took place outside the Catholic Church: that is, over 16 per cent of all marriages involving Catholics. In other words, 1 in 6 of all Catholic marriages in the diocese of Liverpool were thus regarded by the Church as not simply illicit but also invalid – 'no marriage at all'. The effect of this was to solidify the walls of the fortress parish, and the large numbers of Catholics who married outside the Church after Easter 1908 now found that their Church not only denied them its sacraments but also regarded them as living in concubinage. Success – if success it was – in maintaining the boundaries of the Catholic community by controlling the marriages of its members was achieved only at the cost of alienating large numbers of them. The visible endogamy within the 'fortress' parish noted by Hornsby-Smith (1987, pp. 90–94) masked a sizeable exogamonic exodus from the Church.

But what happens to the power to control if people choose not to marry at all? As the Church's legislation becomes increasingly marginal to the real experiences and life-choices of its members, then its power to mould those choices and offer an absolutely authoritative interpretative key to that experience effectively slips away. However, the fortress still has its guardians, and as my fieldwork revealed, discourses over marriage still play a role in manning the residual defences.

The Reforms of Pius X and the Fortress Parish

Simply by exercising their functions within the parish setting, priests were acting as subjects of the power of the Church, and served in turn as its enforcers. This was the case through their administration of the sacraments, in their celebration of the liturgy, and even in their encounters with parishioners in their own homes through the regular pattern of 'outdoor collecting'. (This was the practice, still extant in places until the 1960s, by which the priests visited every home in a parish several times each year. The ostensible purpose was to collect money over and above that given in church collections, but it also of course provided opportunities for both pastoral care and policing of the Catholic community (see Ward, 1965, p. 46).) The same would have been true in different ways of others who occupied positions of authority within the parish community – not least parish religious and teachers. Within the 'fortress' parish there was no relationship between persons, no significant encounter or activity that might not potentially act as a function of the Church's power discourses. This was thanks to the degree to which personal and Catholic identities were so closely melded, and especially because of the extension of the Church's discourses into marriage and family life. It was effectively a 'disciplinary society' in the sense defined by Foucault:

> Not because the disciplinary modality of power has replaced all the others; but because it has infiltrated the others, sometimes undermining them, but serving as an intermediary between them, linking them together, extending them and above all making it possible to bring the effects of power to the most minute and distant elements. It ensures an infinitesimal distribution of the power relations. [Foucault 1977, p. 216]

First communion played a vital role in this whole project, not least because of its constituent discourse of life determination. By bringing forward first communion to an age at which a successful outcome for the ritual could be almost guaranteed, the Church hoped to impress definitively upon the younger children the new disciplinary regime that would pattern their future life course. De Zulueta, a firm proponent of early first communion, used an extended military metaphor to locate the reform in its broader context. Catholics were soldiers who 'must be loyal and strong, all closely united to their invisible King and Leader, and all absolutely docile to the word of command given by His earthly Viceroy in the See of Peter' (1911, p. 7). He continues:

> For this end Our Lord's young recruits must be brought early under His discipline, they must be fed betimes with the Bread of victory, for victory over themselves – that is to say, over those traitors in the tent of their own souls – the natural concupiscences of man, the sad heirlooms of Original Sin ... The sooner sacramental union with Christ is begun, the more strongly will it be cemented by the time the child has to take its place in the fighting ranks, and the less danger will there be of his ever disowning or betraying the flag. Delay

that union in disregard of orders from our Roman headquarters, and we may have to lament, if not a larger number of deserters, at all events the sickly character of a large percentage of our troops. [p. 8]

Socio-ethnic Factors Involved in Assent to Formal Ecclesial Discourses

The first communion celebrations of 1911 offered to the public gaze a spectacle that appeared to guarantee the continuity of the Catholic community as newly reconstituted. It was to serve, as were all future first communions, as a symbol of the success of the entire enterprise – a lens through which the local Church could confidently project its future. That projection, however, was predicated on the presumption that future generations would offer their assent to the disciplinary framework established by the Pian reforms. The numbers of Catholics who ignored the *Ne Temere* legislation ought to have sounded a note of caution. The marriage debate suggested not only a level of dissent from the formal discourses of the Church, but also the illusionary nature of any supposition that a circumscribing wall of ecclesiastical legislation could render the Catholic community immune from external contacts and influences. In a series of studies, Hornsby-Smith (1987, 1989, 1999) has mapped across the late twentieth century a decrease in internal assent, resulting in a greater pluralism of belief within the Catholic community, and a progressive growth in external contacts that has drastically reduced cultural isolation and individuality of the community. These two factors of dissent and progressive homogenization with broader society have undermined the entire reform project.

If, however, the optimism for the reforms expressed by Whiteside has proved false, it was, none the less, built upon expectations that were rooted in the Liverpool society of his time. This is not simply because he could not have foreseen the accelerated pace of change in both Church and society over the coming century, but because assent among Liverpool Catholics to ecclesial discourse was linked to a particular Catholic identity forged in the face of socio-economic factors that had been in play throughout most of the past hundred years. Those factors, no less than the ecclesial, favoured the closely defined, all-embracing community that emerged from the Pian reforms. In this concluding section of the chapter, I wish to consider how two such related factors – the ethnic make-up of the Catholic community in Liverpool and the history of sectarianism there – favoured a broad assent to ecclesial discourses. I shall then briefly bridge the transition between Whiteside's Church and that of the fieldwork by considering two sociological studies carried out in Liverpool in the late 1950s, one of which appears to look back to the situation of 1910 whilst the other prefigures in a number of ways the situations I encountered in the fieldwork.

The Ethnic Nature of the Liverpool Catholic Community

The earliest Catholic chapel in the city of Liverpool was founded in 1701; by Catholic Emancipation in 1829 there were four Catholic chapels in use in the city.[10] Throughout the post-Reformation period Lancashire had maintained one of the highest densities of Catholic population in the country; Bossy (1975) estimates 90 Catholics per thousand in 1641–42 (pp. 404–405), although he is wary about the complete accuracy of his figures. More securely, the 1773 returns submitted to Rome by the Vicars Apostolic and the 1829 report by Bishop Baines to Rome indicate totals of 69 and 82 missions respectively in the county (ibid., pp. 410–13). On the strength of Lancashire Catholicism, cf. also Mullett (1998). However, Catholicism's rapid development within the city of Liverpool was largely due to Irish immigration. Bossy (1975) estimates that in 1834 the total number of Catholics served by the four above-mentioned chapels stood at 30,000–32,500. Of these he reckons between 20,500 and 24,500 to have been Irish in origin (p. 426). The proximity of Liverpool to Ireland and the ease of transport between the city and Dublin encouraged immigration from the early nineteenth century. By 1841 there were 49,639 Irish-born people in Liverpool, making up 17.3 per cent of the city's population (Belchem, 1999, p. 190). However, the failure of the Irish potato crop during three of the years between 1845–49 and the resulting famine led to a massive influx of Irish people into the city. Between 1847 and 1853 around 1,500,000 Irish people landed in Liverpool, of whom 586,000 were formally designated as paupers (Neal, 1997, p. 59). Between January and November 1847 alone, some 278,000 landed, of whom 123,000 remained in the city (Boyce, 1999b, pp. 279–80)· These were not of course the only immigrants into the city, which was growing steadily, but by 1851 over 22 per cent of Liverpool's population was Irish-born (Boyce, 1999b, p. 282).

The impact upon the Catholic Church in Liverpool was dramatic. Whereas throughout the eighteenth century the Church had been sustained largely through the local English gentry and minor aristocracy, the advent of the Irish immigration precipitated significant change:

> Faced with the full force of the famine influx, the Catholic Church redefined its mission: philanthropic and associational provision, along with the recruitment of clerical personnel, underwent a 'hibernisation' more rapid and more thorough than anywhere else in Britain. [Belchem, 1999, p. 203]

In order to cater for the needs created by this population explosion, a number of new churches were built. In 1850 the new diocese of Liverpool had either 79 or 84 churches or chapels served by 113 priests (compare Sweeney, 1950, p. 118 with Hughes, 1950, p. 50). By 1886 there were 21 Catholic missions within the city itself, a number which by 1914 had risen to 24. Of these 16 were located close to each other in the northern part of the city centre (Boyce, 1999b, p. 282).

---

10   For a history of the development of the Catholic community within the city of Liverpool cf. Burke (1910).

Ideological concerns underpinned this apparently philanthropic effort. The establishment of the parish as the natural focus for Irish-Catholic identity and life countered the development of secular Irish associations based around public houses (Belchem, 1992); in another piece, however, the same author writes in more ambiguous terms of the 'complementary rivalry' between Catholic parish and Irish pubs (Belchem, 1999, p. 206). Similarly, the development of Catholic schools must be viewed partly within the perspective of a concern to prevent leakage of children and young people from the community through exposure to Protestant teaching (Burke, 1910). The social and educational structure constructed around each Catholic church provided the Catholic authorities with a mechanism for the diffusion of its own discourses of meaning. The assent given by the Irish-Catholic community to the parish's claim to be the authentic locus for its identity cannot be explained in terms of its own devotion. Whilst the exact causes and date of onset of the 'devotional revolution' hypothesized by Emmet Larkin (1984) continue to be debated,[11] there is a broad consensus that the model of Irish Catholicism characterized by regular Mass attendance was a mid-nineteenth-century creation, and probably post-dated the famine.[12] Even after its arrival in Liverpool and assumption into the parish system, the majority within this community did not conform to expected patterns of church-going: in 1872 Bishop Alexander Goss (1814–72, bishop from 1856), who enjoyed an uneasy relationship with the Irish members of his flock, complained that of a nominal Catholic population in the city of 150,000–200,000, only 50,000 went to Mass. Whilst these constituted 'a vast population nominally', he considered that they were 'growing up forgetful of their duties' (Burke, 1910, p. 203).[13] However, there was a reward to be gained by the Irish-Catholic community in assenting to the parish structure as the focus for its identity and the forum for its life. This reward comes into clear focus when set against the background of sectarianism that plagued Liverpool through into the twentieth century and erupted most violently just twelve months before the promulgation of *Quam Singulari*.

Sectarianism in Liverpool

Gallagher (1985) argued that until the 1830s Manchester was the power-base of Orangism in Britain, and that it was only thereafter that the increased Irish immigration into Liverpool rendered the maritime city a more fertile ground for the movement. However, Bryson (1992) argued that Liverpool's history of sectarian violence pre-dated the phase of major Irish immigration, pointing to Catholic attacks on Orange marches held on 12 July in Liverpool during 1819 and 1820 (p. 109). It appears, therefore, that Liverpool had a history of sectarian conflict that preceded the mass waves of Irish immigration. Later, the waves of immigration heightened the sectarian tensions within the city, not least because Liverpool attracted people from Ulster, Catholic and Protestant alike. (McAuley, 1996). However, the fates of

---

11   For an overview of opinions, cf. the Introduction to Larkin (1984).

12   Cf. also Connolly (1982).

13   These estimates correlate with figures for Catholic church attendance in London at the beginning of the twentieth century: cf. McLeod (1974).

the two communities in Liverpool were very different. Orangism was appropriated by the local establishment, and became the 'primary expression of allegiance, the symbol of inclusive national identity for all Protestants, native and immigrant alike' (Belchem, 1992, p. 10; cf. ibid. 1999, p. 206). In particular, the Orange Movement became closely linked with the Liverpool Conservative Party through the founding in 1868 of the Liverpool Working Man's Conservative Association (Gallagher, 1985, p. 116; Bohstedt, 1999, p. 176). This exclusively Protestant association united the political and leisure activities of its members and forged a link between the non-Irish working class and the Liverpool Conservative party which was to endure well into the twentieth century (cf. Waller, 1981).

There is some dispute over the relationship between sectarian conflict and economic rivalry. Gallagher (1985, p. 110) suggested that the immigrant Irish and the local proletariat were brought into conflict through economic rivalry, with the Irish depressing wages and conditions by working for lower rates of pay. This position was disputed by Bohstedt (1999, p. 201), who argued on the basis of the 1910 Police Report that Catholic and Protestant rivalries were not economic. However, in common with Gallagher (1985, pp. 110–11) and Belchem (1992, p. 13), Bohstedt pointed to an economic factor, founded in Liverpool's particular pattern of employment, that sharpened the sectarian divisions in the city. Because the Liverpool labour market was dominated by casual unskilled work, especially on the docks, the city failed to develop an independent skilled artisanate that would have given rise to self-help associations. Trades unionism remained weak in the city. Consequently, instead of developing independent associations, the Liverpool working class looked instead to their ethnic resources, and these expressed themselves in 'a network of voluntary associations based on nationality and creed, not on class' (Belchem, 1992, p. 13).

In the face of a deeply hostile environment, the Irish Catholics tended to congregate together, particularly in the northern sector of the city centre. This effectively resulted in what one author has described as a 'Victorian apartheid' in the city (Gallagher, 1985, p. 108) with both Catholics and Protestants able to 'live their whole lives in sectarian cocoons in which most of their needs could be created and fulfilled' (Bohsted, 1999, p. 209). These districts retained their separate identity into the twentieth century even though the majority of inhabitants were now locally born. Matters in Liverpool came to a head of 1909, when outdoor processions by two city centre parishes, Holy Cross and St Joseph's, sparked full-scale riots on the streets of the city. The report of the official Inquiry that followed gives eloquent testimony to the reality of the sectarian divide. Priests and laypeople told the Inquiry about acts of violence and intimidation, [14] occasionally reported to have been directed against clergy[15] or nuns.[16] In the aftermath of the riots sectarian minorities who formerly had been living within the 'opposite' community were forced to relocate to, effectively,

---

14   Evidence of Catherine Traynor and Mrs. Connolly; *Police (Liverpool Inquiry) Act 1909*, Questions 21062 and 21085–91.

15   Evidence of Fr John FitzGerald, parish priest of Our Lady Immaculate, Everton (Question 20206).

16   Evidence of Mr Thomas Friery (Questions 21026 and 21031).

their own ghetto.[17] It was in this fevered atmosphere that the Pian reforms of Catholic marriage legislation and the first communion of small children were introduced in Liverpool. The former attempted to draw the sectarian boundaries even more sharply, the latter offered to a beleaguered Catholic community a vision not only of its survival but also of its future strength.

Conclusions: From 1910 to 1999

To its contemporary audience, *Quam Singulari* seemed to give an opportunity to maximize the potential of the parish structure, making use of the life-course-determining capacity of the first communion ritual to progressively increase the percentage of the Catholic population attending Mass. The expected result across a number of generations would have been a deepening assent to the Church's teaching. Especially, the expectation was that attendance at Mass would become the norm, or at least the majority practice, rather than being an exception. However, the coincidence of the broader social needs of the Liverpool Catholic community and the structures established by the Pian reforms only remained in place until the Second World War. Thereafter, a series of educational reforms heralded the emergence of the Catholic community from its relative isolation (Brothers 1964). In Liverpool the identification of Catholicism with Irish identity diminished across the post-war generations (Hickman, 1999), and as the post-war Catholic community entered progressively into the mainstream of Liverpool life, so too it experienced the processes of disaffection and dissent from organized religion that have been the focus of study within the secularization debate (Brown, 2001; Bruce, 1995 and 2002; Davie, 1994 and 2002; Martin, 2005; Swatos, 2000).

Two studies carried out during the 1950s produced sharply contrasting images of the Liverpool Catholic community on the eve of the social revolutions of the 1960s, and of the Second Vatican Council which removed many of the liturgical features and legislation governing diet, marriage and ecumenical contact that had maintained Catholic distinctiveness (Archer, 1986; Gilley, 1999). Connor Ward (1965) in his doctoral thesis surveying life in a Catholic parish, portrayed a thriving community of 2,000 parishioners in 443 households. For 1958, the year he carried out his research, he recorded 56 per cent of these attending Sunday Mass, a figure rising to 76 per cent for Easter Communions. This contrasts with the archdiocesan average for these two markers that he cited for 1957 as 49 per cent and 53 per cent respectively. Not surprisingly, Hornsby-Smith regarded Ward's parish as 'atypical' (1999, p. 7), while Boyce confusingly described it within the same article as both 'typical' and existing within a 'time-warp' (1999a, p. 50). Ward described his subject parish as seething with traditional Catholic activity, with seven key adult societies operative within the parish. His findings contrast with those of Madeleine Kerr's five-year in-depth study of 61 families living in a single city-centre street (Kerr, 1958). Kerr described an inwardly-focused society of chiefly Irish origins, organised matrilocally; married

---

17   On the forced relocation of Catholics cf. the evidence to the Inquiry of Frs Keohan and Clarkson (Questions 20865–910; 20924, 20937, 20932).

daughters lived with their husbands and families either in or near the home of their mother. Thanks to the presence of Church schools, the Catholic Church continued to play a significant role in the life of the children, described by Kerr as 'ardently' religious (p. 135). However, with adolescence, church attendance gradually petered out until it frequently ceased altogether at marriage (p. 136). Kerr considered this as one symptom among many of the matriarchal pull; once married, women withdrew almost completely from all other outside associations, the Church among them. In short, Kerr regarded the primary contact between the adults of the community and the Church as taking place on two levels. First, she found a continuity of acceptance of basic Catholic norms – specifically in the refusal to use artificial contraception. Secondly, there was some active involvement in buying tickets for the pools and sweeps organized by the Church, and in joining processions (p. 137). However, even in the sphere of morality she identified discontinuity. Recourse to contraception was unthinkable, but abortion up to three months was widely accepted (p. 83). Moreover, she suggested that the abhorrence of contraception might also relate to gendered power politics within the community: 'in a community where the woman is dominant the male clings to the vestige of power by refusing to allow his wife to be sterilised or to use birth control methods' (p. 88). It was a development of Kerr's model of a matrilocal community, not Ward's thriving parish, that as we shall see emerged from my fieldwork in two city-centre parishes at the end of the twentieth century.

However, before we can focus on the fieldwork, we need to take into consideration a seismic change in the formal ecclesial discourse on first communion, that was officially implemented in the years between Ward's and Kerr's studies and my own research in the same city. This shift was the adoption by the Second Vatican Council of the construct of first communion as a sacrament of Christian initiation.

CHAPTER 5

First Communion as a Sacrament of Initiation in Vatican II

By the mid-twentieth century, many within the Catholic Church would have identified with an impassioned speech delivered in November 1962 on the floor of the Second Vatican Council by Bishop Luigi Faveri of Tivoli (Italy):

> There is not a parish priest, nor even a bishop, who has not seen girls who, through the folly and vanity of their mothers, come to the eucharistic table for the first time in clothing that is downright contrary to the piety due to the holiness of this sacrament. Girls are dressed up as little queens, with their natural vanity intact. They distract and utterly humiliate other girls who on account of poverty lack such expensive dresses. Of such the Apostle Paul said: 'This I do not praise!' But the mothers and godmothers of these girls spurn the voices of the parishes and perhaps even Church decrees, and almost turn the event into a fashion parade. [*Acta Synodalia*, vol. i, part i, pp. 304–305; hereafter, AS]

The exuberant display that, as we saw in Chapter 3, accompanied first communion before the reform of 1910 had, indeed, continued across the twentieth century. On the other hand, there was little evidence by the turn of the 1960s of that closer affiliation of post-1910 generations of Catholics to the Church which had been eagerly anticipated as the fruit of Pius X's introduction of early first communion. It is thus perhaps surprising that Faveri's intervention was the only direct reference made to the ritual of first communion during all the debates of the Second Vatican Council. Otherwise, the ceremony passed almost unmentioned in its deliberations. Furthermore, despite the prominent role played by the Mass of first communion in the lives of local Catholic communities, it does not directly feature in any of the documents emerging from the Council, which have shaped the formal discourses relating to Catholic life and worship ever since.

None the less, first communion did emerge from the Second Vatican Council with a new identity. From then onwards the moment of a child's first admission to the eucharist was formally understood by the Church as the end point of a progressive and extended initiation into membership of the Catholic community. The initiatory process began with baptism, was continued with the celebration of confirmation and culminated in first communion. This perspective was held as universally valid – irrespective of the age or condition of the recipient of first communion. For adults acceding to the eucharist within minutes of being baptized and confirmed, or for children making their first communion years after baptism, one and the same thing was presumed to be happening: the celebration of a 'sacrament of Christian initiation'.

This revised theological perspective drew the free-floating ritual of first communion into a theological framework that was apparently better focused and more clearly articulated than had ever previously been the case. This ought to have presented the possibility for clarification as to the purpose of the event, and – through the integration of the ritual into a broader catechetical process that stretched back through confirmation to baptism – to provide children and their families with a structured unified ritual experience that was in accord with the mind of the Church. It could be expected, therefore, that the result be a reduction in the tensions implied by Bishop Faveri in the observations cited above. However, the experience of the intervening forty years has proved to be the exact opposite: the ritual still provokes dissent and controversy, and a truly shared meaning that embraces all its participants has, if anything, proved even more difficult to achieve.

This is largely because of the paradox that lies at the heart of the event. In its pre-1910 form the ritual effectively functioned as a rite of adolescent passage, and was therefore indeed infused with a strong initiatory character. The discourse of life-course determination and the debate concerning the 'age of reason' reinforced this sense, although the initiatory dimension did not explicitly penetrate the formal theological and canonical discourses. This link between the sacrament and the natural patterns of human life transition, however, was severely weakened in the wake of the 1910 reduction in the age of first communion. Experientially the event became a celebration of childhood, and no longer held the initiatory character of a rite of passage. The theological vision of Vatican II thus reversed the paradox in the event, rather than removing it. Before 1910 the celebration had been profoundly initiatory in experience, but not in formal discourse. From Vatican II onwards the entire ritual has been understood in terms of a theology of initiation, but because the age for reception set by *Quam Singulari* has been maintained, it has proved extremely difficult to map the new theology onto experience. The resulting mismatch between the experiential and the formal discursive elements is one of the main contributing factors towards the tensions that occur around the celebration of the ritual today.

The transformation of first communion into a 'sacrament of Christian initiation' was the fruit of specialist academic research into the early history of the Roman liturgy carried out in the late nineteenth and early twentieth centuries. A number of those previously engaged on this research were prominent among the liturgical experts engaged first in drafting the documents that emerged from the Council, and then in preparing the revised liturgies in response to the Council's requirements. The Council adopted the resulting historically orientated initiatory perspective. Thus the theoretical model that underpinned the reconfiguration of first communion depended upon a reconstruction of the baptismal liturgies of the first Christian centuries.[1]

This reinterpretation of first communion in the light of research into the liturgical practices of the early Christian community missed two crucial points. First, the ancient liturgies that were now proposed as normative interpretative keys for first communion predated the creation of the ritual by roughly a thousand years. Second,

---

1   This was particularly those found in the *Apostolic Tradition of Hippolytus* (Botte, 1963, pp. 44–58), the *Gelasian Sacramentary* (Mohlberg, Eizenhöfer and Siffrin, 1981) and *Roman Ordo XI* (Andrieu, 1948, vol. ii, pp. 365–447).

and even more significantly, the entire construct of 'sacraments of initiation' is itself dubious. It rests upon the imposition of the scholastic theological category of the seven sacraments onto a reconstruction of patristic liturgy. There is here, therefore, a double false-mapping at play: a ritual of the modern era is interpreted in terms of a classical liturgy, a first-millennium ritual process is interpreted in terms of second-millennium sacramental theology. In somersaulting across centuries of development and at the same time ignoring actual lived experience, the proponents of the sacrament of initiation approach introduced into the ritual the seeds of its own instability.

This instability has been further compounded by the fact that Catholic leaders and communities throughout the world have not implemented the internal logic of these arguments. Most Catholic children today experience first communion as the middle of the three 'sacraments of initiation' rather than as the conclusion of the process. This critically weakens at the level of experience any sense that the ritual closes an extended initiatory process, and undermines the formal discourse. As we shall see, this compromising of the official initiatory line opens a conceptual space within first communion that participants can and do fill with their own discourses of meaning.

This chapter examines the radical change in meaning that Vatican II imposed upon the sacrament, and then considers three very different attempts to translate that meaning into practice across the English-speaking world. The remaining chapters will then turn to my fieldwork in Liverpool to explore from a number of different perspectives the practical working-out on the ground of the revised Vatican II approach to this ritual.

'Sacraments of Initiation': The Genesis of an Idea

The discourse of 'sacraments of initiation' entered the formal teaching of the Catholic Church with the promulgation of Vatican II's Dogmatic Constitution on the Liturgy, *Sacrosanctum Concilium*. The theoretical construct expressing itself in the discourse had by then been in circulation for over half a century. Liturgical commentators have proposed two different sources for the discourse. On the one hand, the French Dominican liturgist, Pierre-Marie Gy (1922–2004) argued that it was to the study of liturgical history in the late nineteenth century – and, specifically, to the work of the French historian Louis Duchesne (1843–1922) – that one should turn for the source of the construct. Gy (1977) identified Chapter 9 of Duchesne's work *Les Origenes du Culte Chrétien* (Duchesne, 1904) as the point of origin of the new discourse. This chapter opens with a phrase that recurs in later works, and became something of a mantra: 'The ceremonies of christian initiation, such as they were described from the end of the second century onwards, consisted of three essential rites – baptism, confirmation and first communion' (p. 292). On the other hand, the American liturgist Paul Turner (2000) suggests that the meteoric progress across the twentieth century of the initiatory construct was due to the increasing attention paid by Catholic commentators to anthropological studies. The truth probably lies between these two positions, as the relationship between anthropological and liturgico-historical studies seems to have been rather more complementary than either commentator draws out.

This complexity can be seen in considering the seminal text for the anthropological study of initiatory rites –Arnold Van Gennep's *Rites of Passage* (1960 [1909]).

This book had enormous influence on the development of twentieth-century anthropological theory. In it, Van Gennep (1873–1957) offered a comparative study of the rituals that accompany human processes of change – whether in terms of a person's social status or as they pass through the different stages of life. Van Gennep categorized such processes as 'initiatory', and argued that in all of the cases that he studied a similar three-stage pattern could be discerned. The first stage marked a person's formal break with his or her previous condition, whilst the third ritualized the definitive entrance into the new state of life. Between the two he found a more or less protracted period of transition, that he categorized as a 'threshold' or 'liminal' period. In preparing his study, Van Gennep relied entirely upon historical and anthropological data produced by different scholars of varying disciplines. His primary source for early Christian liturgy was none other than Duchesne. Consequently, Van Gennep's lengthy and detailed discussion of the early Christian catechumenate is entirely dependent upon *Les Origenes du Culte Chrétien*, as the author acknowledged (Van Gennep, [1960] 1909; , pp. 93–5). So, in laying the foundations for the discourse of sacraments of Christian initiation, Duchesne provided the raw data and Van Gennep elaborated the anthropological theory. Across the twentieth century the historico-anthropological perspective that emerged gradually became the interpretative key within which an essential link between the three moments of baptism, confirmation and first communion came to be understood.

The language of initiation articulated in these two texts soon started to find its way into a number of influential Catholic encyclopaedias and dictionaries published serially in the early twentieth century. These were subscribed to by seminary libraries and individual priests across the Catholic world. *The Catholic Encyclopaedia*, originally published in New York and subsequently in London, bears witness to the gradual and piecemeal entry of the initiatory discourse into the Catholic vocabulary. Its 1907 article on baptism was written by the Jesuit William H.W. Fanning, Professor of Church History and Canon Law at St Louis University. His article is entirely framed in the juridico-scholastic language that had dominated Catholic thought since the Council of Trent, and makes no reference to Duchesne's initiatory approach. The article on confirmation, published two years later and written by the English priest T.B. Scannell is couched much more in terms of Duchesne's approach.

A initiatory approach to the discussion not only of baptism but also of confirmation is to be found in the contributions made to the *Dictionnaire d'Archéologie Chrétienne et de la Liturgie* by the Benedictine liturgist Pierre de Puniet. His lengthy article on baptism (de Puniet, 1910) directly quotes Duchesne's description of the 'three essential rites of initiation', and acknowledges the source (p. 251). In some ways, however, his approach is rather more nuanced than that of Duchesne; de Puniet insists in both the baptism article and his subsequent article on confirmation (de Puniet, 1914) that in the early centuries there was no neat separation of the initiatory process into distinct sacramental units. This restraint on his part ought to have been borne in mind by later authors; unfortunately, as we shall see, the tidy separation of the initiatory process into its constituent elements proved too attractive. Yet de Puniet's article on confirmation also contains an inconsistency that was to recur right up to the debates of Vatican II. Whilst his overall approach is to follow Duchesne's 'three essential rites', de Puniet's treatment of confirmation includes the affirmation that the sacrament had always been considered as 'the logical follow-on from baptism, as the element that completes the Christian initiation' (1914, p. 2515). The eucharist does not feature in this approach. Therefore, there are two unreconciled discourses running through de Puniet's work: Christian initiation as involving the 'three essential rites' and as completed within two intrinsically linked moments. One culminates in the eucharist, the other does not include it at all.

De Puniet's inconsistent approach towards exactly which rituals comprised 'Christian initiation' was also reflected in a work that enjoyed a particularly wide readership during the middle years of the twentieth century. Between 1919 and 1927 the Benedictine Ildefonso Schuster (1880–1954) published in Italian a multi-volume liturgical commentary on the Roman Missal. The significance of this work lies partly in the prominence of its author, as Schuster rose to become Cardinal Archbishop of Milan, probably the second most important diocese in Italy. However, even before his appointment to Milan in 1929 the translation into other languages of Schuster's commentary had begun: the English-language edition was published in London between 1924 and 1930. The engagement with the language of initiation in the work of so prominent a Catholic figure is a pointer to the concept's progressive acceptance across the century. Schuster acknowledges his dependence upon Duchesne, yet states categorically that from its beginnings Christian initiation had been made up of two distinct rites; that is, baptism and confirmation (Schuster, 1924, p. 12). The application of the language of initiation to discussion of the Catholic liturgy in the early twentieth century was, therefore, far from uniform. Duchesne's construct of the 'essential rites' pervades the literature, but there is a lack of clarity as to whether the initiation rituals proper are three or two-fold.

Thus far, the 'sacraments of initiation' discourse had been chiefly used in a historic consideration of the early Christian rites. However, after the Second World War liturgists began to apply the principle directly to contemporary practice, particularly in the French-speaking world. A significant player in this regard was the Belgian liturgist Lambert Beauduin (1873–1960), who cautiously explored the implications for current eucharistic practice of a three-sacrament approach to initiation (Beauduin, 1946). As with previous authors, Beauduin began his argument on the basis of first-millennium texts, but drew also on medieval and Tridentine developments to suggest that initiation could not be considered complete until the eucharist had been received. He saw an organic relationship between baptism and eucharist, and suggested – in the strongest terms – that without the eucharist baptism itself was 'a useless means that lacked its end' (p. 58). Although he recognized that hopes for a restoration of the early practice of administration of the three sacraments in an integrated ritual were 'premature' (p. 72), Beauduin none the less suggested that current rites could be re-envisioned within an initiatory perspective. Whilst he did not discuss the ritual of first communion itself, he suggested that the renewal of baptismal promises at the baptismal font during the *Communion Solennelle* should be understood as expressing the essentially initiatory dimension of that ritual that had assumed the symbolic role formerly played in France and the Low Countries by the pre-1910 first communion ritual. As we shall see, this sense that a renewal of baptismal promises might be used to forge a link between the different 'sacraments of initiation' was to feed into the liturgical reforms of Vatican II – although in association not with first communion but with the other sacrament of the trio, confirmation.

Many of the key liturgical scholars of the first half of the twentieth century were drawn from the Francophone world within which the post-1910 *Communion Solennelle* had developed. Indeed, it was chiefly concern in that world about the *Communion Solennelle* that triggered further exploration of the topic. Alongside the already mentioned Pierre-Marie Gy, the principal figures were Antoine Chavasse (died 1982), Professor of Catholic Theology at the University of Strassbourg from 1956 to 1978, the Jesuit liturgist and musician, Joseph Gelineau (born 1920) and Aimé-Georges Martimort (1911–2000), Professor of History at the Institut Catholique in Paris. These and other liturgists collaborated within an umbrella organisation entitled the Centre de Liturgie Pastorale, of which Beauduin and Martimort were early presidents. These scholars used the various organs of the CLP, including the highly influential quarterly journal *La Maison Dieu,* to publish their work. The 1951 CLP conference, held at Versailles, discussed the 'Pastoral Problem of the *Communion Solennelle'*. Several of the papers delivered at that conference took up Beauduin's theme of rereading the *Communion Solennelle* in an initiatory light – in terms of the overall catechetic process (Garrone, 1951), the traditional pre-Communion retreat (Raughel, 1951), or even of the ritual itself (Robert, 1951). Robert's paper proposed that the Mass should be preceded by an elaborate ceremony that clearly articulated a link between first communion and baptism. The children were to make the physical journey from the door of the church to the sanctuary across three staged rituals. These rituals closely corresponded to the three phases of Van Gennep's model of rites of passage, and were entitled 'the departure from the world', 'the Christian passage' and 'the welcome of the Church'. The proposed rites closely echoed liturgical elements of the classical catechumenate – they included a renunciation of Satan, a solemn profession of faith, and the gift of the book of the Gospels. The entire complex breathed a baptismal air – the children were to be sprinkled with blessed water, they were given a lighted candle, and were signed with the cross on their foreheads.

This was not a purely academic exercise; Robert stated that he based his paper upon an actual event celebrated by Gelineau, perhaps the most pastorally minded of the group. This is evidence of quite radical liturgical experimentation in the pre-conciliar period; the Duchesne-Van Gennep model of Christian initiation was being mapped experientially onto the French ritual that to all intents and purposes was playing the role that first communion had played before 1910.

Therefore, during the years leading up to Vatican II some attempts were made among a highly informed minority to apply an initiatory interpretation to the modern rites. However, the formal discourse of the Church remained unchanged. Moreover, whilst seminary library shelves may have held copies of all the works cited above, the material taught to future priests in the classroom, upon which they were examined before ordination, was produced in a very different theological environment. Once again, the hand of Pius X must be recognized. In pursuance of his concerted attempt to stamp out Modernist tendencies within the Church, he was determined to ensure that the training of future priests should be untarnished in any way by Modernist approaches. He therefore insisted that a strictly neo-scholastic approach should be followed in all seminaries *(Pascendi*, 45). His aim was to ensure that all future priests would be formed for their ministry within a philosophical and intellectual tradition that pre-dated any of the tendencies that Pius and his supporters identified with Modernism. This, he believed, would inoculate the clergy against new, dangerous ideas, and prevent the dissemination of those ideas. The entire neo-scholastic approach was marked by an apologetic and highly defensive style: theses were proposed and defended, and counter-theses discussed and refuted. At all times, the key point of reference was the traditional body of Church teaching, expressed in decrees of Church Councils, Papal pronouncements and Canon Law. Such systems did not reflect the new liturgico-anthropological category of 'Christian initiation', and the sacraments were taught in a rather colourless imitation of the medieval academic tradition. The neo-scholastic method was transmitted through multi-volumed theological manuals that presented a systematic presentation of Catholic doctrine. Because they were written in Latin – the language through which all seminarians were taught – these manuals could pass easily between different countries. It is, therefore, not surprising to find on the shelves of the library of the former seminary in Liverpool a 1946 American eighteenth edition of a manual originally written and published in France in 1935 (Hervé, 1946).

Therefore, even as the initiation language was being explored and articulated more broadly by liturgical commentators, ecclesiastical legislation prevented its penetration into the seminary lecture theatre, and generations of priests and future bishops were educated until Vatican II without reference to it. After 1963, these same men were required to implement a liturgical reform for which they had received little or no formal preparation. The result on the ground was to be a liturgy that neither fully departed from previous types, nor completely integrated the new theological stance.

Sacraments of Initiation and Vatican II

The Build-up to the Second Vatican Council

In 1959 and 1960 all the bishops of the Catholic Church were required to submit to Rome suggestions for issues to be debated at the forthcoming Council. Throughout the bishops' replies, the celebration of first communion was barely mentioned. There was no groundswell of opinion that the ritual should be revised, nor is there evidence that the discussion and experimentation around the *Communion Solennelle* were seriously considered by the bishops. However, the world's bishops did raise two areas of concern that were to feed into the transformation of the celebration of first communion into a rite of Christian initiation. There were the calls for revision of the adult rite of baptism, and of the ritual of confirmation. The eventual response to these requests introduced the discourse of initiation into the teaching of the Council, drawing in its wake the ritual of first communion with surprisingly minimal discussion.

Two factors fed into the perceived need for a revision in the ritual of adult baptism. The first was the enormous social changes that had occurred across the first part of the twentieth century and had been accelerated in the wake of the Second World War. Even in Europe it was no longer possible for the Church to presume that adults who approached it for baptism shared in a common Christian cultural heritage. The catechetical needs of such individuals were more complex and demanding than had previously been understood. They required a rather fuller process of instruction and inculturation than the traditional model of purely doctrinal instruction had permitted. The second, related, factor was the recognition that outside the traditional Christian territories, the human process of transition from non-Christian beliefs to a mature engagement with the Gospel was similarly complex. A progressive and ritualized disengagement from previous belief systems and patterns of life was required. The current ritual, formulated at the Council of Trent, now appeared inadequate because it telescoped the entire process into a single ceremony. By postponing any ritual engagement until the very last moment, the existing baptismal rites failed to offer an integrated liturgico-catechetical process to accompany the convert towards membership of the Church. Furthermore, liturgical studies carried out during the first part of the twentieth century highlighted the extent to which the various elements of the Tridentine ritual had originally functioned as distinct elements within a prolonged, integrated ritual and catechetical process that sustained a carefully articulated transition from a non-Christian lifestyle and world-view into full membership of the Church. Some of the bishops who submitted preliminary reports to the Vatican, therefore, saw a restoration of the original order as pastorally desirable.[2] The Vatican responded by attempting to prevent this becoming a hot issue in the debates of the forthcoming Council. In 1962, on the eve of the Council, the Roman Curia published a reform of the rite of baptism of adults that simply broke down the Tridentine ritual into a number of stages.[3] Significantly, this revised ritual encompassed the two-sacrament approach, and culminated not in the eucharist but in post-baptismal confirmation. The reform was welcomed by liturgists and an entire edition of *La Maison Dieu* was dedicated to it (no. 71, 1962), but the 1962 ritual was swept away in the radical reform that followed in the wake of Vatican II.

The other spur to reform emerged from concerns expressed in the pre-conciliar consultation over the celebration of confirmation. If the Tridentine ritual of adult baptism was condensed, then that of confirmation was positively abrupt. It comprised little more than the core elements of the ritual – that is, a prayer pronounced by the bishop over the candidates and the individual anointing of each candidate. The sacrament was normally celebrated during periodic episcopal visitations of parishes, and was generally administered to large cohorts of children aged roughly between seven and twelve – though in certain parts of Latin America it had traditionally been celebrated at an even younger age. In liturgical terms, the ritual was a relatively

---

2   These included Bishop le Cordier, auxiliary bishop in Paris (*Acta et Documenta, Series 1, vol. ii, part i*, p. 531. Henceforth ADA), Bishop Pierre M. Lacointe of Beauvais (ibid., p. 216), Cardinal Achille Lienart, Bishop of Lille (ibid., p. 305); John Pohlshneider, Bishop of Aachen (ibid., p. 568).

3   For a text of the proposal, see. AAS 54, pp. 315–38.

brief segment of the originally unified patristic ritual – effectively, the bishop's role in the baptismal rite – that had become separated from its original context and had for centuries floated free and independent. Its fragmentary and isolated state was reflected above all in the fact that it contained no proclamation of the scriptures, and was never celebrated during the eucharist – unlike other sacraments such as marriage or ordination. Moreover, as this ritual fragment drifted further and further away from its original setting, it acquired a very different theology to that of initiation: it was now generally understood as the sacrament through which Christians were armed for the conflicts of life, and made 'soldiers of Christ'. This was emblematized very vividly in the way in which, at the end of each individual child's anointing, the bishop lightly slapped him or her on the side of the face.

During the pre-conciliar consultation, the world's bishops had raised a number of concerns over confirmation that ranged from the practical difficulties some of them encountered in confirming between three and eight thousand children in a single celebration to requests for clarification as to what exactly, even in this abbreviated ritual, constituted its most essential elements. There was no single mind among them as to the most appropriate age for the celebration of the sacrament – nor, indeed, as to whether its celebration should precede or follow first communion. Thus, Cardinal Richard Cushing, Archbishop of Boston, asked that confirmation should be celebrated between baptism and first communion (ADA, vol. ii, part vi, p. 283). On the other hand, Archbishop Joseph Rumner of New Orleans argued that confirmation should not take place until at least two years after first communion (ibid., p. 387). The comments of other North American bishops reflect the range of proposed ages: ten or twelve years (James Hill of Victoria, BC, ibid., p. 130), nine years (Stephen Woznicki of Saginaw, MN, ibid., p. 427), or prophetically, at an unspecified 'age of puberty' (Coleman F. Carrol of Miami, FL, ibid., p. 375).

Amidst the concerns over administrative overloads and the difficulties encountered in finding suitable sponsors for confirmation candidates, only four bishops suggested a radical shift in the liturgy of confirmation that was to carry theological implications for first communion – namely, to end the free-floating career of confirmation by anchoring it in the celebration of the eucharist. These four included, however, the highly influential and progressive Cardinal Julius Döpfner (Bishop of Berlin until 1961, subsequently Archbishop of Munich). In this – as in so much else at Vatican II – his line was to prove decisive (ADA, vol. ii, part i, p. 587). However, an even smaller minority within the bishops – a minority of just one – was to expressly request the greatest change that Vatican II was to bring to the celebration not only of confirmation but also of first communion. Bishop Willem Pieter Mutsaerts of s'Hertogenbosch, The Netherlands alone asked whether it would be possible to investigate the relationship between the 'three sacraments of initiation' (ibid., p. 506). He also wished to see discussion of the age at which these sacraments could be administered, and asked whether they should be celebrated together or separately.

The Debates and Documents of Vatican II

The world's bishops as a body were not pressing for an initiatory reconfiguration of baptism, confirmation and first communion. However, the liturgical experts gathered by the Vatican to prepare the draft documents that were to form the basis for discussion at the Council were far more receptive to the idea. The Preparatory Commission included Chavasse, Gy and Martimort, alongside figures such as Bernard Botte (1893–1980), and Pierre Jounel (1914–2004), both of the Institut Catholique in Paris. (At that time Botte was completing his reconstruction of the *Apostolic Tradition*. This text, which offers a detailed description of rites and disciplines relating to the Catechumenate, was thought to be an authentic Roman text of the early third century, and exercised considerable influence on liturgical reform during the second half of the twentieth century.) Not surprisingly, therefore, the draft document that was presented to the Council Fathers on 22 October 1962 explored the sacraments in terms of initiation. Article 55 of this draft said:

> The rite of confirmation is to be so revised that the intrinsic connection between this sacrament and the whole christian initiation should be more clearly set forth: therefore, where convenient confirmation may be conferred within Mass, and preceded by the renewal of baptismal promises. [AS, vol. i, part i, p. 284]

The language of initiation thus entered onto the debating floor of the Council. The Council Fathers generally accepted the construct – only the exiled bishop Vincentas Brizgys of Kaunas in Lithuania made strong objection to it. In a written intervention he argued that:

> It is not possible to say that the actual rite of confirmation in any way expresses a connection with christian initiation. Certainly, in the strict sense, christian initiation is not made through confirmation. Furthermore, I fear lest this proposition has its origins with those people, who go around with protestants and communists At all events, the appellation is not from our liturgy. [AS, vol. i, part ii, p. 349]

Technically, his final point was completely valid; what came immediately before it was a subjective perspective, influenced no doubt by his own experience of fleeing before the Soviet armies at the end of the Second World War. However, whilst the majority of the bishops present appeared comfortable with the expression, their general approach was to limit their application of it to the two sacraments of baptism and confirmation. Thus Karol Wojtyla, the future Pope John Paul II, stated that 'initiation is done through the sacraments first of baptism then of confirmation' (ibid., p. 315). The eucharist was primarily drawn into the debate only in so far as the bishops debated whether or not confirmation could be administered during the celebration of Mass.

This ambiguity was carried into the final version of the draft, which became Article 71 of *Sacrosanctum Concilium*. The revision of the text of the document was carried out between the first (1962) and second (1963) sessions of Vatican II by the sub-commission of bishops elected for the purpose at the start of the Council. The presentation of – and voting upon – the revised version of each chapter of the document was staggered across the length of the Second Session. Thus on 15 October 1963 Archbishop Paul J. Hallinan of Atlanta, GA (1911–68) – a member of the liturgy commission – presented the revised third chapter, which included this article (AS, vol. ii, part ii, p. 567). As Hallinan explained, the article differed from the draft only very slightly. The draft text had placed together in the same sentence references to the celebration of confirmation during Mass and to the renewal of baptismal promises, and subjected both to the qualifying words 'where convenient'. In the final document these two aspects were separated from each other. The effect of this was to strengthen the renewal of baptismal promises, as it was no longer subject to the qualifying phrase 'where convenient'. On the other hand, the link between confirmation and the eucharist was, if anything, weakened: not only did the celebration of confirmation within Mass remain subject to the qualification as before, but the article ended with a new conclusion requiring the preparation of new texts for the celebration of confirmation outside Mass.

Significantly, Hallinan responded in the course of his presentation to a written intervention received from one of the bishops. This intervention had expressed concern that by drawing a close connection between baptism and confirmation the Council might run the risk of creating a confusion between them in the minds of ordinary Catholics ('the faithful'). Hallinan replied: 'On the contrary. It is much to be lamented that the faithful perceive only with difficulty the connection between Confirmation and Baptism (and, in general, between the three Sacraments of Christian initiation.)'

Here was the first mention of the three-fold sacraments of initiation on the floor of the Council. Yet the number three was not included in the text itself. Nor were the Fathers offered any possibility to debate the issue further. The alterations to the article were not considered sufficiently serious to justify a separate vote, and so the new Article 71 and its canonization of the sacraments-of-initiation approach was approved by the bishops when they voted on Chapter 3 in its entirety.

The progression towards the formal endorsement of the three-sacrament approach was completed with the publication of two of the final decrees of Vatican II on 7 December 1965: that on the Missionary Activity of the Church (*Ad Gentes*), and on the Pastoral Life and Ministry of Priests (*Presbyterorum Ordinis*). Article 14 of *Ad Gentes* applies the term 'sacraments of initiation' to the process by which adult converts are 'freed from the power of darkness', highlighting baptism, confirmation and admission to the eucharist. Article 5 of *Presbyterorum Ordinis* reinforces the initiatory nature of admission to the eucharist and establishes that initiatory role as normative not simply in the case of adult converts, but even for those whose Catholic trajectory had followed the more regular pattern:

> Those under instruction are introduced by stages to a sharing in the Eucharist, and the faithful, already marked with the seal of baptism and confirmation, are through the reception of the Eucharist fully joined to the Body of Christ.

Whether a person entered the Church as an infant or as an adult, their initiation, therefore, was not completed until they had been admitted to the eucharist.

None of these three documents cross-references the initiation discourse to patristic texts or to previous magisterial statements. Instead the later documents refer back to *Sacrosanctum Concilium* – thus producing a closed self-referential system. This stands in marked contrast to the general practice within formal Catholic pronouncements of referencing statements to earlier documents – for example

Patristic texts, Papal statements or decrees of earlier Church Councils. Nor do any of these documents explain the expression 'sacraments of initiation'. However, their adoption of the discourse became the justification for a wide-reaching liturgical reform, and subsequent liturgical and catechetical texts ground themselves in these three documents.

It is tempting to draw a parallel across 750 years between the Fourth Lateran and Second Vatican Councils. In each, the formal perspective on the admission of children to the eucharist was shifted as a collateral result of decisions made with regard to other aspects of ecclesial life. As we saw in Chapter 1, Lateran IV drew the question of admission to the eucharist into the 'age of reason' discourse by its inclusion in a legal statement primarily concerned with ensuring that Catholics confessed their sins and received Communion at least once a year. At Vatican II, the ritual of first communion was drawn into a complex construct of Christian initiation because of a pastoral concern to create meaningful processes for adult converts, and a perceived need to revisit the theology and ritual of confirmation. In doing so, the Council formalized the third significant shift in the ritual's history. From the inception of the rite in the seventeenth century until the reform of 1910, it had served as an adolescent rite of passage. In the early twentieth century it was deliberately transformed into a celebration of childhood innocence. In 1963, with the publication of *Sacrosanctum Concilium*, the ceremony was launched upon its new career as a ritual of Christian initiation.

The Implementation of the Reform

After Vatican II all the liturgical texts of the Catholic Church were revised, and the triple-sacramental initiatory construct was then reinforced. The new position was most clearly articulated in the *General Introduction to Christian Initiation*, which preceded the new Orders for Baptism of Children, Confirmation, and Christian Initiation of Adults. This Introduction opened with an unequivocal affirmation that baptism, confirmation and the eucharist together form the 'three sacraments of Christian initiation' (No. 2) The same discourse has since been repeated in the Catechism of the Catholic Church, designed as a compendium of formal teaching (CCC, 1212, 1385, 1322).

Yet, whilst the revised liturgical and catechetical documents bear witness to the entry into formal Catholic thought and praxis of the restored first-millennium initiatory perspective, the Code of Canon Law, revised in 1983 demonstrates the persistence of the second millennium's concerns. Thus, Canon 920 reaffirms the core precept of Lateran IV that once admitted to the eucharist, the 'faithful are obliged to receive holy Communion at least once a year'. Canons 913 and 914 enshrine the core emphases of *Quam Singulari*. Canon 842, on the other hand, brings the Vatican II perspective into the frame by stating that 'The three sacraments of baptism, confirmation and the blessed Eucharist so complement one another that all three are required for full christian initiation'. However, these pieces of legislation are not drawn together into a final unity by a statement that the first communion of children marks the completion of its initiatory process. Moreover, the continued insistence upon the delay in reception until the age of reason imposed by Lateran IV, that most scholastic of Church Councils, effectively privileges the second-millennium discourses by preventing the most logical implementation of the new approach – namely the administration of all three sacraments together in early infancy, the traditional practice amongst Orthodox and Eastern Rite Catholic Churches.

The theological construct of a tripartite ritual process of initiation is further compromised by an almost universal contradiction between theology and praxis. First communion is formally understood as the ritual that 'completes christian initiation' (CCC, 1322). Membership of the Church is completed with admission to the eucharistic community, and full participation in its worship. However, in the overwhelming majority of dioceses across the world, the sacramental process does not culminate with admission to the eucharist; generally speaking, confirmation is celebrated after first communion – frequently, years after. Confirmation in many places has come to assume the role that until 1911 had been played by first communion. It is now the ritual that coincides with adolescence, and offers a Christian rite of passage that articulates life-course transition – exactly as Bishop Carrol of Miami had requested in his pre-conciliar submission. Once again, the seeds of this change can be recognized in *Sacrosanctum Concilium* and the desire of the reformers that the newly formalized link between baptism and confirmation should find liturgical expression. And once again, Lateran IV's concept of the 'age of reason' was a key stimulus for an unintended change.

The draft version of *Sacrosanctum Concilium* proposed that in order to forge a clear link with baptism, the revised confirmation ritual should include the formal renewal of baptismal promises by the confirmands. It was the bishops of Latin America who spotted the implications: in order for a child validly to renew its baptismal promises, that child would need to have attained the age of reason. This would jeopardize their practice of confirming before the age of seven. For a clear statement of the problem, see the intervention of Luis Cabrera Cruz (1893–1967), Bishop of San Luís Potosí, Mexico 1958–67 (AS, vol. i, part ii, p. 181). The concerns of the Latin American bishops fell on deaf ears, however, and the clause requiring the insertion of the renewal of baptismal promises into the confirmation ritual was incorporated into the final version of *Sacrosanctum Concilium*. This inclusion was to have two effects. First, as the Latin Americans had seen, it drew confirmation for the first time into the ambit of the age of reason discourse. This finds its clearest expression in the Code of Canon Law, revised in 1983 in the light of Vatican II: 'The sacrament of confirmation is to be conferred on the faithful at about the age of discretion' (Canon 891). The Canon, therefore, sees a near-coincidence of confirmation and first communion as normative.

There is a second effect resulting from the introduction of the declaration of baptismal faith into the confirmation ritual. This is that the revised rite invites an easy association between reception of the sacrament and a discourse of personal responsibility and individual faith-ownership. This arises, almost inevitably, because Canon Law offers greater latitude in determining the age of confirmation than it does for first communion. Although the Canon just cited pegs confirmation to the age of discretion, it also permits each National Conference of Bishops to set a higher age. As no such permission is granted for first communion, the usual consequence is a reversal of the order of the sacraments, with first communion preceding confirmation.

In fact, this situation had already arisen in many countries even before the code was published. The association of confirmation with a later age maps easily onto a pastoral concern to support adolescents, and has led to the development of an unofficial but widely diffused discourse of confirmation as the moment at which a young person claims for herself the promises of faith that were spoken for her at her baptism.

Within this perspective, therefore, the sacraments of initiation map a progressive movement towards a fully owned faith position across the early processes of human development: from helpless infancy (baptism) to intellectual and moral responsibility (first communion) to early adult self-identity (confirmation). This approach has proved very popular in the English-speaking world – though it is not uncontentious. Thus, when in 2001 the American bishops legislated for the age of confirmation within the United States, they decreed that it should be conferred 'between the age of discretion and about sixteen years' – a reflection of the breadth of practice (and, almost certainly the depth of disagreement) between bishops.[4]

First Communion as 'Sacrament of Initiation' on the Ground

Because Vatican II did not fully integrate theology, canonical discipline and pastoral practice, the Catholic Church emerged from it with a blurred approach to the three 'sacraments of initiation'. Any hope, therefore, that the new guise given to first communion would end the recurrent problems that have marked its history was likely to prove delusory. None the less, those responsible for religious education have attempted to translate the new discourse into action, and a broad range of approaches has emerged. Three very different attempts to link the sacraments of initiation theology with the experience and understanding of young children and their families will be considered here. The first is a parish-based programme: the widely used *We Celebrate the Eucharist* programme, developed initially in the United States by Christiane Brusselmans and then extended across the English-speaking world. The second is a school-based religious education programme, *Here I Am*, followed by most Catholic schools in England and Wales. The third is a diocesesan approach that has been adopted by a number of bishops across the English-speaking world, namely to restore what they describe as the traditional order of the three sacraments by reducing the age of confirmation so that its celebration precedes that of first communion.

We Celebrate the Eucharist

One of the most popular and influential catechetical programmes for first communion to have emerged after Vatican II was *We Celebrate the Eucharist* by Christiane Brusselmans and Brian Haggerty (1986). Brusselmans brought to this project her considerable experience in developing the restored adult catechumenate, and therefore not surprisingly the programme applies principles gleaned from the *Rite*

---

4   United States Conference of Catholic Bishops, Canon 891, US Bishops' Complementary norm, August 2001.

of Christian Initiation of Adults to the sacramental preparation of young children. The scheme treats children preparing for their first communion as catechumens in the classical sense, and maps their progression towards first communion across a series of nine liturgical celebrations that closely echo those of the adult ritual. The process opens with the formal presentation of the children to the community by their parents and the enrolment of their names – derived from the Lenten presentation of adult candidates to the bishop. Similarly, at the third celebration, the children are presented with a copy of the Gospels – as adult catechumens may be at the Rite of Entry into the Catechumenate. Similarly, the signing of the cross on the children's foreheads at the seventh celebration is explicitly drawn from the same ritual. At the same time, elements of the *Rite of Baptism of Children* are introduced into the preparation process. For example, at the opening ceremony the parents renew their baptismal promises, just as they did at their child's baptism. During the second celebration the children receive a lighted candle – just as at baptism.

The effect of these rituals is to stamp the preparation process for first communion with a strongly baptismal character – at least, in theory. *We Celebrate the Eucharist* thereby represents the 1951 Gelineau-Robert ritual for the *Communion Solenelle* developed to its extreme. However, the approach is fundamentally flawed. The participants are not catechumens in the sense intended by RCIA, that is, adults preparing for baptism (Rite of Christian Initiation for Adults). Rather, they are baptized children who for six or seven years have already been immersed in the life of their parish – or not, as the case may be. In the case of the former, the Brusselmans approach is inauthentic; they have already been experiencing many of the realities to which the initiatory process seeks to introduce them. For the latter, there is a real question as to whether the rituals of *We Celebrate the Eucharist* bear much relationship to the realities of their own life and faith.

Here I Am

In England and Wales, as we shall see more fully in Chapter 7, most children are prepared for their first communion through their parish primary school. The core resource for religious education in those schools is *Here I Am* (Byrne and Malone, 1992, 2000). In common with all catechetical material published since 1980 by the English and Welsh Bishops' conference, *Here I Am* draws upon the approach of American educationalists James R. Fowler (1981) and John H. Westerhoff (2000) in envisaging religious education as a lifelong process intrinsically linked to the stages and processes of human psychological development (for an overview of critiques of Fowler's faith development theory cf. Parks (1991); also Moran (1983) and various articles in Dykstra and Parks (1986)). Concepts of faith as a journey and the centrality of story dominate in Fowler's and Westerhoff's approaches. The age of reason discourse can be seamlessly assimilated into these approaches as it is itself an expression of staged psychological development.

The developmental approach is clearly articulated in the overall structure of *Here I Am*. The programme develops a limited number of themes, subdivided into topics, across all the primary years. This permits the presentation of the same material at five different levels that 'take account of the ages and stages of development of pupils in the primary years, as well as the way the National Curriculum is presented in levels' (p. 11).[5] The child, therefore, follows a progressive path through its primary-school religious education, with each year building upon what has gone before and preparing the ground for what will follow. This developmental approach leads to a wariness about introducing reflection on the miraculous at too early a stage. The same wariness is to be found in the programme's treatment of the 'Real Presence' of Christ in the eucharist. Care is taken to avoid demanding a strongly realistic understanding of the eucharist too early. As we shall see in Chapter 7, this terrain is difficult to tread – not just for children, but for their teachers.

Within this overall schema, the discussion of the sacraments of initiation is divided into two distinct blocks. Each autumn term the children study a topic related to the theme of baptism/confirmation, selected by the school from the range 'Invitations', 'Friends', 'Initiation', and 'Signs and Symbols' (Byrne and Malone, 1992, p. 33). Then, during the spring term, the different theme of the eucharist is studied through one of the topics: 'Communion', 'Meals', 'Memories' and 'Thanksgiving' (ibid.). By thus dividing its discussion of the three sacraments, the syllabus only partially applies the sacraments of initiation discourse. Baptism and confirmation are treated within that discourse, but the eucharist is isolated and discussed according to a very different set of concepts. Nor does the idea of the eucharist as a sacrament of initiation occur in the teachers' information. The programme, therefore, does not embed discussion of the eucharist into a schema of initiation; its dominant educational discourse remains that of the age of reason – albeit dressed in new Westerhoffian garb.

'Restoring the Traditional Order'

Both the *We Celebrate the Eucharist* and *Here I Am* programmes operate within the prevailing baptism-first communion-confirmation pattern. However, in recent years an increasing number of Catholic dioceses across the English-speaking world have sought to change this overall ritual process by bringing forward the celebration of confirmation so that the final sacrament to be celebrated in the sequence is first communion. Because of Vatican II's application of the age of reason requirements to participants in the confirmation ritual, confirmation cannot be celebrated before the age of seven; consequently in these dioceses the celebrations of confirmation and first communion are separated by only a matter of weeks – or they may even take place within the same ceremony. In England, only the diocese of Salford has adopted the revised pattern, but in other countries a broader take up has happened. In Scotland a national consultation led to most of the eight dioceses adopting the revised pattern. US and Canadian dioceses that have set out on this path include Cleveland, OH, Fargo, ND, Marquette, MN, Portland, ME, Saginaw, MN, Prince Albert, SK, Prince George, BC and Saskatoon, SK. The dioceses of Brisbane and Adelaide have pioneered the approach in Australasia.

---

5   The five levels treated are Nursery/Reception (3–5 years), Year 1 (5–6 years), Year 2 (6–7 years), Years 3 and 4 together (7–9 years), and Years 5 and 6 together (9–11 years) (Byrne and Malone, 1992, p. 11).

In each of these dioceses, the promoters claim that this revision is a 'restoration' of the traditional order of the sacraments of initiation. Documents issued by diocesan authorities to explain and support the revision tend to read like history lessons – be they Bishops' Pastoral letters (for example, Aquila, 2002), or catechetical materials (for example, Henchal, 2002).

The ritual does come very close to the mind of Vatican II and avoids mapping the child's life-course development onto the initiatory process. However, the question must be asked whether this model represents the triumph of liturgical theory over pastoral practice. Consideration of recent centuries demonstrates a consistent need stretching back to at least the post-Tridentine catechetical reforms for a significant ritual celebration at adolescence. For centuries, first communion fulfilled this role. After Vatican II, confirmation moved forward to replace it. Not surprisingly, therefore, there has been strong resistance to the restored order model within the catechetical field. The American religious sister Kieran Sawyer (2002), for example, argues that the delay of confirmation until adolescence meets psychological and human developmental needs that would be left unaddressed by the restored order. From a liturgical perspective, too, the restoration approach is not without its critics. Paul Turner (1995) points to a theological inconsistency within the project: Rome's continued insistence that children should make their first confession before receiving first communion introduces a solidly scholastic note into this supposedly Patristic reconstruction. Similarly, the fact that both first communion and confirmation are pegged to the 'age of discretion' amply demonstrates the continued persistence of the mindset of Lateran IV.

The 'return to the traditional order' does not, therefore, resolve the tensions created by the adoption of the 'sacraments of initiation' discourse. It continues to require that the ritual straddle two vastly different conceptual universes – even before we consider the question of whether the participants experience it as initiatory: that will be the concern of Chapter 7.

Conclusion

The Vatican II reconfiguration of first communion stands as a stark warning of the dangers inherent in three processes frequently encountered in twentieth-century Catholic liturgical thought, and particularly manifest in the manner in which the rites were reformed after the Council. The first danger is of a romantic and idealized attachment to the view that early Church liturgical structures can be normative – particularly when applied to liturgical forms that only emerged a thousand years after the presumed model. The second process and inherent danger reverses the polarity of the first by mapping second-millennium theological categories – in this case the concept of the seven sacraments – onto the early Church ritual forms. The third danger arises when the early Church Orders are interpreted through a facile application of twentieth-century anthropological categories. Thus, whilst the classic 'rites of passage' process may be discerned in the early Church Orders, it is extremely difficult to map it onto the generally twelve to sixteen years of human development that today span the period across which most children experience the 'sacraments of initiation'.

The experienced result of the interaction of these three dangers is a strong dissonance between sacramental theology and actual praxis. The impact of that experiential gap has been exacerbated by the general failure of the Catholic Church on the ground to execute the internal logic of its own theological arguments: across the world in the overwhelming majority of cases the first communion of children does not conclude the sequence of initiation sacraments. Instead, the ritual is celebrated several years before confirmation finally draws the process to a conclusion. By a curious twist of fate the hopes and anxieties around adolescent adherence to the Church that were once attached to first communion have now been transferred to confirmation, and the age at which the latter is administered has risen to the mid-teens. In spite of the official line, the need for a sacramental marking of adolescence has reasserted itself, and has now become associated with confirmation. On the ground at least, the association of these sacraments with the human life-course has remained irresistible, as an experiential matrix that celebrates transitions through infancy (baptism), childhood (first communion) and adolescence (confirmation) is mapped across Vatican II's three 'sacraments of initiation'. Thus, ecclesial doctrine and practice are out of phase – as, potentially, too are participant experience and formal discourse. As a consequence, first communion in the post-Vatican II Church is, like confirmation, an inherently unstable ritual. How that instability plays out in the parish experience of first communion will be explored in Chapters 7–10, which will draw on the findings of my fieldwork in Liverpool. First, however, it is appropriate to introduce the fieldwork settings and outline the methodology that underpinned my research. That will be the concern of Chapter 6.

The Ethnography of First Communion

In the previous chapters I have traced the story of first communion, mapping the journey from the seventeenth-century French rituals to the catechetical programmes of today. This has not proved to be a tidy history; the study has identified a number of significant shifts in the manner in which the ritual was celebrated, as in the theology assigned to it. Two important lessons can be learned from this history. The first is a warning against the ambitious investment of psychological expectations in ritual processes: the repeated expectations that first communion could determine a child's future life-course have generally failed to materialize. The second arises from the reform of Vatican II, and points to the inherent dangers of easy transference of ritual patterns and theologies from one historico-cultural setting to another. However, whilst this history has undoubtedly proved complex, the book so far has only presented one potential version of it. The various texts I investigated in earlier chapters may at first sight appear diverse: newspaper articles, catechetical texts, formal pronouncements by Church authorities. However, they share an essential common feature. All were produced by people who were committed to the Catholic Church's understanding of the event as it went through its various transformations: Mother Mary Loyola, Pius X, Pierre-Marie Gy, Bishop Faveri, the early twentieth-century editors of the Catholic press. The story I have related thus far had a constant primary point of reference of the Church, its self-understanding, its concerns.

Yet there must be another history to be told about the ritual. This is the story of the children and parents who across nearly four centuries have entered into this ritual – and also of the priests, teachers and catechists who have engaged with them on the ground. What did first communion mean to these people? How – and to what extent – did they internalize the systems of meaning that the Church offered them as they played their part in it? What impressions did it form? What impact did it really have on their lives? The corpus of texts and formal ecclesial statements examined in the first part of the book offer a hint that an alternative history does exist – not least in the severe warnings contained in some of the catechetical material, and in Bishop Faveri's impassioned outburst on the floor of Vatican II, against outward display and over-indulgence, strongly suggesting that non-ecclesial concerns and even ambitions were impinging upon the ritual. However, these indications of a different history remain filtered through the eyes of the ecclesial and catechetical establishment. Another history there undoubtedly is, but it remains inaccessible.

The present, however, is a different matter, and the instabilities that inhere in the current formal understanding of first communion positively invite the investigation of alternative accounts for the celebration of the ritual today. How has this flawed amalgam of patristic motifs, medieval sacramental theology and modern ritual been received on the ground? At the level of parish practice and personal discourse, do the various parties involved in the ritual of first communion today understand themselves to be actors in a ritual of initiation? Or do some of them bring other sets of meanings to the ritual? If the latter is true, then the issue of the interaction between the formal discourse and these informal ones comes into play and spawns a series of further questions. What happens when two potentially competing systems of meaning meet in a ritual event? How do those systems translate into physical expression in a shared ritual space? What issues of power, conflict and compromise emerge? Is it possible to speak of a dissonance around the celebration of first communion between the outcomes desired by those who nominally control the ritual, and what actually happens, so great that it could be termed, at least from the ecclesial perspective, 'ritual failure'? If that is the case, what might be the personal and institutional consequences?

In order to respond to these questions a different data set is required. Instead of written material – as in previous chapters - it is the words and actions of participants themselves that primarily form the texts from which this alternative account is constructed. By listening to participants and by observing their various encounters –in the classroom, during parish meetings for parents or in the liturgy itself – one can not only access and outline a different set of discourses of meaning, but also consider the manner in which those discourses interact, merge or enter into conflict. The account of first communion that emerges does not exclude the official representatives of the Church – clergy, catechists and teachers all feature in this history. However, rather than considering these individuals only as channels of the formal discourse, the text is formed in part by their own perspectives on that discourse, hopes and anxieties. Dress, display, non-ecclesial perspectives are elements not to be criticized, but to be observed; a meaning for them is to be sought in terms of the discourses of the people doing the dressing, performing the display or expressing the different perspective on the ritual. Accessing this different data set requires a different methodological approach; in this case ethnography.

Ethnography and the Study of Worship

A number of recent studies have brought the tools of ethnography to bear on congregational worship. Instead of considering the liturgy simply from an historical or theological angle, these studies have sought to engage directly with the people in the pews. It is their understanding of the liturgical event, and of the manner in which it relates to the rest of their lives, that is investigated. The researcher gathers data by immersing him or herself as far as possible in the worship event, observing it very closely, and by conducting interviews with participants where they are invited to relate their own experience and understanding of the liturgy in which they participate. The data obtained from this type of study is generally categorized as 'qualitative' rather than 'quantitative' – that is, it is not generally reducible to statistical analysis.

By far the largest-scale study in this field has been carried out in Chicago, Illinois, drawing on the services of a large number of researchers to create a city-wide ethnography of Church practice (Livesey, 2000). In Britain, the studies have been on a smaller scale, but there is, none the less, a growing body of research into the study of congregations and their worship. Martin Stringer (1999) compared the experience of worship in four English churches that came from very different traditions. Karin Tusting of the University of Lancaster has conducted research into church congregations in the northern English town of Kendal as part of her university's *Kendal Project* investigating changing patterns of religious life in that town (Heelas and Woodhead, 2004).[1] Other studies in the field include James Steven's work on charismatic worship in the Church of England (Steven, 2002), and two collections that explore the theoretical issues at stake (Arweck and Stringer, 2002; Guest, Tusting and Whitehead, 2004). Three studies of first communion have also been produced that use ethnographic methods. Two of these come from the United States (McCallion, Maines and Wolfel, 1996; Bales, 2005), whilst the third is Irish (Lodge, 1999). Susan Ridgely Bales' work is particularly interesting in the use she makes of drawings produced by the children as ethnographic data alongside interview and observation. This is a useful reminder that there are more ways of expressing a discourse than simply through the spoken word. As my own findings suggest, the ways in which first communicants and their families used dress and other consumer items was as powerful a medium for conveying messages about their approach to the ritual as the words they spoke.

Participant Research

Moving to my own research, the first methodological lesson I learned was that it would be impossible for me to claim an objective stance during my research. This was for two reasons. First, in each location I was identified as a priest, being introduced by title in each setting I entered. I regarded this as essential in order to respect the integrity of the encounter. It was impossible to pretend that as ethnographer I could be divested of my particular status within the Catholic community as an ordained minister. The second reason for not pretending objectivity arose from my personal context of commitment: I remain a practising member of the Catholic Church, a position intensified and institutionalized by ordination. The research was directed towards understanding what is in effect my own faith community, and the issues it raises cannot but impact upon me personally.

I was therefore a participant observer. However, this simple statement requires further qualification, as it masks the multiplex identity I brought to the role of researcher (Davies, 1999; Collins, 2002). I was priest, male, academic, non-Liverpudlian, and a diocesan post-holder. These different facets of my identity featured in my interactions with the various parties, across a spectrum of positions that highlighted the complexity of my insider/outsider status. A fundamental element was my identity as a Catholic, with a personal investment in the Church's future. I had myself taken part as a child in the ritual under study, and for several years I had been responsible for its celebration. In that sense, I was an 'insider', seeking to

---

1   See also the official website at <http://www.lancs.ac.uk/fss/projects/-ieppp/kendal/index.htm>.

understand a reality within whose social network I already belonged. However, I had never been a member of any of the fieldwork communities. I grew up in a small mining village in the northern part of the archdiocese; my accent alone pointed to a certain 'outsider' status as a non-Liverpudlian, and the formative influences in my own childhood faith had been the Lancashire Catholicism of my mother rather than the immigrant Irish tradition of the city centre. Therefore, both the Catholicism I experienced in the fieldwork parishes and the social reality within which it was manifested were subtly different from my own background. To no small extent the historical research represented in earlier chapters grew from my own need to form a broader frame of reference for the religious and social setting I encountered in the fieldwork.

A similar multiplex identity emerges when my relationship to the various parties in the event is considered. The priests were members of my own peer group and generally spoke with me freely and in considerable detail. However, they also related to me as a member of the central archdiocesan structures, and despite my insistence that the research project was entirely personal, the priests in the first and second parishes expressed a hope that my results would in some way feed into archdiocesan policy on first communion. A variant on this issue occurs in Williamson (1999). She undertook to her respondents that she would feed-back anonymously to the diocesan authorities any observations or comments people wished to make (pp. 127–8). She recognizes the ambiguity this introduced into her role, but describes it as a 'trade-off' (p. 152) that enabled her to acquire the data.

My relationship as ethnographer with my subjects was therefore quite complex. It is entirely possible that they fitted what they said to their expectations of me, and that they were using their encounters with me to convey messages to the archdiocese. In that sense, therefore, it is essential to recognize that at least some of the data was constructed from the particular engagement between ethnographer and respondent. With regard to the question of my passing on my observations within the archdiocese, the only archdiocesan forum in which I have made a formal presentation of some aspects of my findings was a conference of thirty priests and a few lay parish workers held at the then Liverpool Hope University College (now Liverpool Hope University) in 2002. The priests of both the first and second subject parishes were present, though I did not identify them as having participated in my research. However, they declared themselves in the course of discussion following my presentation, and affirmed my analysis when another priest challenged my findings as representing a 'bygone age' rather than current realities.

The impossibility of writing myself out of both observation and interview processes is best illustrated by an interview with the priest in the second parish. Reflection on the interview reveals his perception of the impact of my presence as observer within a group of parents. It also highlights the manner in which his musings upon that impact modified his thinking during the interview. The issue turned around the clothes I wore at an observed meeting. None of the priests of the subject parish wore distinctive clerical dress, preferring an open-necked shirt to the clerical 'dog-collar'. This was my normal practice too, but I made my first observation of a parents' meeting in the second parish immediately after attending a diocesan engagement and was wearing a clerical shirt. Commenting on the session afterwards, the priest observed that the level of participation by the parents had been unusually low, and identified my clerical dress as the cause. This led him to reflect in depth on the uneasy relationship his parishioners enjoyed with all systems, figures and symbols of authority. The incident highlighted two ways in which my presence was one of the factors forming the data: whilst the priest suggested that it suppressed engagement within the groups of parents, it also catalysed his own observations. A different ethnographer (say, a non-priest with no link with the archdiocese) might have obtained different data from the encounters. This is not to deny the validity of my data, but simply to recognize its partial nature.

The Fieldwork Sites

From pilot interviews in my own parish during the first part of 1998 I became aware of the delicacy of my own position as researcher. As parish priest, and therefore celebrant of the ritual, I exercised considerable power within the first communion event. It was my policy to place no restrictions on admission to the ritual save that participating children should be baptized members of the Catholic Church. However, I had worked closely with the parish school to determine both the overall content of the preparation process and the shape the ritual should take. On more than one occasion my position resulted in my defending both of these against alternative proposals from parents of the first communicants in the public forum of parents' meetings. It quickly became evident that it was impossible to factor out my status as incumbent in any encounter with parents – or indeed with any parishioner. Above all, there was a very real risk that any responses to direct interviewing would reflect the inequality in status within the parish of myself and my respondents, and that parents of first communicants in particular would be reluctant to make any response that they feared might jeopardize their child's participation in the event.

I therefore decided to look beyond my own parish, and to follow the process of preparation for and celebration of first communion in three different parishes of the archdiocese, focusing on one in each of the academic years 1998–99, 1999–2000 and 2000–2001. The parishes were selected on the basis of their different approaches to the preparation process. In the first parish, there was a significant attempt to involve a group of young mothers, who themselves were to different degrees marginal to the worshipping community, in work with parents ahead of the event, whilst the children were prepared through the parish primary school. In the second, the entire preparation process was entrusted to the staff of the school. In the third, a radically different approach to preparation for the sacrament was being piloted: responsibility was removed from the school, and the preparation of both parents and children was located during and immediately after the regular Sunday celebration of Mass. The first two parishes were in the inner city of Liverpool, the third in a large estate some miles outside the city, built during the 1970s and populated largely by families originating from the city centre. In all three parishes the children received their first communion during their fourth year of primary school (somewhat confusingly referred to formally as 'Year Three'), that is, between the ages of seven and eight. This is a year older than the age at which first communion had been celebrated since

1911: in each parish the change had occurred as a response to the introduction of Standard Attainment Tests in Year Two, which it was felt would, in conjunction with first communion, overload both teachers and children.

In none of these parishes did research proceed as expected. Access was arranged by approaching the parish priest, who therefore functioned as primary gatekeeper in each setting.[2] However, secondary gatekeepers emerged, particularly in the second and third parishes; the headteacher of the parish primary school in the second, and the parish catechetical co-ordinator in the third. The first of these facilitated my access to the classroom, permitting me to observe the encounters between teacher and pupils during the first communion preparation process. The second circumscribed my observations, controlling access to participants, and sought to turn my presence in the parish to her advantage, as will be discussed below.

Research Methods

A qualitative approach was maintained throughout the project, balancing participant observation with unstructured interviews.[3] The pilot interviews had taught me that attempts to access meaning through direct approaches to parents would result in skewed data. Moreover, it became increasingly evident that many parents of first communicants were carefully negotiating their way towards the ritual around a sequence of gate-keeping obstacles controlled by parish authorities. It would have been unfair of me as an (additional) priest to question the parents directly. Furthermore, responses would have been likely to be weighted towards the answer they felt least likely to compromise their way forward. I therefore restricted my engagement with parents to that of observation, sitting in on parish meetings held with them, and being present in the congregation at Sunday masses at which they were required to be present and at the first communion masses themselves.

A variety of recording methods were used. I agreed the use of a tape recorder with the catechetical team in the first parish to record their meetings, with the class teacher in the second parish for observations of his lessons, and with some school pupils whom I interviewed in the second parish as an extension of my observations. The contents of these tapes were fully transcribed after the event. During the first communion Masses I made brief notes supplemented immediately afterwards by written recollections. For all other observed events I made no notes during the event, but recorded my recollections onto tape immediately afterwards. These taped reports were then transcribed *verbatim*.

The celebration of first communion also directly or indirectly involved a number of people who were not seeking access to the ritual for their children and for whom,

---

2   For a discussion of the complex relationship between researcher and gatekeeper, and the manner in which both parties can influence the research, see Fountain (1993).

3   On the broad subject of ethnographic methodology cf. Agar (1980); Hammersley (1992); Hammersley and Atkinson (1995); Padgett (1999). On ethnographic approaches to the study of contemporary ritual cf. Stringer (1999), Arweck and Stringer (2002); Steven (2002).

therefore, a direct encounter with me would be less threatening. These included parish clergy and sisters, a trainee deacon, and lay people actively involved in the running of their parishes. With a number of these in each location, therefore, I conducted open-ended interviews, seeking to discover their understanding of the ritual and their responses to the families who took part in it. These interviews were all recorded on tape. They yielded data that at times contrasted sharply with the observations, and indicated the lines of conflict quite starkly. However, even here I recognized the subjective nature of the encounter.

The First Subject Parish

The first parish was in the inner city of Liverpool, just over a mile inland from the river Mersey. It was founded in 1861, and its present church was built in 1865. Today the church stands on a broad dual carriageway that is one of the major routes into the city. At the turn of the twentieth century, the parish consisted largely of terraces of small houses. These have since been demolished, and have been replaced by several tower blocks and areas of lower-density two-storied housing arranged in four major estates. The 1998 diocesan returns indicated a nominal Catholic population of 1000, and a practising figure of 152. Hornsby-Smith (1989) cautions against over-confidence in statistical data collected by the Catholic community. He is particularly wary of calculations of the overall Catholic population, which he regards as up to two-fifths short of the true total (p. 1). My research suggests that such wariness is justified: when questioned about the manner in which he calculated the figure, the priest in the first parish replied, 'I just go on doing what's been put down before. We never check – how can you check? There's no formula.' The figure for the total number of regular Mass-goers in Liverpool is arrived at with greater precision: on each of the weekends of October every parish is required to count the number of people present at the Saturday evening and Sunday Masses and then arrive at a weekly average to give to the archdiocese. My experience of attending several Sunday services suggests that in the case of this parish, at least, the diocesan figure for the numbers of Mass-going Catholics was reasonably accurate.

The parish priest was in his early fifties. Ordained in 1972, he had served several curacies and one previous appointment as parish priest before his appointment to the subject parish in 1992. In 1997, he was given responsibility for an adjacent parish as well, though he made no attempt to amalgamate the two parishes. There were two celebrations of Sunday Mass in the subject parish – a 'Saturday for Sunday' Mass at 7.00 on Saturday evening and a Mass at 11.00 on Sunday morning. During the five weekends of May 1999, the parish first communions were celebrated during both Saturday evening and Sunday morning Masses.

Preparation of the parents for first communion was led by the priest in conjunction with a team of parish catechists. The team had grown out of a successful community action project spearheaded by the priest several years earlier. This gave them their name: they were the 'A-Team', a title borrowed from a 1980s US television series featuring a problem-solving team of outlaws and desperados. Once the project had been completed, the team re-formed each year for the first communion programme.

The academic year 1998–99 was their sixth year of operating in this way, and there were five female members of the team, all with children of school age. The priest prided himself that these women were not 'regular church-goers'; observation established that this was only partly true. They did, however, occupy a range of renegotiated positions with regard to one major area of dissonance, namely family formation. (Thumb-nail biographies of the A-Team members are given in Chapter 8. Their pseudonyms – Brenda, Josie, June, Nicky, Veronica – will be used in Chapter 7 to aid the flow of the narrative.)

The fieldwork period ran from October to May. From October to December, I regularly attended the Sunday Mass. After Christmas, I attended the meetings of the 'A Team', and the parents' meetings that they led. I observed almost all the ten first communion Masses during May. Meanwhile, across the fieldwork period, I conducted interviews with the priest and key parishioners.

The Second Subject Parish

This parish was just over a mile away from the first, in the heart of Toxteth at the southern side of the city centre. The parish was founded in 1865, and the church built in 1878. The housing stock was a mixture of late nineteenth-century terraces and late twentieth-century council housing. The 1998 diocesan statistics give a figure of 200 Sunday Mass-goers from a total of 2,400 Catholics. Once again, my regular attendance on Sundays during the year of observation suggested that the Mass-going figure was reasonably accurate. This parish contrasted strongly with the first in four aspects – parish involvement in first communion, gender, interests of the priest, and the form of the first communion Masses. First, there was very little direct parish involvement in the first communion process. This parish had no equivalent to the 'A Team'. Instead, responsibility for all preparation (both of the children and of the parents) lay with the school, which also traditionally controlled the first communion Masses. Whereas the chief power-broker in the first parish had been the parish priest; here it was the (female) headteacher. Secondly, there was a difference in the gender of the person with most immediate responsibility for preparing the children. Whereas the first parish had offered an almost exclusively female voice, the class teacher in the second parish was male. This offered the possibility of a different perspective. Third, the parish priest in the second parish had only recently been appointed there, unlike the priest in the first parish who had been in post for several years. Therefore, I presumed that the second priest had not yet stamped the first communion process with his own personality – though I was to learn, despite his statements to the contrary, that he had already introduced significant alterations. These reflected his own keen interest in liturgy – contrasting with the first priest's concerns around social justice. Finally, the first communion Masses themselves took a very different form from those of the first parish, being spread across only two Masses.

As with the first parish, the fieldwork consisted of observation and informal interviews. The former initially focused upon 'regular' Sunday Masses, two meetings held by the priest and headteacher with parents of first communicants, two classroom lessons during the immediate run-up to first communion, and the first communion

Masses themselves. Interviews were conducted with the priest, the headteacher and the classroom teacher. However, part-way into this tranche of fieldwork the focus for research was broadened out in two directions.

First, the head of Religious Education (RE) in the local Catholic secondary school expressed interest in my project, and offered to facilitate an encounter with a group of Year Seven children (aged eleven to twelve), who had recently explored in the classroom memories of their own first communion day. The second expansion happened as I noted the emergence of a new power-figure within the Catholic community. A religious sister, whom I shall call Sister Margaret, had been employed to co-ordinate catechesis across the eight parishes of the deanery of which my subject parish was part (the parish priest was in fact the dean). Her office was located in the presbytery of my subject parish. In that parish she had developed a programme for baptismal preparation. In five other parishes she had also introduced a revised first communion programme, operating with Year Three children in each case. Her programme clawed back into the parish office the responsibility that the parish schools had formerly held for sacramental preparation. It also introduced a requirement that admission to first communion should be subject to attendance by both children and parents at a series of special meetings and Masses during the first two terms of the school year. This approach to first communion differed radically from that of either my first or second subject parishes. Moreover, the fact that Sister Margaret already exercised a catechetical role within the second subject parish introduced an element of conflict. Throughout the period of my observations, she pressed the parish priest to extend her remit there to include first communion preparation. The priest and the primary school headteacher were unyielding in resisting the suggestion that her parish-based programme should be introduced in the parish. Accordingly, I extended my observations and interviews to include Sister Margaret and two of the parishes that had accepted her first communion process.

The Third Parish

The third parish was founded in 1967, when its church was also built, in a new-town development some miles outside Liverpool. The housing stock was poor, consisting of two-storey prefabricated buildings. The 1998 archdiocesan statistics gave the parish a total Catholic population of 4,000, of whom 336 were reported to attend Sunday Mass. It proved difficult to verify this figure, as throughout my period of observation the numbers at Sunday Mass was regularly swelled by the first communicants and their parents. This was because regular attendance was a prerequisite for admission to the first communion ceremony; the preparation sessions were held immediately after Mass on two Sundays each month, making it easy for the parish authorities to check on who had (and had not) attended. The figure of 336 seemed closer to the numbers attending on a weekend at which one of these preparation Masses was celebrated rather on a normal weekend.

Part way through this third period of fieldwork, I concluded that I had to abandon it. The immediate cause for this decision was another form of conflict, whose impact and ramifications I had not foreseen. This was between the authorities within the parish and some of those within the central diocesan administration. The parish was piloting a radically different approach to first communion developed in the adjoining diocese of Salford (cf. Cooke, 1998). Permission for the pilot had been granted by the archbishop, who as Bishop of Salford had introduced it there. The diocesan advisers for schools' religious education believed that they had not been adequately consulted before the decision to pilot was taken, and consequently viewed the project with a degree of suspicion.

That this suspicion may have been mutual is perhaps reflected in the way in which my observations within the parish were closely controlled by the parish catechetical co-ordinator, a religious sister. The catechetical sessions I observed were by design exceedingly brief, and were characterized not by open discussion among parents but by a more or less formal instruction led by lay catechists. Furthermore, over six months I was only able to interview one lay person within the parish, and even that meeting was arranged by the sister and took place in the convent. I learned shortly before the first communion celebration that whilst my operations within the parish were being thus carefully controlled, the parish sister was using my presence there to claim archdiocesan approval of the approach. This mistaken perception of my role, and the resulting misrepresentation seriously compromised my work. I have therefore chosen to disregard the limited results I was in the process of obtaining there. The consequent loss of information was more than compensated for by the extension of focus that had taken place during the second year òf fieldwork, as the attitude of Sister Margaret anticipated many – though not all – of the features I encountered in the third parish.

Having reviewed my research methodology and taken a broad overview of the fieldwork sites, we can now progress to exploring the results in detail. The next chapter will resume the treatment of discourses of meaning that was introduced in Chapter 2 – only now asking what patterns of meaning are at play on the ground. Chapter 8 explores how conflicting patterns of meaning feed into processes of power and gate-keeping in the lead up to the ritual. Chapter 9 balances Chapter 3, exploring in detail the manner in which the ritual itself was celebrated in the fieldwork sites. Finally, Chapter 10 takes a synoptic view of today's ritual, analysing the use of display and consumer goods within the event.

CHAPTER 7

Discourses of Meaning on the Ground

Having considered the parishes in which I carried out fieldwork and the methodology I used in gathering data there, we can now proceed to consider my findings. My initial concern is with the issue of the meaning that participants bring to the ritual. There are two questions that need to be asked. The first looks back to Chapter 5 and asks to what extent the official understanding of first communion as a sacrament of Christian initiation penetrated to ground level. Is this, in fact, how participants perceive the ritual in which they participate? The second question then asks what other discourses of meaning fed into the event in the parishes studied. In order to respond to these questions, it is essential to map out the mechanisms by which the Church's discourses were transmitted within the parishes. This requires an explication of one of the chief peculiarities of English Catholic life that distinguishes it from the American or the continental European experience: namely, the all-pervading role played the parish primary school in the religious education of Catholic children. As we shall discover, the expectations of all parties in the event – and some of the tensions that flare up between them – are tied up as much with the school as they are with the liturgy celebrated in the parish church.

The Role of the Parish School

To a considerable extent, the continuing participation of non-church-going Catholics in the first communion ritual relates to the persistence of denominational schools. The Catholic Church in England and Wales is committed to providing a primary school place to all Catholic children, as far as is possible, and most Catholic parishes have a primary school whose catchment area corresponds to the parish boundaries. These schools differ from church schools in the United States and mainland Europe in that they are fully integrated into the state education system, and are almost entirely funded and maintained by the secular Local Education Authority. The Catholic diocese pays 15 per cent of the capital costs of its schools, and in return is entitled to nominate a majority of 'Foundation Governors' onto the school's governing body. Through this network of foundation governors the Church is able to control the ethos of the school, set a ceiling (usually extremely low) for numbers of non-Catholic students, and exercise considerable influence in the appointment of teachers – especially in the case of head teachers and their immediate deputies. Each diocese also holds considerable autonomy over the religious curriculum, and it is the responsibility of the diocese, rather than the Local Education Authority, to inspect not only the delivery of RE but also the overall ethos of the school. Church schools are generally perceived to be providers of high-quality education and to have a good ethos. This positive status of most Church schools means that most Catholic parents are disinclined to send their children elsewhere. Indeed, a desire to obtain a place for a child in a Catholic school is not infrequently cited by priests as a key motivation among parents for bringing their children to baptism.

The continued existence, then, of the parish primary school provides a focus for Catholic identity that is not predicated upon regular participation in formal Church worship. Education in a Catholic school becomes a highly tangible marker of generational continuity within families, and the school's staff – especially its headteacher – are frequently the most immediate point of contact that parents have with the formal structures of parish life. The headteacher in the school attached to the second subject parish explained that she frequently exercised an intermediary role between priest and parents. This role, she said, became particularly important around first communion when parents who had not attended church for a long time felt unsure about their own role in the ceremony – and about the reception they were likely to receive from the priest:

> But they need to come to you first to see whether he was going to rant and rave – they don't know. So they come to me and say, 'Can I go to Communion when my child makes its First Communion, and these are my circumstances.' Because they think you're Church, and they think you're holy, before they can get to the priest – because they hear horror stories.

The ceremony of first communion forefronts the pivotal role that the school plays in negotiating the relationship between its pupils and their families and the rest of the parish community. This is for two reasons. First, the first communion cohort is identified with a particular year group in the parish school – generally Year Two (children aged 6–7) or Year Three (aged 7–8). Thus, in practice it is enrolment at the parish school, rather than regular participation in Church worship, that is the primary portal through which most children access the ritual. Second, the school normally provides a significant degree of formal preparation of the children for the ritual through classroom RE. The classroom lessons provided during the academic year of a cohort's first communion to differing degrees highlight and develop themes related to the first communion. This preparatory function resonates with the expectations of many within the Catholic community that their schools should play a key role in instructing future generations about, and forming them into, normative Catholic practices and life choices.

However, the majority of pupils who pass through the Catholic school system do not regularly attend Mass. Their families make lifestyle choices (for example, with regard to cohabitation or remarriage following divorce) that do not markedly differ from the rest of society. Consequently, there is a sense among some Catholics that the denominational schools are 'failing', and the religious syllabuses are subjected to frequent criticism (McLeod, 2003). This perception, however, ignores a number of developments that have taken place over the past twenty years, relating both to the organization of contemporary schools and to the rationale that now underpins the school RE syllabus followed in most dioceses. The considerable financial benefits brought through the inclusion of Catholic schools within the overarching state provision are balanced by the requirement that those schools should comply with educational directives. In practice, this means that they have to deliver the National Curriculum, a requirement that significantly impacts upon school organization and the pressures on classroom time. Whilst Catholic schools aim to provide a working environment that embodies Catholic moral and ethical values – not least in the manner in which the school treats its staff and pupils – they do not generally regard themselves solely as instruments for the transmission of Catholic doctrine or practice. Nor, at least formally, would the dioceses expect this of them.

Instead, in its official catechetical documentation, the Catholic Church in England and Wales insists that the parish school is only one player in a three-way partnership responsible for the children's religious education. The other two are the child's family and its parish. The roots of this partnership approach are, at least in theory, well-established within Catholic tradition. After all, *Quam Singulari* had insisted upon a shared discernment by parish clergy and parents of each child's readiness to commence communicating. The partnership vision was more fully articulated through catechetical schemes that emerged during the 1980s – most notably as continental publications such as Wim Saris' programme of family and community catechesis, originally produced in The Netherlands, became available in translation for an English-speaking market (Saris, 1982). From the mid-1980s onwards this position was formalized as a central core of the national catechetical project of the Bishops' Conference – and found its clearest theoretical expression in Purnell (1985) and Gallagher (1986).

The partnership approach is predicated on three factors. The first is that the child should be enrolled in a Catholic school. The second is that the parish itself should have formal catechetical structures in place to complement classroom RE. The third is that the families of the children should be engaged with both parish and school. The only one of these three factors that is generally certain is the first. The other two depend upon the parish's own commitment to provide a sustained catechetical process outside the school and also on the manner in which families choose to practise their faith and relate to the parish.

In practice, the level of commitment to long-term engagement with the local Church on the part of most English Catholics is generally minimal. Furthermore, very few Catholic parishes have sustained catechetical processes that are capable of supporting the expectation laid upon them by this overarching vision. This is to no little extent due to the still widespread expectation among Catholics that a key function of parish schools is precisely that of educating children in the faith; providing a parallel catechetical framework outside the school is generally seen as neither necessary nor practicable. This systemic imbalance between the two institutional elements within the tripartite partnership is reinforced by a general reluctance to match the level of professional competence found in schools with the employment of fully trained lay catechists in parishes. The formal engagement of paid parish catechists across the country has been patchy, and as the second of my fieldwork studies identified their role is by no means clear. This stands in marked contrast with the prevailing situation in much of the United States, where paid parish catechists are frequently encountered. As a consequence, the partnership between parish and school in England and Wales is frequently unequal, with most parishes providing at best a short-term programme ahead of first communion and confirmation. These programmes are generally led by volunteers, who may have received very little formal training – as was the case in my first subject parish. Furthermore, it is now to be questioned how deeply the Catholic Church in England and Wales is, in fact committed to implementing its own vision of a home-parish-school partnership. At the time of writing two English dioceses had recently dismantled the central diocesan structures that trained and supported the work of volunteer laity in this field.[1]

In the fieldwork a number of different approaches emerged to the parish-school partnership. In the first subject parish, the priest attempted to establish a framework within the parish that could support the parents in their role as educators of their children. All preparation of the children themselves was carried out in school, and the parish did not seek to engage the children outside the classroom. However, a series of meetings was set up for parents that attempted to explore on an adult level the same issues that the children were studying in the classroom. The aim was to enable the parents to better fulfil their role in the tripartite partnership: by themselves becoming familiar with the concepts that the children were studying, they would be better able to explore those issues with their children in the home. As we shall see in Chapter 8, however, at times a serious dissonance emerged between the concepts proposed for discussion with the parents and the realities of their family lives.

The second subject parish provided evidence of a system in transition. In the parish itself the school played a dominant role in preparing both the children and their parents. However, this was one of the rare settings that did engage a paid qualified catechist, who was shared with a number of other parishes. In these other parishes she was attempting to raise the profile of the church-going parish in the ritual – and the gate-keeping role it exercised – at the expense of the school. As I shall explore in Chapter 8, this attempt to shift the balance of roles between the various parties in the partnership resulted in conflict and power-play.

Educational/Catechetical Resources

The core programme of RE published under the National Project and followed in most Catholic dioceses of England and Wales is *Here I Am* (Byrne and Malone, 1992; second edition Byrne, Malone and White, 2000). The rationale embodied in this programme has already been considered in Chapter 5. The developmental approach embraced by *Here I Am* leads to a wariness – implicit in the first edition in use during my fieldwork, and explicated in the second edition – about introducing reflection on the miraculous at too early a stage:

> Miracles, therefore, are important but easily misunderstood. Jesus himself was aware of the danger of missing the meaning. Until the age of nine or ten, children have a well-developed magical mentality and a simplistic 'magical' view of Jesus is a very real danger. This may lead to disillusionment and rejection when miracles don't happen for them. [Byrne, Malone and White, 2000, p. 33]

---

1   *The Tablet*, 7 January 2006, pp. 2, 31.

A similar wariness is to be found in the programme's treatment of the 'real presence' of Christ in the eucharist. Care is taken to avoid demanding an over-realistic understanding of the eucharist too early. This caution reflects the position adopted by the hierarchy in Bishops' Conference of England and Wales (1996), which states that it is only at Key Stage Four, age 14, that children are required to study and reflect upon 'the presence of Christ in the Eucharist in word, priest, people, bread and wine' (p. 32).

Different approaches towards *Here I Am* were adopted in the fieldwork settings. In the first parish it formed the basis of all the preparation, of children and parents alike. In the second parish a radically different approach was adopted. *Here I Am* was used for the Year Three children (aged 7–8) for the first term and a half, but during the half-term leading immediately to first communion it was abandoned. An American resource was followed which was designed for parish rather than school use (Leichner, 1992). This interrupted the systematic and progressive approach to RE provided by Byrne and Malone, and led to the isolated treatment of first communion in a self-contained process of religious instruction that could not easily be integrated into either previous or future learning. This lack of integration was manifested both in the rupturing of the educational structure, and in the introduction of precisely those elements of the miraculous and of eucharistic realism that the bishops seek to defer until a later developmental stage. The difficulties created for the children's attempts to understand the eucharist – and for the classroom teacher – will be discussed below.

Leichner opens by inviting the children to consider their own baptism (pp. 12–13). However, whilst the background material describes the eucharist as a deepening and strengthening of the Catholic's relationship with Christ and the Church, this is presented to the children in terms of a discourse not of progressive initiation but of Mass-going and frequent reception of communion as normative behaviour for Catholics.

The process used by the parish catechetical co-ordinator Sister Margaret, in those parishes where she held responsibility for first communion, also undermined the *Here I Am* approach, but in a different manner. The children with whom she worked followed *Here I Am* in their classroom, but their participation in her out-of-school 'lessons' was considered as the normative preparation for the event. She thereby over-layered the *Here I Am* material with resources she had herself prepared. As her material also introduced elements of the miraculous that Byrne and Malone's developmental approach delays until a later age, Sister Margaret, too, disturbed the developmental rhythm of the children's religious education. As with Leichner, her preparation for first communion opened with a treatment of baptism – this time understood as the event through which the children had come to belong to God's family. The eucharist was then presented as a gathering of that family, but no attempt was made to present the eucharist in terms of further initiatory action. A pedagogy of first communion as a rite of Christian initiation was thus absent from each of the settings studied – not least because the catechetical materials encountered there did not forge a link between baptism and the eucharist within an initiatory framework. So did Sacrament of Initiation discourse emerge in the fieldwork sites – and what other discourses of meaning for this ritual were encountered there?

Official Church Discourses of Meaning in the Fieldwork

The Initiation Discourse

Although it forms the theoretical framework within which the Catholic Church today understands first communion, the discourse of initiation did not explicitly feature in the preparation of either children or parents in any of the settings. It was raised, however, on three occasions during the second year of fieldwork, and each time was considered problematic. Two instances emerged in the course of my discussions with individuals who shared a particular context, and this pair will be considered first. The first occurred during an interview with the head of RE in one of the local Catholic secondary (high) schools. This school drew its pupils from a number of inner-city primary schools – including those of both the first and second subject parishes. Speaking immediately after she had attended a first communion celebration in the second subject parish, she said:

> I mean, I looked around today and I've never felt more keenly the whole thing about the divorce between what actually happens and the theory of it being part of the rite of Christian initiation. And I wondered, where's the connection with baptism? Where are the candles they were given at baptism? Parents and godparents coming forward? (And whether they're together as units or not is irrelevant.) But does it fit in with what happened seven years ago in most cases? And how does the ordinary Sunday community, the ordinary Saturday night community, see this as welcoming someone deeper into their membership?

When questioned further about her use of the term 'divorce' to describe the mismatch between theory and practice, she focused on the manner in which it was the child – rather than the explicit content of the initiation discourse – which formed the focus of attention:

> It was all centred on performance – the performance of the child, making sure that their child stood out especially well. It was divorced from faith. Looking well. Walking well. Looking absolutely gorgeous. Carrying their book in the procession. Looking absolutely sweet when they were up on the altar – rather than, 'Thank God we've arrived at this stage: three cheers for Jesus!'

The same teacher facilitated for me a number of group interviews with her own twelve-year-old students. The initiation discourse also emerged during these interviews. Most of the children in each group were Catholic, but the non-Catholic minority took a lively interest in the discussion, at times interrogating their peers concerning the ceremony. Thus, one of the non-Catholic children asked her group, 'Why do you have them, then, communions?' The following answers were given in quick succession:

- To welcome you into God's family.
- No, 'cos you're already welcome into God's family when you've been christened.
- It's another step.

- And then you're in, sir. And then you get, erm, confirmed. Then you get married.

I asked the question of the second group, who replied:

- So we're in God's family.
- To be able to take the bread.
- So you can get communion and get part of God.
- So you can get loads of money.
- So you can have, yeah, so you can have …
- No, 'cos you're a Catholic when you …

There was, therefore, some sense within the group of an initiatory dimension to first communion, but the children found that dimension to be problematic on two fronts. First, to some of the children it appeared to run counter to the discourse dominant in primary school, of baptism as the gateway into the Christian family. Second, whilst several of the children did locate first communion within a sequence of ritual events, the sequence envisaged was broader than the triple sacraments of initiation in the formal discourse. It was several times expressed as baptism – first communion – confirmation – wedding – funeral. It is thus possible that the children were locating first communion in a sequence of life-course, rather than Christian initiatory, rituals. Moreover, it is impossible to discount or determine the influence of their current teacher in placing the initiation discourse in the forefront of their thinking.

Finally, the discourse of first communion as sacrament of initiation was also used by Sister Margaret, the catechetical co-ordinator in the second subject parish. When asked to elaborate, she replied:

> Well, it's the move – I mean, in a church term, it's the movement to being able to take part fully in the liturgy, isn't it … The child has reached this point in their religious life, their spiritual life, of being a full member, able to communicate with the rest of the congregation.

There was no link here to baptism or confirmation, but a strong sense that the ritual marked a gateway into a more complete mode of participation in worship. This expectation for future liturgical engagement placed Sister Margaret on the horns of a dilemma. On the one hand, the discourse of first communion as a sacrament of initiation led her to expect that the enactment of the ritual should lead to practical consequences in the lives of its participants – effectively, regular reception of communion. On the other hand, experience had taught her that the ritual did not in fact serve as a doorway into a new pattern of ecclesial affiliation. She therefore reinterpreted the ritual for the participants, retaining the construct of initiation but transferring its focus away from the Church:

> It is some sort of, I think – well, it is initiation, isn't it. But I don't know if it's initiation into the Church. But it's some, some sort of ritual that, you know, one of today's stages of your life. Marriage has gone, so the next one's your funeral. They're rituals that you have to go through.

First communion, thus perceived, becomes a ritual of life-passage within a broad sequence similar to that understood by the twelve-year-old pupils above.

A similar attempt at reinterpreting the initiation discourse was made by the secondary school teacher quoted earlier. Later in the course of her interview she reversed the polarity of her earlier argument, and directed her complaint not at the families who had failed to engage with the ecclesial discourse, but at the discourse itself and those responsible for promoting it:

> It's a rite of initiation, but forget the 'Christian'. Forget the 'Christian'. It's a rite and it's passage … Let the bishops listen. This is where people are at. This is not where we want them – this is where they are at, where they are. But are we where they are? That's the question! Are we where people are?

She did not explain her understanding of 'passage' in this context. What clearly emerged was her understanding that there was a mismatch between the ecclesial discourse and practice on the ground, and her sense that a resolution of this could fruitfully proceed not from a reinforcement of the doctrinal position but from a serious consideration of the lived reality of those who participated in the ritual. There is a major contrast between the positions of the two women here. The teacher was arguing for a radical review of the discourse in the light of experience, and using the manner in which the event was approached by the first communicants and their families to critique the formal position. Sister Margaret was engaged in exactly the reverse process, an approach which, as the next chapter will show, drew her into conflict with the parish priest of the second subject parish and the head of the parish primary school.

The Continuing Impact of the Age of Reason Discourse

The fieldwork results suggest, therefore, that the post-Vatican II initiatory understanding has not penetrated to ground level in the locations studied. Indeed, it appears to raise more theoretical problems than it resolves. At the same time, however, there was ample evidence that an older discourse associated with the event continues to exercise considerable importance. This is the concept of the Age of Reason that, as we have noted, was wedded through the revised Code of Canon Law to the newer initiatory construct. The concerns about the capacity of children to understand the eucharist expressed in response to the 1910 reform resurfaced during the fieldwork as various parties struggled to express their understanding of the meaning of the event to young children. I shall focus on two fieldwork data sources that illustrate the educational issues: an interview from the first parish with the retired schoolteacher Annie whom we met earlier, and observations of a first communion lesson in the primary school of the second parish. Finally, a section of the interviews with the Year Seven pupils will be used to illustrate their understanding of the issues raised in the primary school lesson.

Annie was in her eighties, but none the less continued to be deeply involved in the life of her parish. One of the greatest supporters of the priest, she shared his passionate concern for justice in the community, but was also forthright in criticizing aspects of the first communion programme. She struggled to reconcile the approach to the event that she encountered in the families of first communicants with those of her own upbringing and her long experience as a teacher in Catholic primary schools. Thus, she compared the methodology of RE that she had employed during her early teaching career with more recent experience in the classroom:

> Now I'm probably going to shock you, you know, but, erm, when we used the old syllabus years before you were born – Bishop Downey's[2] – you *did* the commandments, we *did* the sacraments. The children came to Mass ... I shouldn't be shocked by this but I went back: I go to the parish school (or did occasionally) and help with special needs – just little groups, you know? And one day, first of all - does this really matter, it did to me – erm, how to make the Sign of the Cross at ten? I thought, 'Is this important?' I must change. I mean, I'm pre-Vatican II, you know, and I've had to change.

This goes further than a criticism of the attitudes of the children. The repeated 'We *did* the sacraments' implies that the current syllabus fails to do so. Indeed, she stated that her decision to leave teaching was influenced by changes in the RE syllabus:

> I like things done the right way, and if they're not done the right way I don't swim with the current. You know, it's so easy to sit there and say, 'Well, let me get on with it – it's okay.' And actually what pushed me into an early retirement was the [new] syllabus. [Bullen, 1969]

Yet, she also struggled with the educational issues, and recognized the magnitude of the task:

> If I took a child of seven in a class and started to teach them theology, apologetics, pure and advanced maths, Japanese – you'd say, you know, 'Come on!' But we're doing that in religion. We're taking a semi-baby of seven, even in these sophisticated days they're still only seven, and we're trying to put into them truths that you have been studying and so on. It can't be. It's too, it's too, it's too hard, it's too early.

The difficulties that Annie identified in introducing young children to the concepts contained in formal Church teaching on first communion were acutely highlighted during a lesson I observed in the primary school of the second subject parish. This lesson contained a detailed consideration of the meaning of the 'real presence' of Christ in the eucharistic species. That the class should have been considering this subject in any detail at all this came about as a direct result of the school's decision to replace *Here I Am* with the Leichner resource, as mentioned earlier. By entering into a detailed discussion of this issue, the teacher found himself increasingly in difficulty. He struggled to communicate to the children the content of the formal ecclesial discourse, whilst remaining faithful to his own mediated position with regard to this doctrine. This led him to propose to the children a conceptual stance far removed from the formal ecclesial discourse. He wished to avoid an over-realistic understanding of the eucharist as the 'body and blood' of Christ, and therefore had

---

2   Cf. Archdiocese of Liverpool (1943a & b).

recourse to two strategies. First, he made constant reference to the bread and wine as 'symbols' of the body and blood of Christ, and second, he invited the children to locate any difference between the eucharistic species and normal food not objectively in the bread and wine but subjectively within themselves:

> The difference really, the difference is here [pointing to his head] and here [pointing to his heart.] In your head and in your heart. In what you believe.

This subjective symbolic understanding of the eucharist stands outside the formal insistence upon an objective and real presence of Christ (CCC 1374). Yet the teacher admitted to the children that even this renegotiated position was difficult to understand:

> So you're just seven, eight years old – and, yeah, it is very, very confusing – it might sound extremely confusing. But even in this book here it's telling that no one understands it completely – not even [inaudible] – and nobody does understand it.

A child interrupted, by asking, 'Do you understand it?' The teacher replied:

> To tell you the truth, no, I don't understand it completely. I don't think many people could because it is such a mysterious thing and as I said before, it's up to everybody themselves, really how much they believe in it themselves.

However, the teacher's attempts to convey to the children this symbolic and subjective approach to the Real Presence discourse was in contrast to the realistic approach that they found in the Leichner workbooks. Thus, in leading them through the relevant section, he said:

> Now, this is the most difficult part really to understand, to get a grasp of. Because what happens during the Mass is the priest says a blessing over the bread and the wine, and what happens is it changes into the body and blood of Jesus. But, it doesn't, when you look at it, it doesn't really change at all to look at. But the fact that the priest said this special blessing has changed it. Now we believe that it is changed. I think that's the important thing, that if we believe that that's changed, then it has changed. Very, very difficult to, to grasp. 'The bread and wine become his body and blood.'

There was a tension, then, between the workbook's language of sacramental realism and the rather more nuanced message he was attempting to communicate. The two approaches were contradictory, potentially compounding the children's confusion. The difficulties became evident when he showed to the children the bread and wine used in the Mass; it was only by the narrowest margin that he avoided recourse to the language of magic:

> Now, I said that the wine is just normal wine. Well this here, this bread, this normal, it's just a normal host at the moment. This has not been blessed yet, so would this be the body of Jesus at the moment?
> *[Several children:]* No.

No, it wouldn't. So it hasn't been blessed yet. It's just a normal host. So what would happen in Mass is the father, the priest would bless the bread, and once the bread has been blessed then it becomes the body of Jesus and, of course, is shared out and we receive the body of Jesus. Same again, would this taste any different? Before it's been blessed and after it's been blessed?

[Several together:] No.

No, it wouldn't. But, is it different?

[Several:] Yes.

It is, isn't it. Yes. And remember we said, how's it different? Well, it's up to you really – it's here and here: in your head and in your heart, and what you believe in. And the priest will have said a special blessing to change it from just being a normal host into the body of Jesus. Now, it's, erm, no – I won't use that phrase.

In a conversation after the lesson, he revealed to me that what he had prevented himself from saying was that the eucharist was 'magic'. He explained that sometimes in class he 'felt' as though he was treading in the footsteps of the classic English comedian Tommy Cooper, whose stage persona was that of a failed magician:

Oh, sometimes I feel like Tommy Cooper, or something, you know, like – [imitating the characteristic gesture of the comedian] … Yeah, it's difficult that, you know, if you compare it with a magic trick – to them it's like, 'ta-da' – it's just some kind of show, erm, you know.

When asked if he had ever used the word 'magic' to describe the eucharist to a class, he replied:

I have, yeah, and, I think that's the main thing that stuck with them, that it was magic. I mean, it wasn't really. I suppose – as it says, it's a mystery, isn't it. Nobody really does. Yeah, I, I just sometimes feel that, you know, it's like Tommy Cooper.

The difficulties experienced by the teacher in communicating a nuanced understanding of the real presence illustrates the problems that were foreseen by opponents of the 1910 reform. If, however, we turn to the age group that until the beginning of the twentieth century had formed the cohort for first communion – namely, the rising twelves – then there was evidence from the fieldwork that considerable confusion remained on this point. Once again, I draw on the group interviews of early secondary school children. In all of these interviews, the favoured expression in speaking about the eucharist was 'the bread'. I therefore asked each group if there was anything special about this bread. The following responses were given in quick succession:

It's been blessed.
With holy water *[laughs]*.
It's been dipped.
You're taking part in his body.
It hasn't been dipped.
[Shouting:] You're drinking his blood and, erm …
Skin.
Eating his body.
Skin *[laughs]*.

[Shouting boy, laughing:] You're drinking his blood and – I can't remember the other one. Drinking his blood and …

When asked how they understood this action of eating and drinking, the same group referred to the Last Supper narrative and the action of the priest at Mass:

I don't know, he said 'This is my body – take it and eat it' or something.
Because it's been blessed off, like somewhere, off Jesus 'cos it's like a, a person that Jesus *[inaudible]* to be like a priest and that, and like, he's got the right to bless it.

These comments do express a certain familiarity with ecclesial discourses. The children related the concept of the eucharist to the Last Supper, the Mass and a particular role played by the priest. However, the pupils remained uncertain as to how the concept of the body of Christ in the eucharist related to physical reality – witness the attempt, repeated in the second group, to identify the eucharistic bread with Jesus' 'skin'. Only one pupil directly challenged the formal position, stating that it was not 'really' the body and blood of Jesus – 'because it'd be stale by now'. These particular exchanges were accompanied by considerable banter; whilst only one boy expressed a position of dissent, it was difficult to assess how seriously the other children took the 'body and blood' discourse.

Other Fieldwork Discourses Around Meaning

The evident struggle of the adult parties noted in the previous section to relate the formal discourse of initiation to their experiences of the first communion event points both to the superficial penetration of the discourse into the everyday conceptual framework of the Catholic world, and to the precarious position it holds there. A failure of a formal system of meaning applied to a ritual event to establish a hold in the minds and hearts of participants leaves the way open for other discourses of meaning to establish themselves. In such a case, a ritual event that ignites strong dissonances in the range of meanings brought to it can become a site of competition at the level of meaning. It became evident from the fieldwork that this was, indeed, the case with first communion. In each setting I studied, the formal discourse competed with other meaningful accounts of the event. Four discourses stood out in particular. These were an understanding of the event in terms of generational continuity, as the one special day of childhood, as a substitute wedding, and as a significant moment in the developing relationship between mothers and daughters. In this section I shall discuss each of these in turn; the next two chapters will then go on to consider the manner in which their presence and articulation in and around the rite fed into situations of conflict.

Generational Continuity

Sister Margaret described first communion as 'like some tribal initiation, almost'. By this term she understood the enactment of the ritual to signify the insertion of the child into a framework of ritual experience that had been shared across the different generations in its family. Engagement in the ritual, therefore, conveyed a sense of continuity between generations. To illustrate this approach, Sister Margaret quoted from a conversation during which the mother of one of the first communicants had said to her, 'Me Nan did it for me Mum, and me Mum did it for me. So I'm doing it for my child.' The same discourse emerged in the first subject parish, though without reference to initiation. During the final 'A Team' meeting, one of the catechists reported a conversation in her group during the first parents' meeting. When this catechist, Josie, directly challenged participants by asking why they were there, one woman replied, 'The reason I'm here? Because I want my daughter to be a proper Catholic.' Another catechist interjected, asking, 'And how often does she come to Church?' Josie continued to report the conversation:

> And she said, ''Cos,' erm, she said, 'from my Nan', she said. 'I made it. My Mum was in a white dress – and I've got pictures. I've got pictures of me in a white dress', she said, 'and I'm forty-five and my daughter's seven', she said, 'and I just want - not the same, but the way I've been brought up. So I don't mean 'cos I'm getting her a white dress I want her to be different from everybody else – it's the way I've been brought up to think of it.' So she said, 'If I was to take her to my Nan and say, "She's made her communion and she had the school dress on", my Nan wouldn't understand that. And I just want to carry it on.' That's what she meant by 'a proper Catholic'.

A desire to reproduce the experience of the ritual in one's own children goes some way to explaining the concerns expressed by parents that the current mode of celebration is an unwelcome rupture with their own experience. Some of the accounts of the 1911 first communion celebrations cited in Chapter 3 described enormous groups of children participating in a single Mass. The more usual practice through the twentieth century was for a school class cohort of children (roughly thirty at a time) to receive first communion during a single ceremony. In recent years the practice in a number of locations – including my first subject parish – has been to divide that cohort into even smaller groups, with the children receiving their first communion across a number of weeks during the ordinary Sunday parish Masses. This last point reflects a number of concerns. With increasing ease of travel, first communion celebrations now attract considerable numbers as they become a focus for the gathering of extended families. Smaller churches are unable to accommodate the large numbers that a cohort-wide celebration would attract. However, it is also possible that given the concerns over participant behaviour and dress that were outlined in the Introduction, the smaller numbers are regarded by some as rendering the event more controllable. Finally, the integration of the ceremony of first communion into the Sunday parish Mass introduces a note of 'normality'. The child receives his or her first communion in the liturgical setting that is now expected to be the focus of a weekly experience of communication. The event becomes normative at the level of individual practice.

However, the pattern of celebrating first communion in smaller groups and in a Mass that is celebrated in as 'normal' a manner as possible severs or at least weakens the ties of memory that link the event with the experience of previous generations. Quite simply, it does not feel the same to adult participants. Concern that the re-patterning of first communion was a breach in generational continuity was expressed during one of the parents' meetings in the first parish. Recalling her own first communion, one mother focused on two elements that she now perceived to be lacking – that the entire cohort received first communion in a single ceremony, and that later in the day they took part in a May Procession. The second point was taken up by an older woman in the group, who specified that in her parish the procession had taken place inside the church building (as the ancillary processions of 1910–11 had often done). The response of the priest when this was discussed during the 'A-Team' meeting was to say: 'There was still that kind of hankering after the way – "Why can't we do it the way we did it as kids? That was good – why can't we still do it?"'

For many participants, therefore, their own personal experience of first communion provides the fundamental frame of reference in their understanding of – and expectations for – the first communion of their children. This suggests that the Catholic authorities have failed to convince large numbers of the members of the community of the validity of their revised discourses. Moreover, the threads of emotive memory that the repetition of a ritual invites are at least as important to participants as are the theoretical discourses that surround it. Both the Church-wide theological reforms of first communion and some individual parish attempts to restructure the event have ignored this vital experiential dimension.

The One Special Day

Further light was cast on the theme of first communion as a tradition to be handed down across generations by a concept that emerged during the 'A Team' meetings. This was the notion that the first communion day was a particularly special day in the life of the child. Another catechist, Brenda, located the event within two different sets of significant moments in a child's life. The first was ecclesial: 'It's the first big church event. It's a special thing … It's the first special event, and the next, the next one'll be, you know, your first confession, and then after that, dunno.' The second was familial: 'It's like going on your first holiday – you know, you're never going to forget it, or your best holiday. Everyone can take something from their childhood and the day – or the first meal sat down with adults. You know, everyone says, "Aren't they a credit. Aren't they good."'

Essential to both these elements was a sense that on each occasion a spotlight was turned on one particular child in the family. The first communion was the most significant of such highlighting, as it was prolonged over a period of weeks – indeed, Brenda felt it could even be viewed as the child's year: 'The other children have to accept it's your turn to take a back step because it's their year. It's their year, and they will take it on to pass on to their children, these special things.'

In conversation with the other 'A-Team' catechists, Brenda explained how the event would be extended as the children were dressed in their first communion clothes and taken to visit relatives:

> *Brenda:* They get took round all the family – people who can't get out of the house – go and see them, get a couple of quid, you know. *[laughs]* No, everyone wants to. That's the truth … All the family comes down, or whatever. If there's somebody that can't get out – you know, mine have still got a great-grandmother alive,

and they're very fortunate. They'll go to her ... she takes them round the whole block. No, my children get sent round the whole block.

Nicky: For money?

Brenda: Yeah for money – it was for money *[laughs]*.

Josie: We done that. We got sent round the whole block – didn't you? For money, you know, a few bob?

The sense that the first communion offered a period of intense celebratory individuation of the child was extended beyond childhood by Nicky. In response to Brenda's comments, she said, 'For Catholics it's like your wedding day. It's the biggest day they're going to ever have ... The difference is that on your wedding day you've got to share your wedding day with someone else.' First communion was therefore understood as a unique event – the most significant public moment in a person's life, when he or she was elevated to be the prolonged sole focus of attention within the family setting. Brenda bracketed this elevation with the sense that this was something that the first communicants in turn were to pass on to their own children. Within this perspective the depth of parental resistance to alterations in the ritual process becomes even more understandable. Attempts to reduce the profile of the event risk lowering the stage on which the child could be placed for what is perhaps the most exalted public moment in his or her life.

The Substitute Wedding

Brenda's comparison of the first communion to a wedding day introduces a related discourse: that first communion represents the wedding day that many children would never have. This potentially could heighten the concerns expressed at the end of the previous paragraph, as the event would truly be the 'one special day' in the individual's entire life. The parish priest in the first subject parish outlined the discourse as he understood it:

> I've heard it said – I've no evidence for it – that if people are worried these days that they're never going to see their little one dressed as a bride, so they do it at first communion. Then possibly they're never going to see the lad dressed as a groom, so they do it at first communion. But, I mean, I don't know – I've just heard that said a few times.
> *Who would have said that? What kind of people have said that to you?*
> Some of the mums and dads, among themselves.
> *You've actually heard parents saying that?*
> Yeah, but they usually say it in a putting down – or at least in my hearing – putting down the elaborateness. Because there is some – there's elements of comparison, of competition. Therefore, people will be saying, 'Oh, I'm not dressing our Mary up that way,' and 'All the lads are not getting dressed up as grooms, or brides, that's because I'm never going to see them get married.' You know, you hear them say that.

The priest's report here presents problems on two fronts. First, the phrase 'in my hearing', suggests that the discourse of first communion as substitute marriage may have been modified or even entirely constructed with him as intended audience. Second, he reported the discourse as being used polemically, that is, against a constructed other. It is, therefore, impossible to discount the possibility of elements of exaggeration or, indeed, complete fabrication. None the less, his report establishes that the discourse was present within the community, even if only in his own interactions with certain of its members. The secondary school children provided further evidence of the discourse; the following conversation developed as they discussed their first communion dress:

> *Girl 1:* You like wear a wedding dress.
> *Girl 2:* You're like a little bride.
> *Girl 1:* That's what I mean, erm, like that
> *Girl 3:* It's like getting married when you're little. I had to walk down the aisle with a little boy
>   *Why is it like getting married when you're little?*
> *Girl 4:* Because you've got to wear the big white gown, like. And you've got to walk down the aisle with a lad.
> *Girl 3:* And you get loads of money.
>   *Did it feel like a wedding?*
> *Girl 4:* I had to go up the aisle with a lad – that felt like a wedding to me.

None of the boys mentioned the bridal association, but for several girls the experience of first communion was evidently evocative of their expectations of a marriage ceremony. This bridal association was created by three factors: the wedding-style outfit, the experience of walking down the aisle of the church in procession alongside a member of the opposite sex, and the reception of cash gifts.

A variant on this discourse emerged in conversation with the priest of the second parish. He reported that one of the girls who had received first communion in the previous year had been killed a few months after the event, and had been dressed for her burial in her first communion outfit. Describing his visit to the family to arrange the funeral, he noted that a large number of photographs of the child in her first communion dress had been displayed by the girl's mother. In the weeks before the first communion day she had 'every few nights' dressed her daughter in the first communion outfit and taken those photographs. By way of explanation, he cited a conversation he had held with the headteacher and then a more recent conversation he had overheard between the mother and a teacher:

> The headteacher told me that she had this dress for the girl because she hadn't had a proper wedding. But, and so wanted her daughter to have something almost like a substitute. So hence the many photographs of the girl in it. And yesterday – what was the conversation yesterday? She was going on about, she was psychic – thought something was going to happen, but glad that the girl had made her first communion. So that's the importance of the dress and the occasion in a tragic situation. But the mother – even before the tragic situation happened – you know, this dress had a very great significance.

First communion is here perceived as a substitute not for the wedding that the daughter herself would never celebrate, but for the wedding that the mother did not have.

Mothers and Daughters

At the parents' meeting and in the 'A Team' debriefing there was a gender weighting in this sense of locating a child within the tradition. One of the mothers in the small group had said, 'It's different for a girl. When you're dressing your daughter up for her first communion, you're remembering your own and the way you looked.' Moreover, this sense of identity between mother and daughter did not take as its sole reference point the mother's past – it was understood by the speaker to be part of the progressive induction of the girl into her future world as a woman. The mother continued, 'You're a woman, and she's going to be a woman.' I questioned the 'A Team' about this later, and Nicky replied:

> It definitely is like that for a little girl. And also you're passing all that onto her, aren't you – you know, your feelings and everything. She's getting all keyed up with your feelings and everything, as well.

None of the other members of the 'A Team' developed this theme. Instead, they focused on the pleasure that as mothers they themselves gained from dressing up their daughters for first communion:

Nicky: They really do enjoy getting dress up.
Josie: They love it, don't they – it's part of it.
Nicky: … and the mums enjoy it just as much …
June: You get pleasure out of seeing their pleasure, don't you. And they're excited, and they're all like …
Josie: The dressing's part of it – it's part of it, isn't it, isn't it?

This, the 'A Team' agreed, was an aspect of first communion that the fathers of their children could not appreciate: 'It's a woman's thing', said Brenda. This sense that the event marked an intensification of the relationship between a mother and daughter was contrasted by some mothers in the same parish with their experience of bringing sons to the event. Whereas with girls there was a sense of a shared pleasure in dressing up, for mothers of sons the event could mark the last time that they could persuade their little boy to be dressed as they would like for public display. Symbolically, therefore, the event could mark a loosening in the mother-son relationship.

Gender expectations around first communion held by members of the 'A-Team' surfaced on one other occasion, and reinforced a sense that for them – irrespective of the gender of the child – the primary adult player was female. In the years before I carried out my fieldwork there had been a male member of the team, whom I shall call Pat. There was a general sense of unease among the women that a man should have wished to take part in their meetings. In accounting for his membership of the group, the women chose to ascribe to him a deficient masculinity – 'He was very in touch with his feminine side – a very nice man', said Brenda. They were particularly unhappy about the ease with which he had discussed with them the birth of his children:

Brenda: Every meeting we used to come to, right, he wanted to tell us about how to have
            a baby and all that […] I couldn't stand it. I didn't like it a bit.
Josie: I mean, if his wife hadn't had them children, he'd give birth himself.
Brenda: *[quoting Pat]* 'Oh, she's had about, oh, five hundred and eighty stitches.' *[All
            laugh.]* He says, 'Well, me babies got big heads,' and I said to him, 'You can't
            complain, mate!' He's got a big square head himself.

Pat's interactions with the group did not match their expectations of male gender
performance, especially when he initiated conversations that they felt inappropriate
for men. June said to Nicky, 'I wouldn't like my husband talking like that, would
you?' The group was quick to comment that he and his wife had reversed the
parenting roles prevailing within their community, with Pat taking a greater share of
responsibility for nurturing the children. Finally, Brenda called his masculinity into
question, using a feminine form of his name in speaking about him.

Looking Beyond the UK Setting

It is possible, of course, that what has just been described represents a particularly
British experience, and that the particular configuration of parish and school –
together with the general background of secularization – have created an atypical
set of circumstances. There is relatively little to compare this study with. Lodge
(1999), in an Irish setting in many ways very similar to that in Liverpool, identifies a
number of similar issues. However, her small-scale overview of first communion was
peripheral to her much larger main research project on the issue of gender in Irish
schools. The article (despite its title) does not engage critically with the language
of rites of passage, and there is little analysis germane to my topics. However,
two ethnographic studies conducted in the United States do go some way towards
redressing the balance, and in several ways echo my own findings.

Susan Ridgely Bales closely observed the preparation for and celebration of first
communion in two different North Carolina parishes (Bales, 2005, pp. 2–3). Formal
preparation was given not in a church school setting, but in special catechetical
classes that the parish organized ahead of the event. For many of the children these
classes marked the beginning of their formal religious education (p. 79). Bales
did observe that there was something of an initiatory dimension to the children's
understanding of the ritual – but it was not at all framed in terms of the Catholic
Church's formal discourse of a three-fold sequence of rituals. Instead, it operated
at a sensory level: through the ritual the children were admitted to the sensory
experience of eating and drinking the eucharist that was previously denied to them
(pp. 91–2). First communion removed an 'invisible barrier between the children and
the adult congregation' (p. 93). In the children's terms, therefore, this was a passage
that succeeded – the marginality that they experienced in their parish came to an
end. However, Bales identified that a very significant number of first communicants
never returned to faith formation classes after first communion. She comments:

> The tremendous drop in Faith Formation participation indicates that First Communion
> may fail as a ritual of initiation for most children … For, on the surface, it seems that the

connection that the Eucharist creates between the children and the Church is not strong enough to keep the children interested in maintaining their commitment to the Church – a commitment that should lead a child to participate in the third step of faith development, Confirmation. [p. 80]

As with the familial discourses that I encountered in Liverpool, Bales' analysis suggests that for many of her subjects, the ritual is understood as a one-off event. It did not fulfil the Catholic Church's initiatory ambitions, and any passage made by the child during it was primarily understood in personal rather than ecclesial terms.

In some ways Bales' identification of an initiatory dimension echoes that articulated by Sister Margaret, as seen previously. However, Sister Margaret, operating in an English context of low church attendance, recognized that if she was to apply the notion of initiation to the ritual it had to be in terms that were completely divorced from the Church context. Even then, she did not identify with precision exactly which passage the rite might mark. On the other hand, not only is Bales more earthed in her construct of initiation, but she is able to relate it to liturgical experience for a reason that was completely unavailable to Sister Margaret. It is clear that what Bales is observing is predicated upon at least relatively high levels of church attendance by the children. A sense of exclusion sufficiently powerful to render first communion an initiatory experience in Bales' terms could only have been generated across an extended period of time as children attended Mass with their families. Very few indeed of the children that passed through Sister Margaret's programme would have been in a position to build up such a sense because it was church attendance itself – not just participation in the eucharist – that was a novel experience for them.

McCallion et al. (1996) observed first communion in one parish of the Detroit archdiocese. Their primary focus was not the ritual *per se*, but the manner in which *Sacrosanctum Concilium*'s notion of the importance of 'full and active participation' translated into the practice (pp. 300–301). In their fieldwork site, an attempt by parish personnel to implement this principle resulted in the promotion of a ritual that closely corresponded to what I encountered in my first fieldwork site. Namely, the children were required to sit throughout the ceremony with their parents and families – rather than in the traditional system by which they sat together as a distinct group ('peer seating'). McCallion and his associates analysed the process by which the parish authorities attempted to steer this ritual change through a democratic process that engaged the parents. A very clear split emerged between parents and parish authorities. The former preferred the traditional approach, emphasizing that this was a 'special' day, and that sitting among peers would make the children 'feel special' (pp. 317–18). The parish authorities, however, were more concerned to stress the communal nature of the event, and feared that peer seating would reduce the rest of the congregation to the status of spectators.

The direct issue in McCallion's study was not initiation but the Church's understanding of the Christian assembly, and the role of the children within it. For parish authorities there was a concern to pattern the event as closely as possible on the regular Sunday Mass. For parents, on the other hand, a sense that this was a special day in the life of the child was uppermost. Thanks to the democratic process followed it was this parental approach that prevailed. As we shall see, the same was not true in the parishes that I studied.

Conclusion

The seeds of conflict can be clearly discerned in the picture of first communion drawn by this chapter. On the one hand, the new formal discourse of initiation has not penetrated to local level. This is partly due to the half-hearted way in which the catechetical literature – both official and otherwise – has taken it up. At the same time, the English and Welsh hierarchy has favoured the continuing prominence of the age of reason discourse by embracing a human developmental approach in its formally approved syllabus for RE. On the other hand, alongside these two formal discourses, we can now recognize a number of patterns of meaning that the first communicants and their families bring to the event. These patterns relate rather more to the children's identity within the network of their family relationships than to sacramental theology or ecclesial discipline. The meaning of the ritual, therefore, emerges as a contested field, opening opportunities for power-play and subversion between the various parties who participate in it. The next two chapters will explore two aspects of how the parish authorities in the fieldwork sites exercised the power they held by virtue of their role. In Chapter 8 I shall consider their attempts to present their own constructs of meaning as normative during the process of preparation for first communion. Then, in Chapter 9 I shall consider how each shaped the ritual of first communion around the meaning the event held for them. In Chapter 10, the focus shifts to the families, and the meaning they brought to the event as they used external display and consumption to ensure that their own meanings were not only expressed but also predominated within the ritual.

CHAPTER 8

Power and Conflict in the Preparation for First Communion

Introduction

The previous chapter identified in the fieldwork parishes a failure for the post-Vatican II formal discourses about first communion to penetrate to popular level. As a result, the annual enactment of the ritual was open to conflict between the various parties as each brought to it their own understanding and expectation of the event. In the fieldwork these conflicts surfaced on two broad fronts: the process of preparation during the months leading up to the event, and the celebration of the Mass of first communion itself. On each of these fronts there was evidence of a concerted attempt by parish authorities to establish the formal initiatory discourse as normative. Similarly, there was ample evidence that many families were equally concerned to ensure that the celebration of the ritual realized the expectations bound up with the other, non-ecclesial, discourses outlined in Chapter 5. The juxtaposition of these very different approaches to the same ritual resulted in an interplay of gate-keeping attempts on the part of the parish authorities and corresponding subversive tactics by some of the families. In this chapter I shall consider the attempts by parish authorities to gain an upper hand in the preparation process, and highlight the responses made by the families of first communicants. Chapter 9 will then explore how the same processes played into the ritual itself.

As was noted in the previous chapter, the Catholic Church in England and Wales has officially embraced the concept that the religious formation of children involves a three-way partnership of family, school and parish. Each of the parishes studied in the fieldwork made an attempt to realize this principle in practice as they prepared their children for first communion. The processes they followed were far from uniform, and reflected to a large degree the personal agendas and priorities of key players, such as parish priest, headteacher and catechists. Consequently, across the two years of fieldwork, three very different approaches emerged to preparation for first communion.

The first parish emphasized the preparation of the parents, through a series of three meetings led by the priest and the lay-women of the 'A Team'. In the second parish the responsibility for all preparation, of both children and parents, lay with the school, which also traditionally managed the first communion Masses. So, whereas in the first parish the chief power-broker had been the parish priest, in the second parish the power lay in an alliance between the priest and the headteacher. The situation in the second parish was, however, rather more complex, as that alliance was under threat. The deanery to which the parish belonged, of which the parish priest was dean, had recently been granted funding by the archdiocese to employ a deanery-wide catechetical co-ordinator. This funding was exceptional; it was made available as part of a reorganization package within the inner-city area in which long-established parishes were either closed or amalgamated, with a significant reduction in the number of available clergy. The clergy of the deanery had appointed to this post the religious sister, Sr Margaret, whom we met in Chapter 6. She brought with her several years' experience of running a very different, parish-based approach to first communion preparation in South London. She preferred that all the preparation of the children should be carried out during the Sunday Mass – thereby reducing considerably the role of the school. At the time of observation she had introduced this approach in a number of other parishes within the deanery, and was now seeking to extend it to the subject parish, in which she already had received responsibility for baptismal preparation. I therefore extended my observations to Sr Margaret's preparation of children in two adjoining parishes, and her approach is discussed in this chapter as a third model for realizing the home-school-parish partnership.

First Parish: The 'A Team'

The rationale for the process of preparation for first communion in the first subject parish can be located in the personal convictions of its parish priest. His entire ministry had, he said, been motivated by a deeply held conviction that the community should be engaged with social and political issues, and particularly with questions of social justice. Yet as he looked back across his life since ordination, he vividly identified a paradox. On the one hand he had devoted considerable time and effort to fostering the presence in the Church of a laity with the confidence and authority to engage, in the name of the Church, in their local community. On the other, however, he now recognized the extent to which his entire approach had been rooted in traditional clerical attitudes and power structures. He held both a blueprint for action and the institutional authority to push it forward. However, this could not succeed in effecting change at base level, because what appeared to be lay empowerment in truth still depended upon the hierarchical power-base of his role and identity as a priest:

> I also begin to understand that – and I'm trying to work through for myself in person the kind of journey through the years – it's a part of, for me, I was arriving with the whole dominant – I was arriving with a blueprint idea: this is how they should be; all they need is the opportunity to react like this and they'll see it clearly. And they'll all learn new wisdom, which is, of course, my wisdom – I'll give it to them. And it's a load of bunkum really – it doesn't work.

This insight had emerged as he had reflected on the increasing difficulty of motivating individuals or groups towards social action in the face of greater self-absorption in the Church: a Church, he said, that was diverting the energy of its lay people ever more fully towards sustaining institutions and patterns of ministry as the number of priests declined. This, he felt was exacerbated by changes in British society in the wake of the 'Thatcher years' – individual self interest was now prized above social involvement. He had lost none of his conviction that the Church must be engaged with quality-of-life issues, but was now unsure how far his ordained status permitted him to proceed with integrity. Now acting out of a sense of 'old age [at the time he was a very healthy man in his early fifties], weariness, and being faithfully present to people', he was unwilling to claim that his efforts at social mobilization could in practice lead to a genuine and successful empowerment of people.

The preparation process for first communion reflected that desire to be 'faithfully present'. His aim was not to impart doctrine, nor directly to change the quality of participants' lives. It was, rather, to create a forum within which the parents of the first communicants could consider from an adult perspective some of the themes that their children were exploring at school. His hope was for two outcomes: to facilitate conversations between the parents and children, and to help the adults to relate issues of faith to their daily lives. It is difficult to assess the success of his first desired outcome. It is possible, however, to arrive at a firmer judgement about the second on the basis of observation.

The key to the entire programme was the intermediary role played by the group of women who called themselves the 'A Team', and who worked with the priest each year on the project. Their role operated on two planes. First, they mediated to the priest the realities of life in the local community. All were mothers of young children. Of the five members of the group during the year of observation, three did not conform to the patterns of family formation and regular church attendance that constitute the Catholic Church's expected norm. This range of experiences made them considerably more representative of the body of parents with whom they dealt than the type of catechist envisaged in formal church documents, who are expected to have 'a deep faith, a clear Christian and ecclesial identity' (*General Directory for Catechesis*, 1997, p. 237). The last point certainly did not apply, as most of the team members stood in an ambiguous relationship to the Church and its teachings. The second plane of mediation lay in the fact that they led the group discussions during the parents' meetings and provided input on the Church's formal teachings. The nexus between the two planes was a series of meetings the priest held with them to prepare the parents' meetings. He told me that these meetings operated on two levels, the first structural, the other interpersonal. On a structural level, they determined the shape and content of the later parents' meetings:

> So we get to talk, and we go through the theme, and they'll say whether a particular passage which has been offered by the people who put the syllabus together – they'll say whether it rings bells for them or not. And they're executive at that point, because they – with their pens – and me will cross that passage out.

Interpersonally he thought that all parties were enriched by the experience. Of himself he said that their meetings 'feel like self-indulgence'. He added, 'My God, I thoroughly enjoy their company.' This was the forum that came closest to achieving his vision for a genuine dialogue between faith and life:

> We're allowed to say, 'We're not into pious stuff', and 'pious' has become a shorthand for airy-fairy-Churchy things. If it's about Jesus Christ, and our lives connect – they love talking about the Incarnation. The Incarnation now means that God has touched their flesh

– their humanity is a place where God lives. And they love to discover that afresh. In their relationships and things.

He saw the experience for them as providing not only an opportunity to explore issues of faith and life, but also a place where they could grow in the confidence and ability to articulate their individual positions.

His hope, then was that through the mediation of the 'A Team' the preparation of parents for the first communion of their children could be a genuine mutual encounter between the Church – not least as it celebrated its rituals – and the majority of its local members, who stood on its periphery. He recognized that even this manner of working was not abstracted from the traditional power-role of the priest; that it was quite possible for him to unconsciously use that power, and for the 'A Team' themselves to quite consciously avail themselves of it. However, his hope was that through the process such power could be subsumed into a mutual relationship based on friendship.

From this consideration of the priest's stated aims arise two sets of questions to be put to the preparation process in the parish. First, was a genuine encounter between faith and life achieved? Second, how was power exercised within the process, and by whom? These questions will be asked first of the meetings of the 'A Team', and then of the broader parents' sessions.

The 'A Team' and Their Meetings

In his conversations with me the parish priest was eager to stress that the 'A Team' were 'not Mass-going people'. However, it became apparent that the five members of the team manifested a range of patterns of Mass-going, from regular through occasional to very rare. Similarly, the members of the team also occupied varying positions with response to the Church's teaching on family formation. Two were married, one was a single parent who was not in a current relationship, and the other two were cohabiting. There was a close correlation between marital status and church attendance: the two married women were more regularly at church, the other three less so – though to varying degrees. As was noted earlier, church attendance and family formation within the strict parameters of ecclesiastical law have been the most visible markers of lay allegiance to the Church. Indeed, the 1910 reform of first communion was located within a raft of reforms that sought to strengthen exactly these dimensions of Catholic life. Catholic marriage and weekly Mass-going have also been – and continue to be – key constituents of a 'normative' Catholic identity. However, the breadth of positions that the 'A Team' held on both of these issues is broadly a pointer to the way in which many people have renegotiated their religious and social identity within the Catholic Church. What was remarkable in this instance is that the parish priest was able to sit comfortably with the positions adopted by the women, and regard their leadership with him of the first communion programme as a positive good. As the 'A Team' played such a significant role in the fieldwork, it is helpful at this stage to offer a brief biographical picture of each of them in order better to contextualize some of their responses. All names been changed.

Veronica

Veronica was the quietest member, and attended only two of the four observed meetings. A married mother of three children aged between eight and fifteen, she most closely resembled the type of first communion catechist normally encountered – committed to regular church attendance and living within a stable family setting. She did contribute to the meetings, but was never at the forefront of discussion, and tended to withdraw as conversations became heated or contentious. Despite her apparent conformity with 'formal' Catholicism, she appeared to have no qualms over buying black economy goods when they appeared for sale during the course of one of the meetings. Renegotiating one's adherence to Church teaching could evidently take place across a series of fronts.

June

In contrast to Veronica, June was the most vocal member of the 'A Team'. Like Veronica, June was a regular church-goer. Within the parish she organized the local credit union, and also led the 'Little Church' in the parish. More formally known as 'Children's Liturgy of the Word', this is the now widely diffused practice in Catholic parishes of offering children of primary school age an alternative Liturgy of the Word during Mass. They are generally taken out from the main congregation at the beginning of Mass for readings and activities conducted at their own level of cognitive ability. Whilst evidently a close collaborator with the priest, June none the less would criticize him at times, and in the meetings she constantly introduced a note of realism, objecting strongly to suggestions from him that she did not believe would prove effective. She was particularly insistent that the material used with parents should not be 'too holy'.

Nicky

At 39, Nicky appeared to be the youngest member of the team. In 1999 she was in her third long-term relationship. She had three children; her current partner was the father of the two youngest, whilst the eldest child was in regular contact with his biological father. When the priest first spoke to me about the 'A Team', he singled out Nicky for particular attention:

> There's one particular woman, Nicky, who I think has had the least education than the others. Probably didn't enjoy her own education when she was younger. The others call her: 'Oh, she's the silly one – she always comes out with the silly remarks.' But she always asks the questions that no one dares … And Nicky's particular way of asking her questions is usually recognized quite quickly and used to be something for ridicule – almost a foolish, naïve question. But we've learned to trust Nicky because her questions are from wisdom, from wisdom.

Nicky was an occasional church-goer who explained her sporadic attendance by the discomfort she experienced in attending church with young children:

Tim and Mike – both our children – are very boisterous, very loud. And sometimes people don't always understand, you know, you're doing your best. I've got a son who wants to light candles and, likes, erm, cars – Mike wants to get cars. And it's very difficult, and you feel it's a stressful thing. Instead of looking forward to it, it just becomes an event where – you know – it just causes you hassle. It just, it like makes you – puts the spotlight on you, and you go, 'Oh God, yeah – I feel I can't control my kids and everyone's looking at me.'

Brenda

Brenda was also the mother of three children, whom she had raised for the past few years as a single parent. The priest outlined her story to me:

She's come through a bad marriage. She was battered and he was a gambler – all sorts of debts. She's a real fighter. She has fought her way through, I mean. She's got herself a job, against all the odds really. She's been rehoused so he didn't know where to find her.

During the sessions, Brenda emerged as a realist. Her attitude to life – and, perhaps, the depth of her personal struggle – was reflected when the group discussed the topic 'Freedom and Responsibility' as a possible theme. Brenda took up the statement in the proposed material that 'Circumstances may diminish our freedom to choose', and said:

Circumstances rule your life. You don't have no choices … You know, you don't always have a choice, you know. For a start, you don't ask to be born, do you? You've no choice in that. The way your life goes, the way you think it'll go, the way it does go. I'm not being a pessimist. I'm not saying you can't change it – but you don't always have a choice.

Despite this apparently fatalistic outlook, she showed considerable initiative. She ran a boys' football team, and on occasions would illustrate her thoughts with examples drawn from the game – for example, citing the off-side rule as inducing a collaborative approach within a team.

When Brenda's children had been smaller she had attended church regularly, though like Nicky she had found the attitude of older members of the congregation difficult:

It's very stressful. I used to enjoy coming to Mass – when my youngest was a baby. I could cope with him – bribery and corruption, bottles or something in the pram … It's just a rule, isn't it. At the end of the day I'm not going to get struck by lightning. I understand best what keeps him quiet. But the stress, the stress – especially you get a lot of people that aren't quite able – older people – and the tutting and the stress. And all of a sudden you're sweating and you feel this is no longer pleasurable.

Brenda described how in order to cope with this situation she had started to arrive late for Mass: 'I'd come half-an-hour later. I'd just sneak in, bless myself, and pretend I'd been there. At least I'd been half an hour … At least it was less stressful, half-an-hour. It was an escape route.' Yet in describing this 'escape route', she expressed a further anxiety – namely that she had been under surveillance by the priest, a sense of scrutiny that had been learned from childhood. Nicky reinforced this sense of awareness of his gaze: 'We think he mightn't notice us at the back, but he always does.'

Josie

Josie was the mother of several children, and lived with them and their father in a long-term and stable setting. There was a presumption among the group that she was married, reinforced by references she made in conversation to her 'mother-in-law'. It was therefore a surprise to the other members of the 'A Team' when during the third session with parents she spoke about marriage in open forum in a highly critical manner: 'I've never been married. I don't want to be married. I don't want to lose my identity. I don't want to take his name – that gives him something of me.' This attitude to her partner of nineteen years contrasted sharply with the close relationship she enjoyed with her sisters:

> We've always been close. I couldn't go not one day without seeing our girls, so I ring them. That's the way we been brought up. If I hadn't seen our Bernadette one day, I'd ring her, and go, 'I've not seen you today – what's wrong?' 'Ah, nothing – I've been to work, I've been tied up.' And I know then that she's all right. And she'll ring me.

Josie's core identity was thus framed not within the parameters of her relationship with the father of her children, but within her family of origin, in which her mother was a constant reference point: 'We had a lot of respect for me mum, do you know? What she said went, and the kids were all brought up like that. They still respect that, the kids.' So strong was this identificational link, that to surrender her name in marriage would have constituted for Josie a loss of self and a threat to her identity.

Josie's pattern of church attendance is best described as cyclical: 'I will go for a while, and then I just can't be bothered going.' June suggested that Josie kept returning out of a sense of guilt, but Josie simply replied, 'I just get the urge to go.' Yet despite her non-conformity to the Church's expectations with regard to either family formation or church-going, she was the most vociferous member of the 'A Team' in voicing criticism of other parents at first communion: 'You're all coming here 'cos you want a party. You want the dress and everything'.

How the 'A Team' worked

Having individuated the different members of the 'A Team', we can now consider how they and the priest worked together. The chief task of the meetings of the 'A Team' with the priest was to adapt material contained in *Here I Am* for use during the parents' meetings. The aim was to select three topics from the six covered with the children in school during the autumn and spring terms, and then to adapt the material presented by the syllabus. The first question to be asked, then, is whether this process was for the 'A Team' the faith-life encounter so desired by the priest.

There was a reluctance on their part to engage directly with 'religious' concepts; these they consistently referred to as 'the holy bits', which they regarded as proper to the priest. Thus, within the discussions they maintained a clear distinction between the categories of the sacred and the non-sacred. Indeed, they treated any attempt to pass from the secular to the sacred as an unwelcome intrusion on a fruitful line of conversation. For example, Josie commented on the material proposed by the priest around the theme of memories:

> I don't like the last bit. One bit's good and the other bit's not … 'Memories are powerful. They can heal, divide, sustain, guide and challenge.' That's really good, that – isn't it? That's brilliant. But then 'Christ' comes into it, doesn't he? He spoils it.

However, they were able to relate to a great deal in the material, sometimes with startling results. Material found under the topic 'Special Places' prompted Nicky to muse:

> I was thinking about it … and thought, it doesn't mean special places like somewhere to go. It can mean, like, a special place inside your head *[laughs]* … Yeah, do you know what I mean, like? It feels, like special – like things in your head as well. Not like particular – not like to go to McDonalds or like visiting your mother's grave.

At the next team meeting one of the other members returned to this conversation, saying:

> It's like that 'most people have a special place.' Then you said last week that it could be in your head. Mine's half-past-six with a cup of coffee and a ciggie each morning … But that never goes away. I didn't think till Nicky said last week that her, your special place could be in your head. When I get up at half past six so I don't have to look at the kids and Johnny, and I can have my ciggie there by myself – I mean no offence to him – I can sit there.

The priest was, therefore, justified in his belief that whilst the 'A Team' stood aside from an explicitly 'religious' content, their engagement with the core concepts found in the syllabus was real, rooted in their own experience. However, this was achieved within the special setting of the 'A Team' meetings, and the members doubted that it would be possible to replicate the experience in the larger parents' meeting. This opinion was based on two concerns. The first was that the material with which they were required to work was at times removed from the realities of life within their community. One related an earlier episode when the group had found difficulty in engaging with ideas proposed for a discussion on 'Meals':

> We were talking about meals, like as a celebration – 'cos if you're working all day and your husband works, that's when you sit and talk, isn't it, about how the kids' day's gone and what your husband's done at work, and what you've been doing yourself. We were with this group and some of them – you couldn't, well, I couldn't get any response. And this woman went, 'I don't sit at the friggin' table – have you seen the way he eats? He slobbers and everything!'

The second concern related to the process to be followed in the parents' meetings. The 'A Team' felt that whilst they enjoyed space within their own meetings to tease out the meaning of the material, the broader forum of the parent's meetings did not permit such a positive engagement. Brenda said of the material under review:

'There's good sentences in it, but it's just not, it's just not going to get in, is it? It's just not going to get in'. June responded, 'I can just see them sitting there, going, "You got your frock?" Do you know what I mean? "How's your Mam?" And we're all like standing there reading this really heavy passage. It just doesn't work for me, I mean.' They were concerned that they had only 'one shot' at presenting this material – and the way it was written rendered it largely unintelligible to the parents. Indeed, one baulked at the prospect of reading to the parents a text containing words she was unable even to pronounce, let alone understand. These concerns were not dismissed as such; my observation was that the priest was simply unable to hear them.

This undermines his statement that it was the team who determined the material to be used, and his hope that his institutional power lay more-or-less dormant through the process. Indeed, when he stated this opinion, June exclaimed:

Oh no we don't! Oh no we don't! Peter – this is the truth. We get these and we read them, and he goes, 'Erm, "We are God's work of art created in Christ Jesus from the beginning as he meant us to." So, you like that?' And we go, 'No!' And he says, 'We'll keep it anyway.' That is the truth … He'll say, 'Well, is there any way we could simplify this?' And his favourite saying is, 'Yeah, yeah, could work – but we'll try this way first.' And then he goes, 'Yeah, yeah, yeah, that was really good, that's a really strong suggestion. I'd be lost without youse – but we'll do it this way.'

Another later made a similar comment: 'We take it, cut it up, throw half of it away – but what he done is, "Oh no." *[laughs]* He sticks it back together.' These comments bring into question his assertion that the 'A Team' was truly 'executive'. Its members did, indeed, take some responsibility in selecting the topics for discussion, but in the final analysis the priest retained control over the content, and permitted them little scope to modify it. The content in the syllabus held enormous significance for the priest, and he genuinely believed that the format of the parent's meetings permitted participants to access that content. He seemed unable to pick up the concerns of the team that this was not so, and repeatedly overruled their suggestions about language, content and, indeed, the overall process. None the less, he had succeeded in creating and sustaining a setting within which they were able to explore creatively certain crucial aspects of their life, and this stands in itself as a considerable achievement. The second question then arises, were he and the 'A Team' able to translate that experience into the broader context of the parents' meetings?

The Parents' Meetings: Faith and Life

Unlike the unstructured preparatory meetings, those with parents were highly formal. At the heart of each lay a half-hour discussion in small groups, led by the priest and individual members of the 'A Team'. To illustrate how these meetings operated, I shall focus on how the theme of 'Freedom and Responsibility' flowed through the small group and into the concluding plenary at the third meeting.

The small groups were invited to consider questions taken from the teacher's introductions to the syllabus theme, ending with two questions: What would lead to a loss of your freedom? What would lead to you gaining freedom? The responses were to be fed back when the whole group reassembled. Within the group I observed, a key theme explored was an inequality between male and female roles as experienced by the women within their current relationships. Parenting was seen as having little direct impact upon the father of a child:

> When you become a parent, the man still goes about doing things as normal. If he wants to go out, he goes out. If he wants to go down the pub, he goes down the pub. But for the woman, wherever she goes, she has to take the child with her. That's what restricts her freedom.

The group effectively equated freedom with the irresponsible attitudes they identified as typically male; it seemed that they perceived their own behaviour, springing out of a sense of their family responsibilities, as a lack of freedom. They agreed to report back that freedom was lost when the consequences of action were taken into consideration, but gained by disregarding these consequences. With regard to the second question, one woman spoke about paid work as a doorway to freedom. She explained that the money did not give her freedom; she was not particularly better off than she would have been drawing 'a raft of benefits'. Instead, it was work itself that gave her freedom from the house: 'If I had to stay in the house all day, looking at the four walls, I'd go doolally.'

As the other groups reported their findings to the plenary session, a different theme emerged as dominant. Three of the groups stated that marrying would represent the greatest loss of freedom; one woman described it as an 'entrapment'. The priest appeared genuinely surprised, even shocked at this. He attempted to introduce a positive perspective on marriage by asking the group to consider the companionship and partnership that he understood to be part of it. The response of the majority was to laugh openly: 'That's for men. They get all that – not us.' Another woman said, 'I can't see the point of getting married. I've been with my fellow for twenty years – I can't see the point of a piece of paper. If I got married we'd be divorced in two months.' The priest's attempt to forge a link between his audience and the Church's teaching was definitively undermined when Josie publicly declared her unmarried status. Thereafter, neither the input offered by other members of the team, nor the intended period of quiet reflection, served to return the meeting to its intended course. The remainder of the session was accompanied by a low murmur of discussion among parents – very much as June had foreseen.

A similar thing had happened at the first meeting, during which the plenary session was also diverted away from the intended theme ('Special People') by parental concerns around the exact form that the celebration of first communion was to take. It is possible, therefore, to evaluate the two observed meetings against the priest's own criteria set out at the start of this chapter. As with the preparatory meetings, the parents' meetings did facilitate within the small group setting a remarkably fruitful engagement between participants. In the small group I observed this was due to no small extent to the ability of Nicky, who led it. On the other hand the plenary session of each meeting failed to achieve its aim of bringing out links between life experience and the discourse of faith. Issues were raised during the small group session that would have required considerably longer to respond to appropriately than the brief plenary allowed. Consequently the sessions in fact respected neither the priest's intentions nor the personal agendas of the parents. The ultimate failure of the process – despite the quality of some of its individual elements – served to reinforce a deeper dynamic running beneath it, the issue of who ultimately held power within the process.

Parents' Meetings: Power and Authority

These meetings served as a gateway to the first communion event, providing parents with their only opportunity to finalize the date of their child's first communion. A limited number of places were allocated for the Masses on each of the five weekends of the celebrations, and listed on pre-prepared sheets. Parents claimed these places, first come-first served, by writing their child's name on the sheets. The fact that these lists were only made available to parents during the meetings effectively constrained them to attend, though this was never articulated by either the priest or the team. It became evident during the group work at the third meeting that parents experienced this requirement as an imposition. One mother had been unable to attend either of the two previous sessions through work commitments. She expressed her frustration over her attempts to discuss the date with the priest outside the meeting: 'He just said, "Monday, one-forty-five. Monday, one-forty-five". He's arrogant and horrible.' By the time she accessed the lists, other parents had already had two weeks to take up the slots, and her choice was thus restricted. Some, therefore, experienced themselves as being discriminated against in what at first sight might have appeared (and was surely intended to be) a totally democratic system.

There was potentially a high social cost to be paid by those who lagged behind other parents in securing a date, as another woman in the same group underlined. Having chosen the date on the previous Monday, she then found that she could not book the venue of her choice for the post-Mass party for that date. She had gone ahead and booked for a different Sunday, and had to endure a worrying wait until this meeting before she could try to change the date at the church end. Others in the group confirmed that in booking venues for parties, they were in competition with each other, and with parents in other local parishes, many of whom had been able to choose their dates much earlier. There was a general sense that in being unable to confirm church dates until the first meeting (1 March), they were being disadvantaged within the broader Catholic community.

However, the priest was not the only party exercising power in the debate around dates. The 'A Team' too occupied a privileged position within their broader peer group of parents. They were perceived to have – and understood themselves as having – a role in controlling the dynamics of the parental group. This was particularly significant when situations of conflict existed between individuals within the group. June related a recent incident in which a mother had approached her before the first parents' meeting:

> And she went, 'Can you do us a favour? Can you make sure I'm not in a group with this woman, 'cos I don't get on with her. We don't speak. Don't dare put me in a group with this woman.' So she said to me, 'Have you got a pen – I'll write the name down.' And I

thought, 'I'll remember' ... I couldn't believe it – she nearly run after me across the room, 'Do us a favour, can you make sure I'm not with this woman 'cos we don't get on.' I'm going to put them in a group together – 'Go on, make up!'

The position of the 'A Team' members within the group was, however, unstable – they were, after all, themselves parents and therefore their own actions within the parental group could precipitate conflict. June explained:

> We used to give the dates out at the second meeting, and I heard that Veronica had put her name down, and somebody else – Pat, or someone. And this one went, 'Eh! There's already names on that sheet!' And I said, 'Yeah. We've got kids.' And she went, 'You haven't got more right.' 'But we take time to come and do this all the time. We don't just come and sign up – so why should we wait till the last, then?' She said, 'No, but I mean there's supposed to be a queue.' And I said, 'Yeah – and we're first in it. We just got to be.'

The 'A Team' emerged from the fieldwork as forming a distinct bloc in the parish. They were, indeed, members of the parental peer-group at the school gate, but in the lead-up to first communion their particular association with the priest separated them from their peers. A sense that they formed an established group was, perhaps, reflected in an unwillingness of other people to become members of the team. When asked why he had difficulty in recruiting new members, the priest replied:

> You see it when you go to the school gate after school. There are different divisions at the gate. Some people say, 'We're the ones who stand on *this* side of the gate – and they're the ones who stand on that side.' Or, 'We come from that estate – and they come from another.' These are some of the reasons why some people might not want to join the 'A Team'. They don't fit in where others see themselves as belonging. Or it's a bit like youth groups. The first set are fine, but no one else wants to join them – the group has pissed on all the corners and no one else wants to come and join them, Whether people feel comfortable or not in a group determines whether they will join it.

Paradoxically, then, the priest's success in providing a space within which the members of the 'A Team' could feel sufficiently comfortable to engage with serious life issues had rendered that space uncomfortable and indeed perhaps inaccessible to others.

Second Parish: Focus on the School

In the first parish the chief power-broker had been the parish priest, with the 'A Team' borrowing some of that power to further their own interests. In the second parish, power at first communion resided in a close alliance between the parish priest and the headteacher. Each respected the other's sphere of activity – she his oversight of the liturgy, he her autonomy in preparing the children for the event. Both were aware of the power that their status afforded them *vis-à-vis* the parents of the first communicants; both sought to exercise that power on behalf of those parents and their families. The contours of that power were thrown into relief by the challenge for leadership of the first communion process that Sr Margaret mounted during my period of observation. A discussion of that challenge, and the approach towards first communion that it embodied, forms the final section of this chapter. First it is appropriate to consider the status quo.

The Priest

The priest acknowledged that in the encounter between the parents of first communicants and the parish as institution, the various parties faced each other in an unequal relationship. There were, he suggested, three reasons for that inequality. The first was located in the experiences that had taught the body of his parishioners to mistrust institutional authority of any kind:

> I'd say authority is for them a problem – probably all authority: the police, you know, local councils when they go for benefits. Life is probably a struggle for many of them, and they come across so many barriers where they, erm, wherever they live. Or when they do try to do something, or their attempts to live comfortable lives.

A majority of the parents of first communicants, he said, would locate Church and school alongside other such institutions. Consequently, they expected those who exercised authority within the parish to be negatively disposed towards them, and unwilling to respond positively to requests for, say, baptism or first communion. His second reason flowed directly from early experiences of schooling. Local people, he said, would have difficulties with the concept of attending meetings in preparation for first communion because the very meeting format represented an unfriendly environment:

> There'll be those for whom the thought of going to a meeting – if it's to do with school, particularly if it's to do with the Church side of school, is something with which they would perhaps feel intimidated with. Again, this is partly because of my experience in my previous parish, where there was a similar catchment of those who had not received a very good education, erm, and so school, Church are authority figures. Therefore you know, they're not the sort of people who necessarily would be comfortable in that setting.

The third aspect was specifically Catholic. He recognized that most of the parents did not regularly attend church and as a consequence not only sensed themselves as 'alienated' from it, but also carried a burden of guilt 'because they perhaps perceive that they should be doing something and might expect – I'm sure half of them expect the third degree.'

In response to such possibilities, the priest stated that his aim for the process, therefore, was to render the encounter 'as non-threatening as possible'. Yet, having identified as problematic both the meeting format and the status of schoolteachers as authority figures, he continued the parish practice of holding a series of four preparatory meetings with parents in the school hall. He and the headteacher led these meetings, and the groups in which the parents were invited to discuss issues relating to first communion were led by the priest, the headteacher and the teacher who taught their children. Consequently, discussion was limited and parents were guarded about self-revelation. The priest expressed his own doubts:

I don't know whether it actually works, because in the very act of going in that group – it's not a terribly friendly area in that hall, in that large hall. Also they sit at tables – there are some whose body language is not comfortable. Some are, but you find that in any group. But discussions, it's quite difficult – because they're not used to meetings, they're not 'meeting people'.

However, he had no alternative structures or personnel to carry out this work: the parish lacked trained catechists, there was no equivalent to the 'A Team'. Consequently, the school continued to hold complete responsibility for preparing both parents and children for first communion, in contravention of the formal position of the bishops of England and Wales. None the less, the priest declared a policy of non-interference:

Wherever I've been, I've always worked with what the school has done because I reckon there's no right way or wrong way to do first communion. It all depends where you are, depends on the children, depends on the parents' background and so on. So because of that, I've simply worked with, you know, whatever they've done.

The Headteacher and the School

The dependence of the parish upon the school for the preparation of first communion raised the profile of the headteacher within the event as a whole. In the first parish the 'A Team' performed a mediating role between the priest and parents, even though on occasion they subverted that role by appropriating to themselves the very power that the priest was seeking to play down. In this second parish the headteacher performed a rather different mediation. As with the 'A Team' she was aware that she stood in a relationship of power to the parents, but it was a power that she owned, built on both her professional position and her personal status in the community, rather than an external authority borrowed from the priest. She continued to live in the small house in the parish where she had been born, and she had spent her entire professional life at the parish school. Consequently, she knew several generations of parishioners and had taught many of the parents of her current pupils.

During interview she expressed a passionate concern that the encounter between 'our parents' and the Church should be as positive as possible, and articulated for herself a position of go-between for her former pupils and the Church. She eased their way to the priest at baptism or weddings, and calmed their anxieties around first communion. She contrasted her situation with several of her colleagues in other Catholic schools:

I've been fortunate in the priests I've worked with because I don't know how I'd cope if I had to cope with some of these – I know friends who are having very, very difficult priests, and they are breaking their hearts over it.

Yet, although she was adamant that no child had ever been refused first communion, she did exert pressure on parents to attend preparatory meetings:

If they don't turn up for one or two meetings, having had plenty of notices and letters, I usually write a little note saying, 'Dear Mrs So-and-so, since I haven't seen you at the last two meetings perhaps you're not interested in your child making their first communion. Please let me know.'

She insisted that such a letter was not intended as an ultimatum: 'It's not an "If you don't turn up, you're not going to make it". It's a gentle reminder.' However, given the authority inherent in her role as headteacher, it is difficult to imagine that for some parents, at least, such a letter would not have carried significant weight.

Within the school itself, the exercise of catechetical responsibility impacted directly upon classroom practice. During the final half-term before first communion, the educational pattern of the first communicants was subjected to two major alterations, regarding the approved syllabus of religious education, and the use of curriculum time. In doing this the school departed from both the formal expectations of the archdiocese and the requirements of the National Curriculum. Not only was the authorized syllabus (Byrne and Malone, 1992) replaced during the half-term leading up to first communion by an unauthorized resource (Leichner, 1992), but the time allocated to religious education was considerably expanded, to four-and-a-half hours per week during this half-term. This exceeds the requirement that religious education should occupy '10% of the length of the taught week' that the national hierarchy reaffirmed that year (Bishops' Conference of England and Wales, 2000, p. 9).The additional hours devoted to Religious Education were found at the cost of other subjects, though the teacher justified the practice by comparing it to other cross-curricular foci.

An Alliance Under Threat

The priest and headteacher thus formed a close alliance that maintained the school's hegemony in the first communion process. At the time of observation, however, that control was threatened by the activity of Sr Margaret who, as already explained, had recently been appointed as catechetical co-ordinator for the deanery. Her emphasis upon a parish-based approach brought to the forefront an element of power that had only been subtly hinted at in the headteacher's letter to non-attending parents. In Sr Margaret's programme, attendance at the preparatory sessions was a prerequisite (at least in theory) for admission to the ritual. Had she succeeded in extending her programme to the subject parish the balance of power between parish authorities and parents would have been altered and the role of the headteacher diminished. Stripped of her position of mediation, the headteacher would have watched a new power-base form around Sr Margaret. Consideration of Sr Margaret's approach to first communion in the adjacent parishes offers an opportunity to view a third approach to the preparation and also the strong resistance that both parish priest and headteacher in my subject parish offered to her attempts to implement that process within their parish.

Focus on the Sunday Mass

Sr Margaret's Process

The programme was organized over the course of twelve weekends, running from mid-January to early April. On each weekend, one Mass in each parish was identified as the locus for preparation for first communion, and parents and children alike were expected to attend. Sr Margaret's process built upon the practice of 'Little Church'. In her first communion process, Sr Margaret transformed this adaptation of the Sunday readings for children into a sequence of preparatory 'lessons' (her expression) for first communion. These lessons were written by her, and were led by local lay catechists whom she had trained. On each Sunday, while the children were engaged in their lessons, Sr Margaret delivered a talk to their parents and congregation at the point in the liturgy normally given to the sermon. Finally, two first communion masses were held between 30 April and 15 May in each of the four parishes that had taken up Sr Margaret's package.

The movement of the preparation process into the Sunday assembly had one immediate effect: attendance of children and parents at Sunday Mass assumed the status of prerequisite for admission of children to the eucharist. At the start of the first communion year, all the parents were faced with a choice: if they wished their child to receive first communion during the course of that year, they would need to declare a willingness to attend church with the child during the period of preparation. This choice was given a ritual form on the third Sunday of the series, when the children were formally enrolled as candidates for first communion. Sr Margaret stated that in one parish three or four children had not engaged with the programme from the start, and thus failed to make their first communion that year.

So what was the purpose of transferring the first communion preparation into the Sunday Mass? At the end of the process Sr Margaret admitted to a broader aim than the preparation of the children and their parents for the event: 'I suppose my hidden agenda was to get people to realize, you know, "We can come and worship." I know deep in my heart it's not the be-all-and-end-all of everything, but I would like to have seen a little more response.'

The movement into the Sunday liturgy, therefore, was an attempt to draw into regular church attendance a body of people whom Sr Margaret described as 'faith people', but not 'church people'. She expressed her aims in positive terms. However, they were not perceived as such by all within the community. The parish priest of my subject parish described it as 'compulsion', and believed that it would be counterproductive; it would generate resentment on the part of the parents and stifle any movement to attend Mass out of a genuine sense of free choice. Indeed, Sr Margaret's aims were frustrated from the start. Narrating an encounter with a group of mothers at the beginning of the programme, she reported one as saying:

'After the sixth of May we don't have to bother.' So I looked, and she saw my face and said, 'Oh, I'm just being honest' ... She will not be there – and she made it very clear – after he's made his communion. And there were some mums who looked askance, but I had the feeling they looked askance because this woman was honest, not the fact that she wouldn't be there. She was expressing in all honesty, 'I'm only here for the beer', sort of thing. And I think that would be general.

At the end of the programme, Sr Margaret expressed disappointment and confusion. She felt that the programme had successfully engaged the parents:

> They were very much involved. They came to the Mass, you know. They followed the programme. As far as I could see it was going well. The catechists were pleased, and when we evaluated it with the parents, yes, it had been lovely.

However, once the first communion had been celebrated, none had returned: 'Afterwards, the usual – nobody's there.'

However, Sr Margaret later qualified her statement that the parents came to Mass by admitting that levels of attendance had not been as high as she had hoped: 'There were some whose attendance was, I would say, quite poor.' Yet, despite the repeated insistence that attendance was obligatory, reinforced by the keeping of registers, she declared that no child enrolled in the programme had failed to receive first communion at its end as a result of a poor attendance record. This contradicted the perception of the priest in the subject parish, who believed that several children had been refused first communion on those grounds. It would also have disappointed a group of mothers, as Sr Margaret reported: 'Some of the mums in that particular school were hoping that would happen – you could see it in one of the meetings: "And if they don't attend, are they going to be refused?"'

The use of the word 'hoping' suggests a tension among the mothers – with a possible resentment by those who had remained with the process towards those who had proved rather more easy-going in their participation. In discussing the latter, Sr Margaret's tone was more belligerent than usual. Drawing a comparison between her current situation and her previous parish in South London, where she had organized a similar programme, she said:

> I know that in London they wouldn't have got away with it. But when you're just starting I don't think it's the time to put your foot down. Well, you could, and that would teach them all a lesson, but that's not the – I don't see that as the process here. The process is to try to get people to come.

What lesson would it have taught them?

> Well, if you want to make it, you know – as they do – then you've got to be there. So they would have jumped through the hoop.

It had, therefore, been the practice in her previous setting to refuse. The effect would have been that of enforcing Mass attendance ('the hoop') upon parents. I have noted this practice elsewhere in the Archdiocese of Liverpool (cf. McGrail, 2004). It appears that the aim of such schemata is to pattern non-practising families into the discipline of regular Sunday worship.

Because the threat of exclusion from the event – real or perceived – hangs over the preparation, the issue of Mass attendance is drawn into an equation of power: if the parents are to access the first communion ritual, then they must submit to the requirement of regular attendance. Running through this is a dialectic between two very different constructs of the event. In terms of the formal discourses of the Catholic Church, the ritual is part of a process, the start of a life-long series of repeated receptions of communion. Within that perspective, an attempt to enforce a pattern of attendance before the ritual is utterly comprehensible, as is the insistence upon parental responsibility to continue attendance after the event. This insistence even found its way into the first communion Mass itself. In one of the parishes that had implemented Sr Margaret's programme, the priest in his homily on that day admonished the families:

> We hope this first communion day is not the children's last communion day. Sadly, a lot of parents forget that tomorrow is Sunday. We all say that we pray, but we need to pray as a community – and Sunday is our day for that. We cannot expect children of seven or eight to come to church on their own – these days we know that children need to be escorted everywhere. This is your duty and obligation – you should take the opportunity to bring your children to church each week. Please do not send them on their own accord – we do not want that responsibility. It is your responsibility to bring them.

For many of the parents, on the other hand, the event is oriented towards a set of reference points other than the ecclesial expectation of repeated communion, and these locate the event within a considerably slower cycle of repetition. For the majority, the conceptual framework within which the rite takes place is not the weekly cycle of individual church-attendance, but the cycle of ritual enactment from one generation to the next. It is not the reception of the eucharist that is repeated, but the enactment of first communion itself. Within this longer cycle, the goal is that each child should take part in the ritual; and the overwhelming majority of parents remain willing to pass through Sr Margaret's 'hoops' to achieve it.

The dialectic between the two very different cycles of repetition ultimately subverts attempts such as Sr Margaret's to establish a discipline of attendance. Indeed, as the priest in the subject parish noted, policies of compulsory attendance also risk alienating parents who recognized coercion for what it was and rendered any voluntary attendance less likely. This would be especially true if the insistence upon weekly attendance precipitated a conflict with other weekend commitments.

The Response of the Subject Parish

The reality of such commitments was recognized by the priest in the second subject parish, and was, indeed, a factor in his determination not to implement Sr Margaret's programme there. Whilst acknowledging that weekends were frequently given over to sporting activities, he also recognized that enforced Sunday attendance might impact upon family relationships. He cited the case of children who spent alternate weekends with non-cohabiting parents. In such cases an insistence upon attendance risked jeopardizing the delicate balance of carefully negotiated access arrangements and could precipitate further conflict within families. This he was not prepared to countenance.

He was supported in this position by the headteacher, who was strongly opposed to any first communion policy that excluded any children. Speaking of 'her' parents, she said:

> They would sell their souls, for want of a better word, that their child has the very best for first communion. They feel as though they've done their bit for their children. The worst thing that can happen to them is *[whispers]* that they're not allowed to make it … It's never happened here, never. I would, erm, how could I put it? I couldn't condone that – not that it's ever been raised. But I couldn't work with that.

Equally, the class teacher echoed this outlook. He understood automatic admission to first communion to be an expression of the school's declared ethos of providing equal opportunities to its pupils. He thus located the event on a continuum that extended through all dimensions of school life:

> I think that that, what counts for the ethos of our school really is that it's, we are all-embracing and everybody has a fair crack of the whip and everybody's treated equally, that everybody in this class here has the opportunity, an equal opportunity to prepare for communion, and we, we're all, erm, treated in the same way together, and we receive communion together, and so what if you miss a meeting, your parents didn't come one night, or you've been off for a week from school, you know. You're not suddenly going to be kicked out.

As has already been noted, the priest preferred to defer to the school on first communion policy. Unlike Sr Margaret, he had no difficulty with the school's taking sole responsibility for the programme. He regarded sacramental preparation as a continuing function of Catholic education, not least because the school was the only forum of encounter between the majority of Catholic families and the Church. He could, therefore, find no enthusiasm for Sr Margaret's approach, and despite her repeated requests was not prepared to implement it in his parish.

Conclusions

This chapter has illustrated how concerns over the meaning invested in the ritual fed into the processes of preparation and generated processes of gate-keeping. These processes were at their weakest in the second parish, in which the priest and headteacher had consciously opted for an open approach. None the less, they engaged with parents at first communion from within the institutions of parish and Church that already invested them with significant power. The gate-keeping processes were at their strongest in Sr Margaret's approach. She controlled access to the ritual through a preparatory process that attempted to imprint a meaning for the event upon the children and their families, framed in terms of weekly Mass attendance rather than a generational cycle. Between the two approaches stands the line taken by the priest in the first parish. Whilst not attempting to enforce a formal ecclesial discourse, he was none the less concerned to facilitate the parents' engagement with Church teaching. By refusing to allocate dates for first communion outside the meetings arranged for that purpose, he wittingly or otherwise made participation in those meetings a condition for access to the ritual. At all times he retained a position of considerable power – not relinquishing it even in his encounters with the 'A Team'. Yet, by developing that team he had introduced into the equation another set of power-brokers.

However, the potential for conflict, and questions of power and gate-keeping, were not restricted to the preparatory process, but spilled over into the first communion Mass itself. This will be the subject of the next chapter.

CHAPTER 9

Different Ritual Patterns in the First Communion Mass

Introduction

The potential for the parish authorities to control the first communion event was at its strongest during the hour spent by the children and their families in the church for the ritual itself. Then the priest and his collaborators could stamp their own understanding of the event onto the ritual pattern, and could use that pattern as an attempt to control the meaning that participants derived from the event. Therefore, this chapter will consider in detail the way in which the first communion Mass was celebrated in each of the two subject parishes and also when managed by Sr Margaret. Just as three distinct patterns emerged from a consideration of the preparation processes, so three clear modes of celebration could also be discerned. In the first parish, the emphasis on adult participation was reflected in a concern that the first communion should take place within an 'adult' Mass. In the second parish, the priest's liturgical sensibilities and the headteacher's concerns for the sensitivities of the parents created a relatively simple celebration in which the schoolteachers played a significant role. By contrast, the celebration developed by Sr Margaret was designed to maximize the direct involvement and visibility of the children. The ritual structure of each will be considered in turn, and cross-referenced where appropriate to comments drawn from the interviews conducted with the twelve-year-old school-children, several of whom had received their first communion in these parishes.

A Regular Adult Mass? The First Subject Parish

The first communions of 47 children were celebrated in the parish across the five weekends of May 1999, during the established parish Masses on Saturday at 7.00 pm and Sunday at 11.00 am. The children were divided into groups of no more than ten for each Mass. The aim of the priest was that these Masses should interrupt the pattern of regular Sunday worship as little as possible, so he had not adapted the liturgy to be more suitable to children. Instead, he advised the parents at the start of each celebration that this was 'adult worship', continuing the normal pattern of Sunday liturgy, and thereby affording the weekly Mass-goers a role in welcoming the first communicants and their families to their regular worship.

However, four concessions were made to the presence of the children. They were displayed to the congregation at the start of Mass, they took part in an adapted Liturgy of the Word ('Little Church'), they joined the priest at the altar for the Lord's Prayer, and their reception of communion was especially ritualized. In the light of the priest's explanatory remarks, these 'little ways of making Mass special for the youngsters' raise a structural question: what was their cumulative effect on the liturgy as a whole? Did they in fact compromise its status as a 'regular adult Mass?' Furthermore, how did the regular congregation respond to their role of welcoming the children and their families? To answer these questions, let us consider the four concessions in turn before addressing the broader issues.

The Initial Display of the Children

At the start of Mass the first communicants were seated with their families in the body of the church. After the priest had processed into the church, he asked, 'Would all those smart young people come out here now, and show themselves?' The first communicants moved to stand in a line across the altar step, facing the congregation. The children were not individually introduced nor were they presented to the congregation; they were silently offered as the object of an adult gaze that was held for a few seconds before the children were led from the church for the second concession.

The 'Little Church'

As in Sr Margaret's parish, so too the regular practice at the 11.00 am Mass was to hold a 'Little Church'. For the five weeks of first communions, the practice was extended to the Saturday evening Mass. Immediately after their 'showing off' at the start of Mass, the first communicants were accompanied into the sacristy by other children, some of whom would have been regular church-goers whilst other were siblings or cousins of first communicants from non-practising families. Once there, one of the members of the 'A Team' led a series of activities based around the Gospel reading for the day. The aim was to offer the children a calm period in which they could focus on the spiritual nature of the event in which they were taking part, but this was subverted by the first communicants themselves. They were clearly highly excited – reinforced by the experience of being paraded to the congregation that had immediately preceded the 'Little Church'. It proved virtually impossible for the leaders to hold the children's attention for any sustained period, and conversations broke out again and again between the children about the parties to follow and gifts that had been received. At one celebration the question of how much money they had received was the dominant theme of conversation between the children of both sexes; one boy punctuated the 'Little Church' with a constant sung repetition of the opening line of the Abba song, 'Money, Money, Money' as he repeatedly and ostentatiously counted the ten- and twenty-pound notes he drew from his pockets. On that day, the leader's exasperation with the children boiled over: 'Excuse me. It's hard work standing here doing this. So shut up and give me a chance.' The aspirations the priest had held for this period as a time of sustained reflection before the children returned to church for the eucharist were not fulfilled. On the other hand, their absence from the church for the first half of the Mass permitted him to develop his theme that this was a 'normal, adult' Mass, and to preach the type of sermon he would have given on any Sunday. Whether this held the attention of the majority of the congregation who did not regularly attend Sunday worship is open to question.

At the end of the 'Little Church' session, the children made their way to the back of the church, where the first communicants were handed the vessels containing the bread and wine to be used in the eucharist. These they carried in procession to the priest, who stood in front of the altar. All the children then returned to their places. A formal procession to the altar with the bread and wine is a feature in most Sunday Masses, as is the practice of its being carried by the first communicants at their Mass. In this parish the action took a simple form, in keeping with the priest's desire that the liturgy should be as 'normal' as possible.

The Lord's Prayer

At the close of the Eucharistic Prayer, the priest once again called the first communicants to the front. He invited the children and the congregation to gaze at each other, saying to the first communicants, 'Can you see them? They can see you.' Then immediately he asked everyone to close their eyes in order to say the Lord's Prayer. Not surprisingly, this directive was largely ignored. Given the care lavished on the dress and appearance of the children, and the fact that the priest had brought them onto the raised platform of the sanctuary (effectively, that is, onto a stage) and encouraged the parties to look at each other, it seems almost naïve for him to expect that people should then disengage from that gaze. To him the meaningful recitation of the Lord's Prayer was a priority, but his lead-up to it had keyed into a different set of priorities in his congregation.

After the Lord's Prayer, the priest offered the Sign of Peace to each of the children, and directed them to return to their places and exchange that peace with their families. During one of the 'A Team' sessions, June related an occasion that drew out the mismatch between the priest's attempts to ritually translate the event into terms meaningful to those present, and the actual level of participation of some in the congregation.

> I come one Saturday night, and there was communions as well, and there was a little lad. The priest took him up on the altar. When it come to the Sign of Peace, the priest shook his hand, and then said, 'Go back to your parents.' And so this kid walked up to his Mum, and she was going, 'Where's me Mam?' And the kid was standing like that, and she was going, 'Mother!' And this poor kid was standing waiting for his mother to turn round – I thought, you know, my heart was going out to this poor kid who was just stood there waiting for her. 'Mam! All right, lad.' And the kid got shoved, and it was just – and I thought, 'Ah, God love him', you know.

The priest explained that this was because 'we sometimes ask people to do things they're not familiar with at all', and did not engage with June's reiterated sense of outrage that however unfamiliar the mother was with the pattern and meaning of Mass, she should have been more attentive to her son.

The Ritual of Reception of Communion

The priest described the moment of first communion during an interview:

> The child comes up first and they surround the child, and just before the child receives communion, I would say, with as many of the family who can surround them – horse-shoe fashion – and I've normally said to them beforehand, even if they're not Catholics, or even atheists, to gather round the child … I get the child to look around at everybody, and there's usually a couple of smiles created by the process, then I try to get the child focused on me again, and I say, 'Why are all these people smiling? It's because they love you and you love them.' Sometimes there's a tear in a mother's eyes, or whatever, and then I lift the host and say, 'The Body of Christ – God's come to you because he loves you.'

Two aspects of the ritual as I observed it were absent from that description. First, when the family had gathered, the priest – holding the vessel containing the hosts for communion – sat on his haunches so that he was at eye-level with each child. Second, each child 'looked round at everybody' by turning through 360 degrees. During the same interview he explained the ritual, which he said was of his own devising, in the following terms:

> Because part of what we're sharing is that the child's loved by God, loved in a special way in which God manifests himself. Therefore, the real expression of this for the child, or the … family around them: they love you, your family, and therefore God loves you too … I have in the back of my mind that the sacramental presence of God is to affirm these children.

But was that the experience of participants? The Year Seven interviewees included a number of twelve-year-olds who had previously taken part in this ritual. They recalled an experience markedly different from that intended by the priest. One girl said, 'and he made everyone stand round me, so I felt ashamed.'[1] Another said, 'All your family were sitting round – were standing round you in a circle, a circle, and you were in the middle.' A third remembered being asked to turn around: 'You gotta, while your family's around you, you've gotta turn round and look at your family.' However, when I asked why they thought this had been done, none of the priest's reasoning was articulated. Three boys spoke almost simultaneously:

> Don't know – it's just …
> Just the thing that's done …
> To see what, *[pause]* just *[pause]* just to look at what they, who they're looking at.

When asked if they could remember how they felt at this point, the following responses were given in quick succession by the boys, with some bantering between themselves:

> Scared.
> No. All my cousins were making me laugh.

---

1   A Liverpool usage, meaning 'embarrassed'.

Loved. I felt loved.
Ah it's his first time – got to be drunk!
Eh, yeah! *[Brief confusion breaks out]*
Nutt'n …
I felt weird.
I felt sick.
I was dead nervous.

Most of these memories appear far removed the sense of affirmation intended by the priest. Many of the first communicants I observed in 1999 were indeed smiling broadly as they turned through 360 degrees within their family circle. Others, however, appeared rather less comfortable, looking down as they turned rather than into the faces of their families. As the interviews with the older children suggested, a ritual action that was intended to be positive could prove unwelcomed and even frightening.

After the child had received communion, the priest offered it to the family members who stood around. In each family, only a minority responded to the invitation. The family returned to its place in the congregation as a body. The ritual was repeated for each child, and when the last family group had returned to its place, the rest of the congregation came forward to receive communion. The Mass then continued to its normal conclusion, after which many families remained in the church to take photographs, posing the first communicant with different family members, and sometimes the priest, in front of the altar. The families then left for their various parties.

Welcomed to a Regular Adult Mass?

The priest admitted to misgivings about the Masses, but these were not about whether an 'adult Mass' had been retained. After all, neither the prayers of the Mass nor the scriptures had been adapted; the homily each weekend was based as normal on the readings of the day and directed towards the congregation as a whole. He was, rather, concerned that the majority of people there might have been unable to 'cope' with the liturgy in this normal form. Of the children he said, 'I think the liturgy is wonderful, but it needs unpacking. It's certainly not for a seven- or eight-year-old child.' He was also aware that the adult members might have been 'swamped' by the event, because the majority of those who accompanied the children to the Mass would not have had the benefit of the parents' meetings. Yet, was it a 'regular' Saturday evening or Sunday morning Mass that he had offered to them? The use of the 'Little Church' was an adaptation of a normal feature of the parish's worship, but the double parading of the children and the extended ritual of holy communion were far from the norm. As these focused on the children and their families they probably created the most enduring impression for most participants, as is borne out by the vivid recollections of the event by the Year Seven children. Moreover, the regular congregation experienced the first communion Masses as anything but normal. The priest acknowledged to the 'A Team' that the period of first communion represented 'six weeks of disruption' to many worshippers. Annie, who in most things was one of his closest collaborators, expressed it more strongly; it is her complaint that is quoted on the first page of the Introduction.

Balloons and Liturgical Law: The Second Subject Parish

The first communion Masses in the second parish were also celebrated as the parish Sunday morning eucharist. However, in almost every other key respect they differed from the pattern of the first parish. Instead of attempting to retain the Sunday Mass more or less intact and incorporating the ritual of first communion into a 'regular adult' celebration, the priest in the second parish used the opportunities afforded him by Catholic liturgical law to adapt the celebration to the age and cognitive abilities of the children. (A range of adaptations is offered in the *Directory on Children's Masses*, 1973). The resulting liturgy had clear outlines and a minimum of movement. However, he superimposed upon this reduced ritual structure an unorthodox and playful element that served as a vehicle for his own exuberant celebratory style.

The Arrangement of the Church

The cohort of 34 children made their first communion across two Sunday mornings. The school allocated the children to the two groups according to the initial letter of their surnames. There were some exceptions to this rule: cousins were placed together, and children who had siblings in one of the years taking Standard Attainment Tests were all placed in the first group because the tests began on the day after the second celebration. This final point was explained by the headteacher's concern that no child should either miss the test or be suffering from a hangover when they sat it. The front benches of the centre aisle were reserved for the children and their immediate families. The children themselves were seated at the end of the bench, on the centre aisle. Eight large helium balloons had been tied to the ends of benches along the length of the centre aisle. These bore the mottos: 'Congratulations' (x3), 'Thanks for a job well-done', 'Thanks for the hard work', 'Hang in there', 'Thanks a bunch', and 'Welcome home'.

The Ritual Process

The priest's desire to celebrate a Mass in keeping with the formal guidelines on Masses with children resulted in a reduction in the number of scripture readings from three to two, the use of simplified texts for them, and a homily appropriate to the children's age and cognitive ability. A further option is allowed; one of three official Eucharistic Prayers adapted for use with children may be used. The priest, however, used Eucharistic Prayer II, the shortest of the standard set of prayers.

When first interviewed, the priest explained that he had made 'slight changes' to the previous pattern of first communion Masses to achieve this type of liturgy. However, it later emerged that he had transformed the liturgy by significantly reducing the active role the children played in it. Whereas under his predecessor as parish priest, the children had proclaimed the readings and led the prayers of General

Intercession following the homily, they now performed no active role whatsoever in the liturgy. No child was asked to come forward to read, sing or pray before the assembly. He offered me two reasons for this change in policy. The first was pastoral: asking the children to perform such liturgical functions would be 'another thing for them to worry about, whereas getting there to communion in their dresses or whatever, you know, is enough in itself'. The second was liturgical: he judged such a degree of elaboration inappropriate.

As regards the pastoral concern, one of the first communicants had expressed anxiety when I visited the school about 'singing' at her first communion day:

> I'm nervous – I don't want to sing.
> *Why not?*
> I don't wanna – I feel ashamed.
> *Why do you feel ashamed?*
> I don't know.
> *[Boy:]* Because my cousin always skits me, and she'll probably do it again.

Such concern resonates with the memories of the Year Seven children, several of whom recounted the discomfort they had felt at performing such actions in the liturgy. Perhaps this is partly due to simple embarrassment. To find oneself the object of the congregation's gaze was not welcomed by all the children; one girl said: 'I felt ashamed when people kept looking at me.' However the children's memories – and particularly those of the girls – may also have been coloured by the experience of attempting to negotiate steps in procession whilst wearing unaccustomedly long and full dresses; a note of ordeal begins to emerge from these comments:

> Yeah. Like, I was, like, we all had to go on a stage, right, where you could sing this big hymn thing, right? And there was this lad in front of me, and this lad behind me stood on my dress and I tripped and banged me mouth on the lad's foot who was in front of me. And I had a big lip on me, I was like crying singing the song. I was.

The priest explained his second, liturgical, reason for reducing the children's involvement:

> I've been in situations where the children have done everything, and also because there have been too many children for the things to do, like in terms of the readings and bidding prayers – they've added things like introducing the Mass. In my other parish here they did the Opening Prayer and then final Thanksgiving Prayers, so it wasn't a liturgy – it was an assembly. It was the equivalent of a school assembly where every child does something. Whether you can tell what the child is saying or not was irrelevant.

These two concerns led to a stripping-down of the liturgy to a simple form that made few demands on the children. They all remained with their families throughout the first half of the ceremony, and then they moved as a body, guided by and subject to the scrutiny of the school staff. Thus, after the Bidding Prayers, the children moved to the back of church where two of the teachers were waiting for them. These distributed among the children the various items to be brought to the altar in procession. Two children carried the bread and wine for the eucharist; each of the remainder carried his or her 'family album' – a scrapbook, carefully covered in shiny wrapping paper, in which the children and their parents had pasted photographs and other items to track the story of each child's life:

> I've seen the most amazing things in these books: the scan when the mum was pregnant, the little tape around the baby's hand when they were in Oxford Street Hospital, the first curl that the child had cut from its head, the first tooth that the baby laid. And then photographs in, in ,in – certificates from school, certificates from, erm, it's saying, 'I love this child. This child is very precious to me.' [Headteacher]

As the children reached the entrance to the sanctuary, the headteacher and their class teacher directed them to the priest. Standing immediately in front of the altar, he received from them the books, which he placed at the foot of the altar, and the bread and wine. The children then remained within the sanctuary, some flanking the altar, others facing inwards from the top of the steps leading to the altar, their backs to the congregation. The headteacher and class teacher moved into the side chapels that communicated with the sanctuary. From this position, masked from the congregation by the chancel arch, they maintained discipline by holding eye contact with the children and, on occasion, through discreet hand gestures. They moved around to the front of the sanctuary after the Sign of Peace to direct the children through the process of receiving communion.

The children remained in position on the sanctuary through to the time of communion. They did not exchange the Sign of Peace, therefore, with their families, nor was the reception of communion itself elaborated into a family ritual as in the first parish. Instead, when the time came, the children moved from their positions within the sanctuary to receive the host from the priest, who stood in front of the altar. They then passed to the bottom of the sanctuary steps to receive from the chalice at the hands of two lay ministers of the eucharist, and thence returned to their families. After the children had all received, the priest moved to the head of the aisle to distribute communion to the congregation. The children and their families thus received communion at two distinct times. This, the headteacher explained, was to avoid placing the adults in a position where they felt either pressurized to communicate or embarrassed because the circumstances of their life rendered them unable to do so – for example, as a result of cohabitation or remarriage after divorce. (CCC 1650 and 1655)

The Balloons

The controlled, sober quality of the ceremony was relieved twice by the priest himself: during the homily and at the end of the Mass. At the start of the homily he moved to the head of the centre aisle, and asked, 'Children, do you like the balloons? What would happen if we cut the string on one of them?' The children were slow to respond, but eventually one of them suggested that the balloon would rise to the ceiling. The priest then asked, 'Shall we try it?' He released one of the balloons, and waited for it to drift to the rafters while the children followed its path:

You were right! Now some people think that God's up there, where that balloon is heading, but he's not. He's here *[pointing to himself]* in you and in me. And God is with you in a special way in holy communion. So will you remember that, while you're having your party at home: God's in you?

At the close of the Mass the priest returned to the head of the aisle, and asked: 'One final thing, children. What is the most common word on our balloons? "Thank-you". So every time we come to Mass we say "Thanks" to God. So let's say "Thank-you" this way.' He walked down the aisle and released all the balloons – thereby sending a message of thanks to the very place where earlier he had told the children God was not. The exuberance of his use of the balloons contrasted with the controlled pattern of the rest of the Mass. Did it detract from the moment of communion? Later he said to me, 'Today all they'll remember is the balloons.'

Something for Everyone to Do: Sr Margaret's Ritual

The first communion ritual created by Sr Margaret contrasted sharply with the simple ceremony desired by the parish priest just discussed. Indeed, she had included all the elements he had sought to remove. While she reduced the number of scripture readings before the Gospel from three to two, in accordance with the permissions stated in the *Directory on Children's Masses* (p. 267), she made no further simplification in the structure of the Mass. Her chief goal throughout the first communion process was to draw the first communicants and their families into regular participation in the eucharist, so she created a first communion Mass that accentuated the level of participation of the children. As in the second subject parish, the classroom cohort of around thirty children was alphabetically divided into two groups for first communion. During the Masses – held across two Sundays – each first communicant came forward to proclaim a reading, a prayer or a commentary. Each participated in at least one of the several processions during the liturgy. The result was a complex, restless ritual that constantly paraded the children before the public gaze. The ceremony adapted the rite of Mass at three levels, which will be considered in turn before attention is given to a particular question arising from the administration of holy communion itself.

The Adaptation of Standard Ritual of the Mass

In accordance with normal practice the children proclaimed the First Reading and announced the General Intercessions (Bidding Prayers). These elements were shared between a number of children: two read the scripture passage, and each of the five intercessions was announced by a different child. At the start of both elements, the priest named the children who were to take part in it and called them forward as a group. He then held the microphone for each child in turn; none of them returned to the congregation until all had spoken.

Allocation to Children of Roles Normally Exercised by Priest

In order to achieve Sr Margaret's intention that all the children should have a speaking part during the liturgy, they were allocated certain elements normally said by the priest. There were two categories: presidential prayers reserved to the priest alone in the formal liturgical texts, and sections which in common practice fall into the priest's remit, but which may be delegated. The first of these categories comprises the Opening and Concluding Prayers and the Prayer over the Gifts. These formulae, together with the preface to the Eucharistic Prayer, form the classical block of presidential prayers in each Mass of the Roman Rite; they change according to season and celebration. Their delegation is never formally permitted. Before each one the priest called children forward by name to read the prayer: two each for the Opening and Concluding Prayers, one for the Prayer over the Gifts. The second category comprised the Introduction at the start of the Mass and the invocations of Christ within the penitential rite; considerable latitude for adaptation and delegation is afforded to these within the liturgical texts. Once again children came forward when called by the parish priest: one to read the Introduction, three for the Penitential Rite.

Significant Ritual Adaptations

Sr Margaret did not limit her liturgical adaptations to distributing the various prayer formulae among the children. She also elaborated three processional moments in the early part of the liturgy: at the entrance, before the Gospel and at the Presentation of Gifts (Offertory). Whereas the adaptations considered above provided opportunities for each of the first communicants to perform a solo, spoken role within the liturgy, the three processional moments displayed the children to the assembly either *en masse* (Entrance and Offertory) or in a small group (Gospel).

Before the Mass began the children were taken to the room in which their 'lessons' had taken place each Sunday during the time of preparation. Each was accompanied by a family member. In most cases this companion was the child's mother, though several were with their fathers, and one girl was accompanied by what appeared to be her elder sister. When the priest had joined them, the musicians began the opening song, humming the melody rather than singing the words, while the children and their accompanying adult processed into the body of the church. When they reached the sanctuary the children moved onto the steps and turned to face the congregation, their hands joined, whilst the adults returned to their benches. The priest brought up the rear of the procession, and moved to his usual place behind the altar. Sr Margaret took her place in the left front bench, facing the children. The whole action had been precisely timed, so that at the end of the hummed verse everybody was in place. The verse was then repeated, this time with the words added. The children accompanied their singing with choreographed hand gestures, taking their lead from Sr Margaret. They remained in full view of the congregation throughout the opening rites of the Mass, performing similar hand gestures at the 'Gloria', and only returning to their families at the scripture readings.

During the reading, Sr Margaret began to prepare the second processional element. She led four children – two boys, two girls – to the rear of the church, and gave each a lighted candle set in a low stand. She then formed them into a procession, the two girls to the front with the boys to the rear, and between the two pairs a catechist holding a copy of the Lectionary. The procession moved down the aisle to the lectern during the singing of the Alleluia. The catechist gave the lectionary to the priest who placed it on the lectern and read the Gospel with the four children standing around him. At the end of the Gospel, the priest took the candles from the girls and placed them on the top of the altar, between two altar candles that had been there from the beginning of Mass. The boys returned to the back of church, where they gave the candles to Sr Margaret. All then returned to their places.

No explanation was offered as to why only two of the candles had been placed on the altar. However, the candles returned to the rear of the church reappeared at the head of the third processional moment, which involved all the children once again. This time the candles, again carried by two boys, were placed between the others on the front top of the altar; the heights of the six candles that now stood there had been carefully calculated so that together they formed a symmetrical concave arc. The other children processed behind the candle-bearers, each carrying his or her workbook. These were not the scrap-books as in the second parish, but a bound series of worksheets produced by Sr Margaret to be completed by the children after each Sunday lesson. These were presented to the priest, who placed them on the altar. At the rear of the procession two mothers brought forward the bread and wine. Immediately after presenting the objects they carried to the priest, the children and the two mothers returned to their places.

Communion

Compared to the elaborate and carefully controlled processions of the early part of the ceremony, the reception of first communion was performed in an almost perfunctory manner. The families were directed forward in turn by one of the school teachers, but the priest did not wait until everyone was in place before he administered communion to the child. Consequently, several children had already received communion before all the relatives had left the family bench. The speed at which communion was administered was amplified by the fact that very few of the children received from the chalice which was offered by Sr Margaret. She later expressed her surprise, as she had explained to the children that they were to receive under both kinds. However, several of the Year Seven pupils stated that they had chosen not to receive from the chalice at their own first communions. One had explained 'I didn't drink the wine because I didn't like wine at the time', while several had agreed that they 'never had the wine' – meaning that they did not on that occasion.

Conclusions

The effect of the multiple voices and near-constant activity at this Mass was to fragment the flow of the liturgy, and reduce the priest's role in it. The major adaptations also considerably affected the ritual balance within the Mass, adding weight to the opening rituals and to the processional elements before the Gospel and at the Offertory, without offering any counterbalance later. In contrast with the elaboration of these earlier liturgical sections, the ritual of communion itself was conducted in a somewhat haphazard manner, with neither the formalized family ritual of the first parish nor the more remote but controlled process of the second. The ritual itself, therefore, whilst aiming to encourage the maximum visible participation of the children, reinforced a static reading of the event; the moment of communion was lost in a series of other words and gestures that encouraged a focus upon the child. What mattered was to see the child, but not to see its communion. Paradoxically, the ceremony supported an interpretation in terms of the slower, familial cycle of repetition rather than the ecclesial weekly cycle.

Conclusion: The 1910–11 and Contemporary Rituals Compared

When these three rituals are compared to the ceremonies performed in 1910–11, four significant areas of difference become apparent. First, whereas the 1910–11 first communion Masses had been celebrated in the early morning, the modern rituals were held at varying times across the day. This is due to significant changes in Catholic legislation regarding the celebration of Mass and reception of communion. In 1910, Mass might not begin later than one hour after midday, and the early twentieth-century children were subject, like their elders, to the obligation of fasting from midnight before receiving communion. The significant relaxation of both these disciplines during the course of the century permitted the celebration of evening Masses and the reception of communion after just one hour's fast.

The later celebration and the removal of the midnight fasting requirement lessened the importance within the wider ritual of the first communion breakfast taken by all the first communicants in school following the Mass. In the second subject parish, the teacher explained how the tradition had fallen into disuse only two or three years before my observations:

> I think the last two years we haven't actually had one because it got to the point where – it's terrible, saying about the parties being the most important thing – it got to the point where the children were all, were all coming in (or some weren't even coming in at all – they were being whisked away to wherever or whatever they were going to do), and the parents came in to 'Don't eat too much!' or 'hurry up, hurry up, come on because we've got to get to ours, to get to …'. And really it was not nice for the ladies who'd spent so much time getting everything ready for the children. It wasn't really appreciated what, what they did. So that, that's one tradition that, that has fallen by the wayside.

None of the rituals I observed was followed by a group meal; instead all the children made their way to family parties.

Second, the liturgy of the contemporary Masses was more creative than the earlier ones. Whereas the celebration of the eucharist until the Second Vatican Council was highly controlled, with no variation to the set texts permitted (Bouscaren and Ellis, 1946, p. 818), the current practice for widespread adaptation within the liturgy was manifested in the creative freedom exercised by the two priests and Sr Margaret

– although whether Rome would recognize that its current legislation in fact permits such freedom of adaptation is debatable. In the first parish, the four concessions to the presence of the children not only heightened their presence, but introduced a new visual element that superimposed a dissonant ritual rhythm onto the traditional structure of the Mass. The second priest, on the other hand, took pains to respect the formal structure of the Mass within the guidelines for adaptation permitted by the Church. Yet his balloon-play similarly introduced a novel visual element that would, in his own admission, remain the lasting memory of the Mass for the children. Finally, Sr Margaret produced a celebration that not only introduced new ritual elements, but also redistributed some of the priest's functions among the first communicants.

The third difference between the two celebrations was related to the second. Given that they enjoyed no latitude to adapt the Mass, the celebrants of the 1910–11 liturgies poured their creative energies into non-eucharistic secondary rituals later in the day, such as the renewal of baptismal promises, dedication to Mary and evening processions. The long-standing incorporation of these rituals into the first communion celebratory complex was noted in Chapter 3, yet over the course of the twentieth century they have almost disappeared. However, they can remain a focus of nostalgia; during the parents' meetings in the first parish, several parents strongly expressed the opinion that the ritual should be performed for their children in exactly the same way as it had been for them.

The reluctance of priests and catechists today to bring the entire cohort of thirty-plus children together and process them around the church as a body is part of the fourth significant difference between the two sets of rituals. In 1910–11 the children partook in the event – including the supplementary rituals – as a body. Their frame of association was the school cohort. The celebrations of the last years of the century reflect the growing concern in the Catholic catechetical community that the preparation and celebration of the ritual should involve the children's families more fully. Thus in each setting a greater emphasis was laid upon the family; in none of them were the children separated from their families, and, in the first and third celebratory models particularly, the families played an accompanying role.

The new emphasis upon the role of the family raises questions of authenticity. Did the part the parents were invited to perform in these rituals correspond to the reality of the relationship with the Church and the conceptualization of faith that they communicated to their child? Or were they, through their participation in the ritual, expressing other concerns that potentially went in the face of the carefully constructed ritual discourse of the parishes, concerns that related rather more closely to the non-official discourses of meaning identified in Chapter 7? The final chapter will examine these questions by using theories of need and consumption to analyse the ritual from within the non-ecclesial discourses.

X family replaces school

CHAPTER 10

First Communion and Consumption

Introduction

Chapter 7 identified four related non-ecclesial discourses that emerged from the fieldwork: generational continuity, the one special day, the substitute wedding, and mothers and daughters. From the fieldwork it became evident that these discourses are not articulated in verbal form only. Also, and indeed most powerfully, all four find expression through the world of symbol: through dress, gift-giving, and eating and drinking. As a consequence the ritual of first communion designed to sustain a series of symbols and gestures that express fundamentally Christian concepts also serves as the framework for a very different symbolic language. One and the same ritual space comes to contain two symbolic universes. The parish clergy and their associates may have corralled the first communicants into a ritual that in structure and spoken texts conforms to an ecclesial norm. However, as the first communicants enter the building with their families and guests, they introduce into that carefully regulated ritual space a very different modality of symbolic performance, and one that exerts a powerful counterpoint to the expected movement of the liturgy. Moreover, once the Mass has ended, the opportunity for parish authorities to control the meaning within the event comes to an end, whilst the performance of the first communicants and their families spills out from the Church and is prolonged in the family home, in the pub or even in the parish social centre.

On the day of first communion, the key symbolical carriers of the non-ecclesial discourses are consumer goods – the clothes that the first communicants and their families wear, the gifts the children are given, and the food and drink that they consume. The prominence given to consumer goods at first communion and the costs incurred emerged as a matter of criticism and regret for clergy and regular church-goers, frequently dismissed in terms of an unneeded extravagance. I suggest, however, that the problem for the Church posed by the use of these goods is far more serious than the parish authorities recognise: that use expresses a rival account for the event that claims space even within the ritual itself. If the use made of those goods is analysed in terms of the meaning they carry for the families, then a social purpose can be recognised in their consumption that, contrary to the perception of parish authorities, does correspond to a real need. The first communion offers the child's family an opportunity to convey a sense of its identity and worth to the local community through the ritual display it constructs using goods understood as carriers of shared meaning. Rather than being 'needless', the expenditure may serve a vital purpose in establishing, marking or sustaining status within the local community. Similarly, a poor or incorrect display might have negative social consequences.

In considering these issues, this chapter is divided into two parts. The first part draws upon the fieldwork to explore discourses that emerged in the observed parishes about the use of consumer goods. I shall begin by identifying relevant comments made by the 'A Team' and their priest before going on to consider attempts by other respondents to theorize the use of consumer goods. In the second part of the chapter I shall analyse the use of consumer goods as it emerged from the fieldwork, through recourse to a sequence of theoretical approaches. This second part opens by problematizing the concept of 'need', and moves to considering the use of consumer goods in ritual perspective. Finally, and at greatest length, I turn to a developing tradition within the field of consumer research, which since the 1950s has been gradually and with increasing sophistication drawing upon anthropological and sociological approaches to analyse the symbolic use of consumer goods.

Discourses of Consumption in the Fieldwork

Describing Consumption: the A Team and their Parish Priest

According to the 'A Team', expense was incurred on two main elements of the first communion event: the child's – especially the girl's – dress, and the party that followed. A number of anecdotal illustrations were offered. Brenda told of a mother who, despite being on income support, had spent £500 on her daughter's dress, and would have hired a horse and carriage to transport the child to church had her friends and family not voiced their objections. The priest similarly related his experience of an extended family in which the daughters of two sisters were making their first communions in the same year:

> I knew that one of these sisters is addicted to substances, and I knew that she wouldn't have the cash even to compare with her own sister's child ... I said to this woman, 'Look, I've got three or four dresses that to be honest with you are worth hundreds of pounds.' And I said to her, 'You don't have to spend hundreds of pounds', – not saying, 'I know you can't afford it.' And she said, 'Don't worry about that side of it, Father, because the family have got together – she's going to be beautifully dressed that day.' That woman's been in gaol since.

The initial response of the 'A Team' to these accounts was negative; Brenda suggested that underpinning the situation she had recounted had been an attempt to use the first communion to 'over-compensate for not giving, not putting input, basically, into the child'. The priest's concern lay with the debt incurred:

> I've actually said – don't go and repeat this in public to my friends, Peter – but there's only one sin left in the Church, and that is to go into debt at first communion. And you really mustn't. You've destroyed what it's all about if you go into debt.

However the 'A Team' recognized this as unrealistic, and a more moderated position emerged. Josie challenged him: 'You stand up and say that in every meeting, every one. You say, "You're a sinner." So everyone is a sinner in that room – they're going to do it. You stand there, and they're going to do it'. Indeed, 'A Team' members agreed that they, too, would incur debt to pay for the first communion party, though they claimed greater restraint than their peer group with regard to dress.

The 'A Team' voiced their criticisms of other parents in terms of competition. They perceived an anxiety on the part of parents that their child should not be seen to be dressed less lavishly than its peers. Josie noted: 'You get some people that like a price tag and want to brag about it.' June elaborated:

> I think they've gone daft! Well, that five hundred pounds one. And this girl was on her own, and she went, 'Oh, I've seen her dress – and it's five hundred pound.' Stupid cow! Five hundred pound! My wedding dress didn't cost that.

June explained that such price comparisons would be made by mothers as they dropped off or collected their children at the school gate. Both she and Josie expressed concern over the pressure under which this spirit of competition placed parents. This was particularly true if the first communicant was a girl, as there was an expectation that each girl should be dressed in a unique manner. Team members explained the lengths to which local retailers complied with – perhaps exploited – this concern:

> *June*:   There's shops won't sell – if I went in one day and Brenda went in the next, they wouldn't sell you the same dress.
>
> *Josie*:   Why?
>
> *June:*   Why? Because they could all have the same dress – I mean they all look different.
>
> *Brenda*:   Oh they – all those shops now, all the Liverpool shops, even the market in Great Homer Street – they'll all ask you the school and the date because the mothers are so competitive. There's murder if two of them dresses go out.
>
> *Nicky*:   They want to know what date your communion is. No one else has got that in the school.
>
> *Brenda*:   It doesn't matter if it suits your child, and she grabs it and she wants it. You can't have that dress. The shop won't sell it you. That's the script now. Even Great Homer Street Market, they'll ask you, 'What school? What church? What date?'

Brenda located the competition at first communion on a continuum that extended through other aspects of life in the community. She drew a parallel between the female competition among mothers concerning their daughters' dress and the aggressive competition she observed amongst parents – most especially fathers – as they supported the boys' football team she ran:

> You get big angry dads, and they're ... just shouting one name, which is their child. And the aggressiveness, it's incredible – oh, shouldn't even be there. I mean, it's a privilege to be a parent, I feel – even more of a privilege to watch your child. It doesn't matter if they're absolutely rubbish or bottom of the league, or whatever they're doing – gymnastics or whatever. It's a privilege for you to be there watching them – to these dads – and some mums are like that. They've all got this negative aggression towards their child. And they're wondering why their child isn't doing well! The kid's not doing well because it's not learning anything positive from its parents.

Whether on the football field or in the first communion event, then, the child became the vehicle for adult competitiveness within the community. In either case, the children were usually the willing participant, though as the Year Seven interviews suggested, they could experience certain aspects of the first communion event as an ordeal.

There was general agreement amongst the 'A Team' that boys' dress at first communion need not be as great an issue as that of girls. Brenda said, 'If anyone dresses a boy for over sixty pounds there is no need, it's not necessary. But what some people do is they'll go to town and they'll get a tailor-made suit. Well, that's their fault.' During the first parent's meeting several mothers in Nicky's small group expressed the opinion that the entire business of dressing up was a source of embarrassment rather than pleasure to the boys, and that some would need to be coaxed into wearing special clothes for their first communion day. One grandmother spoke of her own son as hating to have compliments paid to him on his appearance – and especially his clothes – when he was a child. This observation received a murmur of agreement from those present, who agreed that whilst girls developed a strong sense at an early age of what they would or would not like to wear, boys were less interested in formal dress.

Two Theories from the Second Parish: Heart and Head in Conflict, Generational Continuity

The protagonists from the second subject parish voiced contrasting approaches to the twinned issues of dress and expenditure. Both Sr Margaret and the primary headteacher identified the issues as problematic, but their attempts to rationalize the expenditure led them in different directions. Sr Margaret had used a questionnaire to invite parents to prioritize the importance of different aspects of the first communion event:

> We said, 'We don't want you to put down what you think we want, but what are your worries at this time.' And we went into the discussion groups and, you know, we kept saying, 'Please don't put what you think you ought to put, like the Mass. Put what really is the basic worry.' And they sort of insisted that the dress and the party were not the priority, and when we almost tried making them say that, because that's what we felt [was] their priority, they just wouldn't have it. They claimed they were not the priority. And in two schools they were quite concerned about the cost of the dresses – the girls really – and they didn't want this bill to be left with them, and they weren't interested in the dresses.

Sr Margaret demonstrated awareness of the possibility that parents might return the response they expected her to be seeking. This was, after all, a potentially crucial moment: a group of authority-wary individuals being asked to declare their motives for seeking the ritual by its effective gate-keeper. It is impossible on the basis of this interview alone to judge the extent to which – despite their reported protestations to the contrary – they may have been stating the 'expected' view. Furthermore, Sr Margaret's account is confused about the directions given to the group – was their focus to state their priorities, or their concerns? It is significant to this chapter that she perceived the cost of the event to have emerged as a prime issue. Yet as her account continued, it became evident that even that concern was overridden by the interaction of two other discourses – first, a variant of the mother-daughter discourse, and then the discourse of social competition identified by the 'A Team':

> One of them said, 'Well, I' – she'd had two boys, and – 'I've got a little girl now, and I want to give her the best.' And I said, 'Well, the best isn't always the most expensive, the best is what she's going to be comfortable in, and look pretty in.' And other mums were really against her, and what they were saying was, 'If we all say the same thing, then we don't have to go overboard.' ... A lot of them go into debt for it, and we try explaining that it's just not worth it, that it's not the important thing. And in their heads they know that it's not the important thing. But in their hearts, because they don't want their kid to look any lower, or whatever – any different to other children .... .

Drawing upon this interaction and her experience of directing first communion programmes elsewhere, Sr Margaret constructed a theory of the relationship between the faith stance of the parents and the expectations of the parish community. The parents' stated priorities revealed that they placed 'the faith side of it first'. For her, this pointed to their having 'a very deep faith and a relationship with God', although without a sense of commitment to Sunday worship. There was a paradox in this. She could hold this essentially positive attitude to the faith of such parents (she described 'feeling very small' whilst discussing faith with their counterparts in her previous positions), whilst at the same time imposing a preparation process for first communion that accentuated exactly the dimension (weekly Sunday Mass) that did not feature in the faith life she constructed for them.

A different interpretation was developed by the headteacher. She spoke of one attempt made by parents to recoup some of the cost of the day:

> I have great difficulty with parents. They pay a hundred and fifty, two hundred pounds for a dress. Then they come to me and say, 'Do you think you could sell this for me?' And I say, 'Did you buy it second hand?' 'Oh my God, no! I wouldn't have my child ... ' So I say, 'So who else is going to buy it second hand? Let's pass it on to some mission, or somewhere where people won't know.' But yes, they'd sell their souls, for want of a better word, that their child has the very best for first communion. They feel as though they've done their bit for their children.

This evidence of the reluctance of parents to countenance using second-hand dresses at first communion echoes the data from the first subject parish.

As has been seen, Sr Margaret incorporated the issue of expenditure into a discourse about faith, and saw it as subordinate to an optimistic perspective on the parents viewed from an ecclesial standpoint. In contrast, the headteacher located this lavish expenditure within a discourse of generational continuity. She used as her reference point a piece of local autobiography (O'Mara, 1933):

> This little boy who was writing – he's gone to America now – he was writing his memoirs. But he said they were very poor, the father was often drunk and mum worked hard and they had no money. And he was worried because it was coming up to his first communion. Mum went and worked terribly hard. He had a new pair of boots, a new pair of trousers, a new shirt and a tie. And when he went she scrubbed him clean. When he made his first

communion he was as good as everybody else. The next day she pawned the lot. But it was their way of celebrating the one ... of their life that they can celebrate joyfully. It's nothing to do with – people criticize them that they make this great fuss. But their lives were so awful that this was one way of celebrating their child's first communion. And yes, it's traditional. And so it goes on.

The expenditure, for her was a sign that today's parents, like the mother of O'Mara, wanted 'the best' for their children – as had their parents before them.

Community Display: A theory from the First Parish

The most sustained attempt to theorize the significance of expenditure and display at first communion was made by a respondent in the first subject parish, whom I shall call Linda. A founding member of the 'A Team', she no longer took part in first communion preparation, though she remained a highly active member of the parish community. Brought up in a middle-class background, she was widowed at a young age, and had raised two children as a single parent with the support of state benefits. Although she shared the relative poverty of her neighbours, she was none the less 'observing' (her own word) them as an outsider. In sharing her observations, she was, therefore, 'writing culture' for them (cf. Wagner, 1981).

Linda suggested that the extravagant display encountered at first communion stood at one end of a continuum that included all use of external display within her community, such as the insistence upon designer sportswear and big bicycles for children, or mobile phones and cars for adults. These external displays were used to buy status and credibility within the community – especially by those who lacked social status or power within society as a whole:

> People – it's not, a middle-class idea: you see the middle classes dressing their children in rags, really, because they've got plenty of money in the bank and, you – they're fairly well-assured. But in the sort of families whose, who really live from hand to mouth, they don't look very far ahead, so they're just looking at what ... I suppose it reflects, if their, if people laugh at their children, and, 'Oh, look at who's dressed in those stupid clothes', I suppose it, they feel slighted. They feel it reflects badly on them, on their egos, on their self-esteem. So I don't know how they get their money. Maybe they go into debt, so nobody will laugh at their children so they'll feel a bit water-tight against being humiliated and laughed at.[1]

She understood first communion to be an illustration of this function of the children's dress as a vehicle for acquiring parental self-esteem. She gave a particular illustration, linking the bride-like display of one child with the projection of self-esteem on the part of her unmarried mother.

Linda then linked this continuum of display to the issue of competition Brenda had identified. Relating her own experience of poverty to a sense of disempowerment,

---

1   For a consideration of the use made by children of consumer goods, cf. Walkerdine (1997).

she suggested that the exuberant display of first communion gave families a sense of empowerment within their community:

> Maybe it makes them feel a bit powerful for a day when they're having their communion and, you know, throwing their money about and buying their children dresses and things, do you think? ... Well, maybe, maybe just everybody looks at them and thinks, 'Oh well, you look nice today and you've made a great effort.' You know, the host of a great, of a nice party with plenty to drink, and nice food. People look at that, that child and say, 'Ah, look at that beautiful little dress – doesn't she look lovely.' And, you know, it gives them some sort of lift, some self-esteem which everybody needs, don't they? ... It's just, you know, to be somebody, to be in that community – I mean out of that community, you know. But in that community they have some status for that day, and people maybe remember that holy communion day as a good day, a good party. You know – a good time.

If it is indeed true that the first communion of their children is used by members of deprived communities to 'buy' esteem and even power, then an inadequate display could be regarded as a failure to maintain status, with negative social consequences. This might explain the manner in which mothers and children so obviously compared their own display to that of others. It might also be one of the factors that lie behind the wishes reported earlier; the desire to return to the 'old' system by which an entire cohort of children received their first communion at one celebration is a plea against the constant insistence of the Church upon less lavish celebrations and the now almost universal practice of dividing each cohort into small, manageable groups. The stakes in a whole cohort setting would be much higher than in the small group: the social rewards for a successful display would be more significant, whilst the consequences of failure would be more acutely felt.

Conclusions

A number of core ideas, therefore, emerged from the fieldwork comments on expenditure and display. First, whilst parish authorities often experience unease over the expenditure incurred at first communion, there are other – primarily social – drivers that exercise considerably greater leverage than ecclesial directives in determining familial choices. Second, those drivers may be expressed in terms of the discourses of continuity in family tradition, the substitute wedding, the child's special day or the mother-daughter relationship. Third, a further significant driver relates to the highly public nature of the event: because of the opportunity it affords for competitive comparison within the peer group of families, it stands as a high point on a continuum of display that helps to determine the family's status within its local social hierarchy. In order to draw these core ideas into a coherent theoretical whole, we turn to the consideration of a number of theories about the role played by consumer goods in social interactions.

Theorizing the Use of Consumer Goods at First Communion

In analysing the fieldwork, theories drawn from four broad fields of study will be brought into play: political (Slater, 1997), anthropological (Douglas and Isherwood, 1996), sociological (McCracken, 1986) and commercial. This last category embraces the work of a number of people active in the field of consumer studies, who analyse consumer trends in terms of the symbolic use that consumers make of the goods they buy. These various studies will be used to explore the function of consumer goods in terms of goods and ritual, self-image, 'symbolic interactionism' and gift-giving. First, however, it is necessary to examine the use of the concept of 'need' often brought into play to criticize the use of consumer goods at first communion.

Problematizing The Construct of Need

As has been noted, several times during the fieldwork the view was expressed that parents did not 'need' to go to the lengths that they did. To thus frame the question of consumption at first communion in terms of needs may be a genuine expression of pastoral concern, but it is none the less problematic. Most immediately, it fails to take account of the views of the participants: suggestions that a mother did not 'need' to buy a new dress for her daughter were met with universal incredulity. At a deeper level, such a definition of the needs of one group in society by another has ramifications of power and disempowerment. In framing a discourse of needs in terms of the formal discourses relating to the event, and imposing that discourse as a yardstick for judging the approach taken by families, priests, catechists and active parishioners are engaged in a process of recognition or non-recognition, validation or non-validation, of the meaning which families invest in the ritual.

The challenge is to identify where need is located. The anxiety over expenditure found in the fieldwork operates on two levels. The most immediate expresses financial concern – there is a genuine disquiet over the levels of debt incurred at first communion. However, the proposed response ('They do not need to spend that money') moves the issue to another level: the formal ecclesial discourses that locate the event in terms of personal religious involvement. On the other hand, the families of first communicants may well share the concern about expense, but frame it within a very different discourse, locating the event more within a social context. This generates a very different set of criteria according to which the need for expenditure could be determined. Hence, a conflict that appears to operate at a relatively simple level of economics, is in fact a conflict over meaning.

To pull the question of need and meaning into a sharper focus, let us consider the argument of Don Slater (1997) against externally constructed statements of need. Slater inveighs against the

> ... terroristic and totalitarian potential of any statement of needs which grounds metanarratives in a transcendental truth of the human, in the name of which actual humans can be legitimately coerced into conforming to regimes of truth. [p. 54]

His language is polemic, the coercion of people into 'regimes of truth' is a much more complex matter than his argument would suggest. However, in challenging any construct of needs built upon metanarrative, Slater gives a voice to the tensions experienced at parish level. The position held by the gate-keepers to first communion can indeed appear 'totalitarian' to the families, whilst the families' approach can seem to lack the underpinning values and challenge the ecclesial metanarrative that forms the bedrock of the community's 'reasoned' appeal to the 'real need'.

Instead of rooting needs in metanarrative, Slater proposes that

> ... subjective preferences can be assessed from the point of view of needs which have a validity with respect to achieving visions of a good life – of 'how we should live' – and with respect to the socially available means for achieving such a life. [p. 53]

Significantly, he locates such needs within a social perspective. Thus, needs are formulated at the level neither of the individual nor of the universal, but in terms of 'the intersubjective meanings and institutionalised norms of groups – the meaningful patterns of social life within which alone needs can be defined and made sense of' (p. 59). In other words, in a given setting, a series of historically evolving sets of core values that respond to the question 'What is the good life?' give rise to a sense of what is needed (p. 57).

Slater's argument is not unproblematic, but it is useful in his insistence that need should be understood intersubjectively. The fieldwork evidence suggests that the 'good life' includes the establishment or maintenance of position within the community. In that case, the use of consumption goods to present the appropriate external display would be justifiable in familial terms as the embodiment of a recognized value; it would meet a real need. Furthermore, the various encounters around first communion do indeed constitute a debate about 'values, priorities and power'. The situation is made more complex by the fact that there is an overlapping of core values. This is not a case of two distinct social blocks facing each other, or of one metanarrative schema opposing another; many of the Mass-goers will be grandparents of the first communicants, the catechists may themselves be parents. Perhaps it is the very proximity of the parties in this debate that can render it so painful.

Goods, Meaning And Ritual

Slater locates 'need' at the intersection of interpersonal relationships and social context. How, then, are we to understand the use of consumer goods in first communion in that intersection? Three theoretical approaches are summarized below, and then their findings are applied to the fieldwork evidence.

Douglas and Isherwood: Goods and Information

Douglas and Isherwood (1996) offer a parallel to Slater's concern to discuss need at the level of the interpersonal. Exploring the social role played by material goods, they focus on the cultural context within which the goods are used. Goods are perceived as bearers of messages; the 'overriding objective', therefore, of the consumer is a concern for information (p. 67). Goods are thus bits of information, the 'visible part of culture' (p. 44) to the extent that they function as 'markers for classifying cultural categories' (p. 51). Through the relationships between the individual goods a sensible world can be constructed (pp. 47–8).

Douglas and Isherwood, however, note a problem: cultural categories can be fluid. How does one know whether or not a good continues as an adequate marker, or whether meanings have been changed? There is a need to agree upon conventions for selecting and fixing agreed meanings; for Douglas and Isherwood, rituals supply such conventions. It is not simply that consumer goods play a part within human ritual activity; because of the fluidity of the process of classifying cultural categories, it is essential that the individual who has arrived at a particular set of judgements should rehearse them before other people. This is done by inviting others to share in a ritual within which the goods are highlighted:

> By inviting others to share his rituals, the consumer obtains a judgement from them of the fitness of the choice he makes of consumer goods for celebrating particular occasions, and a judgment on his own relative standing as a judge, as well as a judgement on the fitness of the occasion to be celebrated. [p. 45]

Just as importantly, the consumer needs to be present at other people's rituals of consumption 'to be able to circulate his own judgements of the fitness of the things used to celebrate the diverse occasions' (p. 56).

Rook and Levy: 'Everyday Behavior Ritualization'

Within the field of consumer studies, Rook and Levy (1983) also attempt to link the use of consumer goods to ritual behaviour, though their field of meaning for the ritual is broader than that of Douglas and Isherwood. Rook and Levy locate ritual in a conceptual continuum extending from elaborate public occasions, through rites of passage, to 'the everyday behavior ritualizations that may be either public or private (prayer, grooming) or more interactional and public (the weekly visit to the "beauty shop")' (p. 329). Rook further clarified his concept of ritual in a later article (Rook, 1984). Here, rituals are described as 'formal behavior systems' comprising four elements: actor-participants, an audience, scripted behaviour episodes and ritual artefacts. Rook and Levy's insistence upon grooming as a preparation for social role and social acceptability has a bearing upon our discussion, as we shall see.

McCracken: Goods and the Ritual Transfer of Meaning

A third linkage of the concepts of ritual and goods is made by Grant McCracken (1986). He locates the significance of goods beyond their purely utilitarian character and commercial value; it lies rather in their 'ability to carry and communicate cultural meaning' (p. 71). He further elaborates the notion of the transitory nature of cultural meaning, and constructs a thesis to illustrate the trajectory followed by the meaning of goods. Cultural meaning for McCracken is located in three places:

in the culturally constituted world, within the goods themselves and in individual consumers. Within these three locations, he identifies two points at which meaning is transferred: between the world and the goods, and then again between the goods and the individual consumer.

We have already seen that Douglas and Isherwood (1996) construct their anthropology of consumerism around the notion that goods make visible the categories of culture. McCracken expands on this by considering how material goods can be used to represent materially the various categories of culture – 'objects are created according to a culture's blueprint and to this extent, objects render the categories of this blueprint material and substantial' (ibid.). In rendering solid and material the categories of a culture, however, such goods also signify the meanings, or 'cultural principles' that 'allow all cultural phenomena to be distinguished, ranked and interrelated' (p. 73). It is impossible for goods to signify cultural categories without also signifying cultural principles. McCracken understands this to be a double process of transfer – first from the broader culture into the goods through the agency of advertising and fashion, and then to the individual consumers through the use they make of the goods.

In the latter phase of the process, McCracken makes use of the concept of ritual, distinguishing between four types of rituals used for the transfer of cultural meaning from goods to individuals: rituals of exchange, possession, grooming and divestment. Each of these forms involves (or, in the final case, concludes) a relationship between the individual and the consumer goods through which the consumer appropriates for him/herself (or divests him/herself of) the cultural principle expressed by the object. The cultural meaning is thus moved out of the goods and into the lives of its consumers. The concern with which people display, clean, and compare their possessions are attempts by the consumer to claim possession of the goods and thereby to draw from them the transferred qualities.

Application to First Communion

If these theories are brought alongside the fieldwork data, they bring into focus two contested areas that are generally expressed negatively: consumer goods as distracting from the ritual, and inappropriate dress. First, by attempting (with differing degrees of success) to locate the use of consumer goods within a ritual process, all three theories invite a broadening conceptualization of the ritual framework for first communion beyond the church service alone. This wider vision casts a different light on the criticism that consumer goods are a distraction at first communion. Instead, and particularly when we consider the theories of Douglas and Isherwood, it suggests that every element in the event both inside and outside the church offers the participants a ritual stage on which they can make sense of their world. The church ceremony thus takes its place within a ritual complex that also involves family feasting, gift-giving and the ritual visiting of relatives as described by the 'A Team'. Consumer goods function across this ritual continuum, serving as testing and tested markers of cultural categories. The dividend for a successful ritual would be confirmation not only of the correctness of one's world-view within the community, but also of one's standing in that community.

Second, a key aspect of that testing process is the manner in which grooming is used to dramatize key players. Here Rook and Levy's consideration of the effects of grooming comes into play. Time and money, they argue, are invested in dramatizing the body and achieving the 'perfect look' in order to elicit a particular response from others – echoing, in terms of personal appearance, Douglas and Isherwood's concept of the ritual use of goods. However, with regard to first communion this approach to grooming assumes a subtly different force, as the child is groomed by another, usually its mother. This invites the question whether in lavishing such care upon her child, the mother might be expressing something of herself and of her desire for a response from others. A positive response would be given by Annette Kuhn (1995), who explores photographs of her own childhood to interrogate her relationship with her mother. Starting from the unease with which she recalled her mother's attempts to dress her up, Kuhn went on to discuss the care mothers lavish upon dressing up their little girls. She speaks of the particular investment of desire, fantasy and identification made by the mother:

> The mother's identification (in which she cares for her little daughter as she would be cared for herself, and produces the baby in herself as a beautiful little girl worthy and deserving of love) rests upon a degree of projection, the baby is its object, its screen. In the processes of projection and identification, the baby is fantasized as part of the mother – who can simultaneously have, and be, the baby girl. In both senses, the baby becomes her mother's possession, and the play with femininity involved in dressing her up part of the mother's own involvement with femininity and its paradoxes, its ambiguities and its masquerades. [p. 52]

Kuhn's work offers a viewpoint external to the fieldwork that offers a similar focus. The story related by the priest in the second parish, of the mother using her daughter's first communion to substitute for the wedding that she herself never had, and Linda's resonating account, have already been noted. The implication in both cases is that the carefully contrived bridal appearance is not a deliberate and defiant flaunting of the mother's unmarried status in the face of the (perceived-to-be) disapproving Catholic community, but is something rather more positive.

However, the fieldwork also established that at first communion the mother's own appearance received careful attention – and negative comments from parishioners and clergy. At this point, McCracken's thesis of the transference of cultural values can be brought alongside Rook and Levy's observations on grooming. The greatest criticism of the dresses and accessories chosen by mothers at first communion was levelled at those that accorded with contemporary fashionable summerwear of bare arms, low necklines and high hems. McCracken's thesis suggests that whilst some church-goers were scandalized by the outfits, they had been chosen with a mind to the cultural values relating to advertising and fashion that the mothers were seeking to appropriate for themselves.

Self-Image and Consumption

The final point above introduces a significant concept within the symbolic consumer behaviour material: that consumer goods are used to communicate to others an image of self. Grubb and Grathwohl (1967) argue that the self-concept of the individual will be sustained and buoyed 'if he believes the goods he has purchased are recognised publicly and classified in a manner that supports and enhances his self-concept' (p. 25). In other words, purchases are used to 'transfer' certain socially attributed meanings of symbols to the individuals who purchase them. Schenk and Holman (1980) refined this model further, developing a theoretical framework within which the effects of social stimuli upon the consumption behaviour of individuals could be incorporated. In place of the simple and monolithic construct of 'self-image', they proposed the 'situational self-image' – 'the meaning of self that the individual wishes others to have of him/herself' (p. 611). This would include the attitudes, perceptions and feelings that the individual wishes other individuals in a particular situation to formulate about his/her character and appropriate behaviour. This expresses itself in 'Social Role Performance' – the actual behaviour of an individual within a particular setting. The authors argued that 'the individual will attempt to match his/her performance to the social expectations if this permits the individual to reach some goal within the position occupied' (ibid.).

At first communion, the family has the possibility of carrying out a highly visible and very public performance. Linda dwelt on the use made by the family of the event to demonstrate to their community that they were a 'strong family', and Kuhn (1995) argues that the way a mother turns out her daughter can be a way of proclaiming to the world that she is a 'good' mother. The use of display through visible consumption of goods across the first communion ritual continuum outlined above can thus be understood in terms of the 'situational self-image' of the participants and of their desire to receive particular positive reactions from other participants. Frequently, the families are met by a church-going community that does not offer such a favourable response to their self-image; however, in many settings the priest, catechists and school are not the intended audience. Rather, it is other parents, neighbours and family members. Concerns expressed by Mass-goers over the dress of the adult female participants or the amount spent on the child's outfit thus miss the point entirely. Ecclesial criticism may prove a significant irritant, but there are more significant critics to be met.

The consequences of failing to satisfy the demands of those critics through a misjudgement of the expected performance can be illustrated through a further reference to Rook and Levy and to an incident narrated by one of Sr Margaret's catechists. Rook and Levy consider the manner in which grooming is used to classify and evaluate others:

> Grooming is, first of all, sanctioned behavior … There is a widespread recognition of prescribed norms for personal appearance, and of (sometimes severe) sanctions that ensue when the rules are violated. Grooming is seen as directing outcomes in both the vocational and romantic arenas, and it is used to assign individuals niches in the social hierarchy. [pp. 331–3])

Sanction, generally taking the form of ridicule, can follow violation of the rules. Thus, the catechist spoke of an adopted girl who had been brought up as an only child particularly doted upon by her parents:

> We all wondered how she would appear at her first communion. She wore a plain white dress, but over it she had a shawl with a long frill, and it was tied at the front with a brooch. On her head she had a straw hat – and of course it kept slipping off one way and then the other. And everyone was looking at her, and you could hear them saying, 'Eliza Doolittle'.

The child's parents had wanted her to stand out in the crowd, and the shawl was described as very expensive, but the violation of the community's expectations of what constituted the appropriate display was too severe. A note of disdain remained in the catechist's voice as she related the story.

Gift-giving and Identity

Thus far, attention has focused on the use of consumer goods in personal dress and display. However, consumer items also enter into the event as gifts. During the fieldwork period, the children received items such as mobile telephones, clothes and computer games, in addition to considerable amounts of money; the first communion outfit might itself be a gift – frequently made by a child's grandparents. Just as the consumer behaviour literature explored dress in terms of identity construct and projection, so its exponents also considered the role of gift-giving in the same processes. For example, Schwartz (1967) examined the manner in which gifts could function as 'generators' of identity, both of the giver and the recipient. The gift reveals the idea that the giver holds of the recipient. In doing so, the same gift also serves to indicate the donor's self-identity, as any publication of ideas of the other is simultaneously an act of self-definition: 'giving imposes an identity on the giver as well as the recipient' (p. 2). Thus, in displaying the gift received, the recipient broadcasts the status claimed by the donor. Writing in the late 1960s, Schwartz identified a societal shift as women moved into the economic rather than simply the social sphere, with the consequence that then it was children who increasingly assumed the role of family status representatives.

This role was accentuated in the fieldwork communities, where the predominantly middle-class nuclear family presumed by Schwarz was to a significant extent absent. Within a shifting pattern of adult relational formation, the children had become the primary message-bearers of relational continuity within the family group, rather than the husband/wife partnership. They were the platforms on which the enduring values and aspirations that bound the extended family together could be displayed. The involvement of family members in the event – not least through gift-giving – reinforced the mutual identities of members of the family group.

Schwartz also considers the use of certain gifts as ceremonial tokens of status:

> Status gifts are objectifications of past or present social relationships. The ceremonial display of such objectifications (Christmas cards, for example) is a powerful tendency in

social life: persons invariably seek to make known their social bonds in daily encounters. [p. 7]

One of the greatest gifts is the clothing worn by the child. The fieldwork identified a trend for grandparents to pay for the girl's dress – but even if it is bought by the mother it still represents a lavishing of precious resources on the child in a display that publicly underlines the child's social connectedness and therefore also makes a statement concerning those with which it is related. Hence the impossibility of families considering borrowing, or buying second-hand, the first communion dress of somebody else's daughter.

A Symbolic-Interactionist Understanding of Consumption

A cluster of related themes is beginning to emerge, focused on the question of identity expressed through the symbolic use of products within social interaction. By the 1980s, these themes were being discussed by consumer researchers in terms of 'symbolic interactionism'. The concept was a little older, and is generally traced back to Herbert Blumer (1901–87). According to Blumer, the symbolic interactionist approach rested on three premises. The first was that human beings 'act towards things on the basis of the meanings that the things have for them', be those things physical objects, other people, institutions or the activities of others (Blumer, 1969, p. 2). Second, people come to ascribe meaning to things as they interact with other people in a social setting. Blumer explains:

> The meaning of a thing for a person grows out of the ways in which other persons act toward the person with regard to the thing ... Thus, symbolic interactionism sees meanings as social products, as creations that are formed in and through the defining activities of people as they interact. [p. 4]

However, no meaning is fixed for ever – hence Blumer's third premise. As people interact with each other they constantly revisit the meanings that they give to things. As a result, the meanings we give to the things we encounter and use is subjected to a constant reinterpretation.

A sustained exploration of the implications of Symbolic Interactionism for consumer research is offered by Solomon (1983). He draws that discourse into the consumer studies field by criticizing a tendency he perceives amongst marketing theorists to focus upon the processes that affect purchase behaviour rather than those by which a consumer actually uses what he or she has bought. In other words, product acquisition is regarded only as the satisfaction of some need. Solomon argues that the reality is more complex: 'Under some conditions the learned cues inherent in product symbolism drive behaviour, either by facilitating or by inhibiting role performance' (p. 322f). This reverses the usual understanding of the product as need-response. A consumer item does not only say something to others about the person who bought it (or for whom it was bought). It can also directly impact upon the behaviour of those who use it as they match their behaviour to the meanings that society invests in the item.

Can both of these dimensions be recognized within the first communion event? I have already commented on the extent to which the need to portray an image of 'the close family' or 'the good mother' can be satisfied by the lavish care spent on dressing the child – especially the daughter. Solomon invites consideration of a further question: what is the effect of the use within the celebration of goods that have already been endowed with symbolic content within the cultural context? Specifically, how does the use of bridal dress (for the girls by imitation, for the boys increasingly literally) act as a stimulus for behaviour at first communion? How does it affect the attitudes and interaction of the participants? For example, does a mother dress her little girl in a bridal gown because she knows that within her cultural and economic setting it is extremely unlikely that the daughter will ever walk down the aisle as a bride? Or is the bridal outfit so much a given at first communion in certain communities that its use is not interrogated along the product selection-process, but rather the events of purchasing and using the outfit at first communion stimulate a process of identity reinterpretation and related responses?

Thus far, focus has been on the situational self-image projected by the first communicants and their families for the benefit of their peers. However, it is also possible that individuals are projecting a self-image for the Church. Unfamiliar with the setting of parish worship, many feel themselves disadvantaged there. This is especially the case if, as may well happen, a pattern of conflict has been established between parish community and parents in the months leading up to the first communion. So there is sometimes an attempt to 'put on' a strong religious show. This can be helped by a school drilling process, as the children are taught to join their hands in prayer far more than one would normally encounter in a Sunday Mass congregation, or to enter their bench with a slow genuflection, accompanied by the Sign of the Cross, that contrasts strikingly with the quick up-and-down bob seen in most Sunday Catholics. It may also be seen in the custom encountered in my subject parishes of the children (including the boys) displaying a rosary worn round the neck on first communion day. It is a Catholic symbol – but the use made of it is 'wrong', though increasingly fashionable. Undoubtedly there will be an element here of gift-display, but is this an example of what Solomon identifies as a way in which a lack of experience in satisfying role expectations leads to a heightened reliance on relevant material symbols? Is behaviour (here, bodily ornament) being driven by product symbolization?

However, perhaps more useful than these particular illustrations is the underlying thrust of the Symbolic Interactionist viewpoint. Writing out of a background in psychology, Rochberg-Halton (1984) draws out the relational concept of self that he recognizes from a Symbolic Interactionist perspective. For him, the self consists of a 'communicative dialogue of signs rooted in an environmental context and requiring cultivation for its emergence and continued growth' (p. 360). The meaning of self is to be found 'in its contributions to the community of discourse, both externalised and internalised' (p. 345). As a consequence, and in opposition to a Freudian perception of self, Rochberg-Halton understands the foundation of self as being a social self-dialogue rather than 'an asocial reactor core of libido' (p. 345).

In this perspective, the various interactions that take place at first communion among the various players are not limited to the interplay of previously established positions. As they interact, all the parties are engaging in the process of self-understanding and definition. The history of the rite is a story of constant change and reinterpretation as the Catholic community faces differing social, economic and religious challenges: this is no unchanging tradition. The priests and active parishioners are re-evaluating and redefining their Catholic self-understanding in the light of the current crisis over declining membership, ageing population and reduced numbers of priests. The encounters with the first communicants and their families frequently catalyse this process. Finally, the interactions between parents and with the parish community shape the self-understanding of the first communicants and their families. The conflict frequently sparked by these interactions further serves to define both sets of self-identity as positions become entrenched.

Conclusions

Drawing together the various perspectives outlined in this chapter, it becomes evident that consumption at first communion is neither a 'needless' extravagance nor an element peripheral to the event. It is, rather, a semiotic device through which the participants' identity, values and aspirations are both reinforced and proclaimed to their peers. Dressed in their elaborate costume and laden with gifts from their family, the children become the bearers of messages through which each family conveys its self-understanding to its neighbours and stakes a claim to its desired position within the local community. By attempting to minimize the potential for external display within the ritual, parish authorities jeopardize this social function. The consequent familial resistance to attempts to restrict the field of meaning to the purely religious is, therefore, understandable. For the first communicants and their families, identity as Catholics is only one constituent element within a broader social construct of identity, in which the use of consumer goods articulates the four non-ecclesial discourses outlined in Chapter 7. It is that construct that they bring to the event, rather than the more narrowly defined ecclesial conception of Catholicism with its expectations of ritual practice and family formation. Current discomfort and conflict around the use of consumer goods at first communion draws into the sharpest possible focus the failure across the twentieth century of the reform project of Pius X. It is not simply that the ritual has failed to realize the expectation of generations of Catholics who practise their religion and conduct their lives in accordance with Church teaching. What the ritual event reveals is the failure of the Church to control the systems of meaning out of which its members construct their identity and determine their actions.

Conclusion

Across its history, and in very different circumstances, the ritual of first communion has acted as the focus for the structural aspirations of the Catholic Church – particularly at its most local level, the parish. The perception that the future of the Catholic community is in some way bound up with this event has been a constant theme between the late seventeenth and early twenty-first centuries. As the age at which the ritual has been celebrated has changed dramatically, the formal ritual processes have also been, and continue to be, adapted, and the theological meaning given to the event has undergone significant development. The community has staked its future on the successful performance of the first communion ritual at every turn in that ritual's history. At the same time first communion offers the clearest possible indicator of the success or failure of the strategies that are meant to deliver those aspirations. This is so particularly because it has served as the stage upon which the radically different discourses of meaning prevalent within the Catholic community are spotlighted.

Because so much has been gambled on the ritual, a great deal may be lost in it. If, as many church-going Catholics today fear, the investment in the ritual of so much hope for the future has been a failure, then the structural consequences may be devastating. Contrary to the hopes and expectations of the supporters of the 1910 reforms of first communion, today's ritual has become a lens to view not the renaissance of the traditional Catholic parish but its structural decline.

In fact, first communion probably never could have delivered the results that have been sought from it. Today it may be the glaring inconsistencies between ecclesial discourse and pastoral practice that subvert the attempts to implant the Church's current expectations for the ritual in the minds and hearts of its members; but the ritual has been unstable since its inception. The current situation mirrors earlier difficulties, and the laments of today's church-goers only echo those of previous generations. There is, indeed, a dynamic operating in this ritual – but it is not necessarily the life-course determination that underpins so much of the ecclesial discourse. Rather, it is a very human dynamic: the interplay between ritual performance, meaning and institutional power. First communion exemplifies the complexity of the relationship between a ritual and its performers, and startlingly illustrates the cost of ritual failure for the Church – as well as the prizes of success for other parties. Let us now examine that dynamic. We shall thus bring into focus the very real problems inherent in this ritual, and hence arrive at a clear understanding of its current condition.

The dynamic at play in first communion has three interrelated dimensions. In the interplay of meaning and ritual, first communion graphically illustrates how the same ritual can be invested with different meanings – not only across history, but even among participants in a given place and time. The second dimension flows from the first: contested meaning can lead (perhaps inevitably) to conflict within ritual, with the consequent establishment of both positions of power and strategies of subversion. Finally, structural consequences flow from ritual performance.

Ritual and Meaning

As we have already seen, ever since its conception the first communion ritual has attracted to itself an extraordinarily broad range of discourses of meaning. These have included constructs of ecclesial identity, hopes and fears concerning the life-course trajectory of young people, articulations of the network of social and familial relationships, and formal statements drawn from sacramental theology and Canon Law. Brought alongside each other within the celebration of the ritual, these discourses have at times coexisted reasonably comfortably. At other times the claims encapsulated by these discourses have entered into fierce competition, and their ritual enactment has generated considerable controversy. It is that second state that now prevails in Catholic communities across much of the English-speaking world. As we conclude, we must ask what it is about these discourses that renders so difficult their peaceful co-existence within the framework of the ritual.

The answer lies in the fact that so many of these discourses express aspirations for the future. The parties who generate and invest in these meaningful discourses fall roughly into two camps. The first comprises parish clergy, catechists and church-attending parishioners. The second is made up of the families of the first communicants, who for the main part are not themselves regular church-goers. For the first group, the aspirations contained in the first communion event are bound up with the parish's hopes and fears for its future existence. The ritual of first communion must establish a pattern of weekly reception of communion that will ensure that the Sunday congregation is constantly rejuvenated, and be the clearest possible sign of the adherence of successive generations of Catholics to the formal teaching of the Church. For the second group, which comprises the majority of participants in this ritual, the aspirations that find their ritual expression in first communion do not primarily (or perhaps at all) relate to the future of the liturgical assembly. Rather, they focus upon the family, its identity and its status within the local community. On the one hand, the fact that the ritual has been performed for successive generations makes it an ideal vehicle for expressions of family identity and continuity. On the other, the ritual's highly public nature provides the family with an opportunity to project its self-image and to externalize its broader social aspirations.

There is nothing new in the use of this ritual to express strongly divergent aspirations. The eighteenth-century attempts at St Sulpice to enforce order on the ritual, and the occasional diatribes against lavish display found in the nineteenth-century catechetical texts, bear witness to the potential that the ritual has always had for exciting conflict. However, through much of the twentieth century, the aspirations of the two discursive blocks of parish authorities and of families do appear to have co-existed more or less happily within the ritual. This may have been a reflection of the broader socio-economic circumstances within which the Catholic community existed; in the Liverpool of 1910 – as in so many parts of the Irish diaspora – the religious aspirations of the Catholic community were bound up with the social and economic structures of a tight-knit ethnic minority. Consequently, one and the same ritual could comfortably serve to express the aspirations of all parties. Yet even in that situation of symbiosis, there was none the less a fundamental power imbalance between the various parties, which might well erupt into conflict once the external circumstances were altered. This leads to consideration of the second element.

Ritual and Power

The people associated with the two discursive blocks do not stand on an equal footing as they approach the ritual. The parish authorities possess the capacity to exercise a gate-keeping role, holding the power to grant or deny access to the rite. The profile of this gate-keeping role has not been uniform across the twentieth century – there is, for example, no significant evidence of its exercise in England at the time of the *Quam Singulari* reform. However, the closing decades of the twentieth century have witnessed a decline in the social distinctiveness and institutional self-confidence of the Catholic community. The earlier comfortable co-existence of familial and ecclesial aspirations became strained as Catholics moved out beyond the clear community boundaries that had been maintained at the start of the twentieth century by a combination of ecclesial command and social restrictions. This new orientation of its members in turn exposed the Catholic community to those broader social trends that are generally discussed in terms of secularization.

Whilst today's first communicants and their families retain the construct 'Catholic' as constituent to their identity, the majority of them make little or no personal investment in the future of the Church as liturgical community. It is very difficult, therefore, for those Catholics who continue to regularly attend church and who contribute on a weekly basis to parish finances to avoid the sense that the ritual is being celebrated with and for people who are contributing to the decline of the parish institution that they hold so dear. In this setting, it is not surprising to find that a more severe pattern of gate-keeping has emerged. If the families do not attend church, or if the modes through which the non-ecclesial discourses are expressed run counter to the declared values of the Catholic community – for example, in extravagant consumerism or in the use of 'inappropriate' fashion – then increasingly a negative response is elicited from the gate-keeping authorities. Parents of first communicants may consequently discover that arranging for their child's first communion involves a delicate process of negotiation with ecclesial gate-keepers whose understanding of the event and its desired outcomes differ substantially from their own.

This might at first sight suggest that the balance of power within the ritual remains straightforwardly in the hands of the parish authorities. The situation is, however, considerably more complex than that. The advantage given to parish authorities by their ability to exert power as gate-keepers is counterpoised by an imbalance in the enactment of the ritual itself weighted in the favour of the families rather than the parish. Put most simply, despite the attempts of parish authorities to enforce a celebration of the ritual in terms of their own discourses, families frequently succeed in experiencing the event on their own terms. This success is due to two key factors. First, once access to the ritual has been obtained, families may ensure that the elements of display that express their own discourses find their way into the liturgy – subverting the pleas of parish authorities for 'restraint'. The second factor relates to a fundamental difference in the desired outcome that the two parties seek from the event. The Church reads the event in terms of the formal, one-hour liturgy of the Mass of first communion itself, and its projection onto future Mass attendance. For the overwhelming majority of participants, however, the liturgical celebration is only one (albeit crucial) moment in a broader complex of activities that stretch out beyond it, extending over an entire day at the very least. The parish's stake in the event as these participants approach it is limited to the Church service; priest, catechists, regular Mass-goers can only stand by, powerless, as the familial celebration in its full sense then unfolds. It is this broad construct of the event that permits a 'successful' celebration even for the families of those children who, for example, are required to make their first communion wearing their school uniform. The celebration of the ritual really can fulfil the aspirations of participants and their families. It does – in their terms – produce the desired outcome. For the families, the total experience is that the ritual has 'worked' – often in the face of attempts by the parish community to remove from it the authentic content that the familial discourses bring.

To a large extent this contrary imbalance in favour of the non-ecclesial discourses redresses the balance of power. Whilst the aspirational discourses of the children and their families can be authentically expressed through the ritual as understood in their broader sense, those of the parish authorities are very unlikely to be realizable in experience. Indeed, the annual enactment of the ritual itself can all too painfully reveal them to be delusional in nature. Despite the best (or worst!) attempts by parish authorities to maintain their control over the event and its meaning, the odds are stacked in favour of the event 'working' for the families.

The Structural Consequences of Ritual Failure

The bleak picture here painted of the first communion celebrations and their impact on the parish and community is surely not universal. There must be parishes where the priest at least is happy with the outcome. Those, I suggest, are likely to be largely parishes where minimal gate-keeping has been exercised, but where the celebration is held outside the normal parish eucharist, with few or no members of the regular worshipping community present. There are perhaps also parishes where priest and regular congregations alike are happy. Those, I suggest, are likely to be where the sacrifice of numbers has been made, and strict gate-keeping has restricted the first communicants to the children of regular church-goers only. In the first case, all the children are being 'initiated' into the worshipping parish community – who are not present. In the latter, the community is there, but it is only a small and heavily selected number of children who pass through the ritual. In two different ways the celebration falls short of its own logic. In the former, the link with the worshipping community is broken. The latter raises the question as to why the Church is willing to begin the process of initiation with baptism, but then is content to block the process part-way through for most children.

Except for such parishes as considered above, what many parishes experience at first communion is ritual failure. On first communion day, many priests and congregations stand by and watch as a successful outcome is achieved in terms of exactly those discourses that they have sought to suppress. Moreover, the Church's desired outcome – namely, regular Mass attendance by the first communicants – is rarely achieved. This state of affairs is given a cruel further twist by a combination of the formal ecclesial discourse and contemporary social realities. By interpreting this event in terms of initiation, the post-Vatican II Church continues to set the ritual against a backcloth of its own continuation. Yet, the reality is that in the majority of cases those who are further 'initiated' through this event are no more likely to participate in the regular structural life of the Church after their 'initiation' than they were before it. Paradoxically, the initiation discourse has cast a cruel light through the lens which for Whiteside showed so optimistic a vision for the future of the Church. Rather than crowning the renewal of local parish structures and life within them, the first communion of infants has exposed the weaknesses in the whole system.

This is a painful experience – and a human response is to seek scapegoats. The general response within parishes has been to lay the responsibility for this failure at the door of the families and their inadequate allegiance to their Catholicism – as evidenced both in liturgical practice and in personal lifestyle. Not surprisingly, therefore, there are those within the Church who call for access to the event to be restricted to the children of those who demonstrate regular church attendance and contribution to the life of the parish. The aspirations contained in the 'initiation' discourse would, after all, be most likely to be fulfilled in the case of such children.

However this position loses sight of the historic breadth of the Catholic community. A drastic reduction in the numbers of first communicants would weaken the cultural framework of Catholicism, further reducing it to a liturgical congregation and effectively disenfranchising the majority of its members. In doing so, it would risk finally severing the bonds that link to the worshipping community those whose Catholic identity does not include regular participation in Sunday worship. This would be, above all, the negation of the generational link that is a core element within the familial discourses around First Communion. The Catholic community cannot afford to take that step; its survival depends on the breadth of its membership.

Furthermore, the aspirational crisis is to some extent of the Church's own making. Across history, the very discourses that Catholic theologians and catechists have used to explain the event have proved consistently flawed, and close examination of them raises the question as to whether this ritual could ever 'work', at least in the terms understood by the Church. This book has explored ecclesio-catechetical discourses through three broad historic phases. These articulate successive attempts to map a theological understanding onto the ritual. First, post-Tridentine Catholic catechesis understood the event partly in terms of its potential for determining the future life-course, and, indeed, eternal destiny, of participants. Then, in the early twentieth-century reforms of Pius X, we saw the harnessing of this potential to lock the Catholic population at an early age into a pattern of religious observance that would endure through life. Finally, the post-Vatican II formal discourse of the event as an initiation ritual repackaged these expectations, so that now the event is formally understood as constitutive of the entire Christian life. As such, it continues to carry expectations for the individual's future relationship with the Church, with a particular mode of eucharistic practice presumed as normative.

Each of these aspirational approaches is seriously flawed. The earlier life-course determination model is far too mechanistic an approach to be adequately mapped onto human experience. It leaves no room for personal growth and development – nor, in theological terms, does it allow for the action of grace at a later stage in an individual's life. Passing to the second approach, the twentieth century has witnessed that not even reducing the point of reception to a very young age can realize the potential for individual life direction and institutional consolidation that generations had seen – or hoped to see – in the ritual. Similarly, the ritual authenticity of the post-Vatican II yoking of the event to a theology of initiation is highly dubious: the experience of participants moves too easily out of phase with the formal discourse for that discourse to claim to be normative in practice. This is largely due to two factors. The first, as we saw in Chapter 5, is the sharp divergence between the Church's theory and its practice. Admission to the eucharist is stated to be the culmination of the three-fold initiatory process, but in most cases it is sandwiched between baptism and confirmation. The second factor is the difficulty in sustaining an initiation process across the first twelve to sixteen years of a child's life. If the process concludes not with first communion but, as in most cases, a pubescent confirmation, then in practice the period during which initiation is incomplete spans the most intense period of engagement of the child within the community. The completion of initiation thus paradoxically brings that engagement to an end rather than a beginning.

The failure of these discourses raises the question whether the ritual can ever sustain the aspirations that the Church has invested in it. Quite simply, in ecclesial terms, is the Church expecting too much of the ritual and those who participate in it? Can its enactment ever realize the intentions of the Church?

The answer is probably not. The celebration taps far too easily into underlying tensions within the Catholic community that extend far beyond the purely ritual sphere. Despite appearances, the event does not primarily create problems – rather, it catalyses them. Ultimately, the problem lies not with the ritual itself, but the very different accounts of 'being a Catholic' that now compete for space within the first communion event. These different accounts – and the anxieties that they generate – are not associated with the first communion ritual only. They permeate the life of the local Catholic community. They are played out in concerns over the baptism of non-practising parishioners, over school admissions, and over parish closures and amalgamations. The competing discourses have the potential to spark off conflict every day, as non-practising Catholics present themselves for marriage, or request baptism or admission to the parish school for their children, or seek to adapt the form of the funeral ceremony to more closely reflect the preoccupations of a loved one – which may have had little to do with the preoccupations of the Church!

However, all of these are relatively private events, and if conflict erupts around any of them it generally remains hidden. It is the public and collective nature of first communion, allied to the symbolic weight it possesses in the Catholic community, which renders it different. The power that first communion holds to draw all the underlying issues into focus lies in the fact that its annual enactment invites the broad range of negotiated positions within the Catholic community into a single and highly visible ritual. By placing the non-practising majority at the centre of the ritual stage, the event makes evident to practising Catholics that they are, in fact, the minority within their parishes. The majority bring their own constructed relationship with the parish to the central weekly act of Catholic worship. They stake their own claim in the event. They subvert and overwhelm the formal ecclesial discourses. They fill the event with their own systems of meaning.

In doing so, they highlight the failures that run through the parish structures set so confidently in place with the reforms of Pius X. It appears that on the ground a majority of Catholics fail to find in their Church's official teachings a meaningful account of life. The social distinctiveness of the Catholic community across Western society has progressively dissolved. This dissolution has considerably enlarged the breadth of meaning that today's Catholics bring to their encounters with the leaders of the parish community and with its liturgical events. Catholics now have access to a wider range of 'scripts' than previous generations from which they can construct meaningful discourses of themselves and their families. The Church's discourses concerning regular Mass attendance, family formation and doctrinal submission, which were so central to the construct of the parish that emerged from the early twentieth-century reforms, no longer receive the assent of the general Catholic population. The effect has not only been to place the discourses themselves into question; as dissent from the formal teaching has been translated into action with regard to life-choices, ritual participation and relationship with the institution, then the very structure of the parish itself has become jeopardized. The first communion ritual, therefore, that for Whiteside and his contemporaries had projected confidence in the future of the Catholic community, has become for future generations the clearest possible expression of its decline.

This suggests that there can be no response to the first communion 'problem' without a fundamental reassessment by the Catholic Church of the nature of the local congregation and of the role of ritual within it. Just as the 1910 revision of first communion was welded into the framework of an overall theologico-structural revision, so, too, attempts today to resolve issues with regard to this ritual without addressing the broader structural issues will fail. First communion will remain problematic until the Church's aspirations regarding its outcome are seriously re-examined, in the light of changing social patterns, the multiplication of diverse constructs of Catholic identity, and the renegotiation on the part of so many Catholics of their personal adherence to formal ecclesial discourses. Such an examination would be challenging in terms of the way in which the parish is imagined, and the role of liturgy within it. It would also be intensely painful. The choice would be between a drastic shrinkage in the construct of the local Catholic community, or a willingness to embrace a much wider understanding of the boundaries between that community and the secular world, and of their permeability. In the current climate, such an examination would be difficult, and violently contested. However, unless some such radical self-scrutiny is undertaken, then first communion will almost certainly continue to be an occasion of angst. It will remain an annual reminder of the extent to which the parish system and the account of Catholic life it contained is crumbling, without offering any glimpse of hopeful future possibilities.

APPENDIX

Index of Newspaper Accounts of the Celebrations of First Communion in 1910–11

These are listed in alphabetical order of parish within town or city. All references to the *Catholic Times* are to the New Series; the term is therefore omitted for brevity. All discussion of this material is in Chapter 3.

Birkenhead

Our Lady: *Catholic Times*, Liverpool Edition, no. 2,279, 14 April 1911, p. 5.

St Werburgh: *Catholic Times*, Liverpool Edition, no. 2,279, 14 April 1911, p. 5.

Birmingham

English Martyrs, Sparkhill: *Tablet,* Supplement to vol. 116, no. 3,686, 31 December 1910, p. 1082.

Bolton

Ss Peter and Paul: *Catholic Times,* Manchester Edition, no 2,280, 21st April 1911, p. 5.

Hindley, Lancs

St Benedict: *Catholic Times*, Liverpool Edition, no. 2,280, 21st April 1911, p. 5.

Liverpool

Holy Cross: *Catholic Times*, Liverpool Edition, no. 2,277, 31st March 1911, p. 5.

St Charles, Aigburth: *Catholic Times*, Liverpool Edition, no. 2,275, 17th March 1911, p. 5.

St Peter, Seel St: *Catholic Times,* Liverpool Edition, no. 2,274, 10th March 1911, p. 5.

London

Bow Common: *Catholic Times*, London Edition, no. 2,274, 10th March 1911, p. 5.

Custom House East:	*Catholic Times,* London Edition, no. 2,277, 31 March 1911, p. 5.
Forest Gate:	*Catholic Times*, London Edition, no. 2,274, 10 March 1911, p. 5
German Church:	*Catholic Times*, London Edition, no. 2,281, 24 April 1911, p. 5.
Our Lady and Holy Souls, Kensall:	*Catholic Times*, London Edition, no. 2,278, 7 April 1911, p. 5.
Franciscan Church, Peckham:	*Catholic Times*, London Edition, no. 2,277, 31 March 1911, p. 5.
Ss. Peter and Paul, Clerkenwell:	*Catholic Times*, London Edition, no. 2,278, 7 April 1911, p. 5.
St. George's Cathedral, Southwark:	*Tablet,* Supplement to vol. 117, no. 3,698, 11 March 1911, p. 395.
St. Mary, East Finchley:	*Catholic Times*, London Edition, no. 2,280, 21 April 1911, p. 5.
Servite Church, Fulham Road:	*Catholic Times*, London Edition, no. 2,277, 31 March 1911, p. 5.
West Battersea:	*Catholic Times*, London Edition, no. 2,277, 31 March 1911, p. 5.
Westminster Cathedral:	*Tablet,* Supplement to vol. 117, no. 3,698, 11 March 1911, p. 392.

Manchester

Corpus Christi:	*Catholic Times*, Manchester Edition, no. 2,274, 10 March 1911, p. 5.
Holy Name:	*Catholic Times*, Manchester Edition, no. 2,278, 7 April 1911, p. 5.
Loreto:	*Catholic Times*, Manchester Edition, no. 2,275, 17 March 1911, p. 5.
St Alban:	*Catholic Times,* Manchester Edition, no. 2,276, 24 March 1911, p. 5.
St Casimir:	*Catholic Times*, Manchester Edition, no. 2,274, 10 March 1911, p. 5.
St Joseph, Patricroft:	*Catholic Times*, Manchester Edition, no. 2,276, 24 March 1911, p. 5.

Norwich

St John the Evangelist:	*Tablet*, Supplement to vol. 117, no. 3,697, 18 March 1911, p. 435.

Storrington, Sussex

Premonstratensian Priory:	*Tablet*, Supplement to vol. 116, no 3,685, 24 December 1910, p. 1042.

Bibliography

Section A: Published Works

An Abstract of the Douay Catechism Published with Allowance 1697: Douay, publisher unknown.

Acta Apostolicae Sedis 1909– . Rome: Vatican Polyglot Press.

Acta et Documenta Concilio Oecumenici Vaticano II Apparando. Series Prima (Antepraeparatoria). 1960–61. Rome: Vatican Polyglot Press.

Acta Sancta Sedis 1865–1908. Rome: Sacred Congregation of *Propaganda Fidei* Polyglot Press.

Acta Synodalia Sacrosancti Concilii Oecumenici Vaticani II. 1970– . Rome: Vatican Polyglot Press.

Agar, Michael 1980: *The Professional Stranger*. New York: Academic Press.

Albion, Gordon 1950: The Restoration of the Hierarchy 1850. In Beck, pp. 86–115.

Allison, A.F. and D.M. Rogers 1994: *The Contemporary Printed Literature of the English Counter Reformation between 1558 and 1640*. Aldershot: Scholar Press.

Andrieu, Michel 1948: *Les Ordines Romani du Haut Moyen Age*. Louvain: Spicilegium Sacrum Lovaniense.

Aquila, Samuel 2002: *Send Forth Your Spirit: Pastoral Letter to the People of Eastern North Dakota on the Sacrament of Confirmation*. Diocese of Fargo. On-line version at: <http://www.fargodiocese.org/EducationFormation/Evangelization/Confirmation/confirmation.pdf>

Archdiocese of Liverpool 1915: *Syllabuses of Religious Instruction*. Liverpool: Rockliff Brothers.

Archdiocese of Liverpool 1943a: *Handbook to be Used in Conjunction with the Syllabuses of Instruction for Schools*. Liverpool: Rockliff Brothers.

Archdiocese of Liverpool 1943b: *Syllabuses of Religious Instruction for Schools*. Liverpool: Rockliff Brothers.

Archdiocese of Liverpool 2000: *Towards Pastoral Regeneration in Liverpool City Centre: A Report to the Archbishop's Council and the Council's Response*. Published privately by the Archdiocese of Liverpool.

Archer, Anthony 1986: *The Two Catholic Churches: A Study in Oppression*. London: SCM.

Arweck, Elizabeth and Martin Stringer (eds): 2002: *Theorising Faith: The Insider/Outsider Problem in the Study of Ritual. Birmingham:* University of Birmingham Press.

Aubert, Roger 1981: 'Pius X, a Conservative Reform Pope; The Reform Work of Pius X; The Modernist Crisis', in Hubert Jedin and John Dolan (eds), *The History of the Church Vol IX: The Church in the Industrial Age*. London: Burns and Oates, pp. 381–480.

Bales, Susan Ridgely 2005: *When I was a Child: Children's Interpretations of First Communion.* Chapel Hill, NC: The University of North Carolina Press.

Banks, Sharon K 1978: 'Gift-Giving: A Review and an Interactive Paradigm', *Advances in Consumer Research*, 6, pp. 319–24.

Barmann, Lawrence F. 1972: *Baron Friedrich von Hügel and the Modernist Crisis in England.* Cambridge: Cambridge University Press.

Bazin, René 1928: *Pius X.* London: Sands and Co.

Beauduin, Lambert 1946: 'Baptême et Eucharistie', *La Maison Dieu*, 6, pp. 56–75.

Beck, George Andrew, ed. 1950: *The English Catholics 1850–1950: Essays to Commemorate the Centenary of the Hierarchy of England and Wales.* London: Burns Oates.

Belchem, John 1992: 'Peculiarities of Liverpool', in John Belchem (ed.), *Popular Politics, Riot and Labour: Essays in Liverpool History 1790–1940.* Liverpool: Liverpool University Press, pp. 1–20.

Belchem, John 1999: 'Class, Creed and Country: the Irish Middle Class in Victorian Liverpool', in Swift and Gilley, pp. 190–211.

Belk, Russell W. 1976: 'It's the Thought That Counts: a Signed Digraph Analysis of Gift-Giving', *Journal of Consumer Research*, 3 (3), pp. 155–62.

Bellenger, Dominic Aidan 1981: 'The English Catholics and the French Exiled Clergy', *Recusant History*, 15 (6), pp. 433–51.

Bellenger, Dominic Aidan 1986: *The French Exiled Clergy in the British Isles after 1789: An Historical Introduction and Working List.* Bath: Downside Abbey.

Bellenger, Dominic Aidan 1999: 'Religious Life for Men', in McClelland and Hodgetts, pp. 142–66.

Benigni, Umbert 1911: 'Propaganda, Sacred Congregation of', in *The Catholic Encyclopedia*, vol. 12. New York: Robert Appleton Company, pp. 456–61.

Bishops' Conference of England and Wales 1996: *Religious Education Directory for Catholic Schools.* London: Catholic Education Service.

Bishops' Conference of England and Wales 2000: *Religious Education in Catholic Schools: a Statement from the Catholic Bishops' Conference of England and Wales.* London: Catholic Media Office.

Blom, Frans, Jos Blom, Frans Korsten and Geoffrey Scott 1996: *English Catholic Books 1701–1800: A Bibliography.* Aldershot: Scholar Press.

Blumer, Herbert 1969: *Symbolic Interactionism: Perspective and Method.* Englewood Cliffs, NJ: Prentice-Hall.

Bohstedt, John 1992: 'More than One Working Class: Protestant–Catholic Riots in Edwardian Liverpool', in John Belchem (ed.), *Popular Politics, Riot and Labour: Essays in Liverpool History 1790–1940.* Liverpool: Liverpool University Press, pp. 173–216.

Boisgelin de Cucé, Jean de Dieu Raimond [Archbishop of Aix] 1799: *Discours Pour la Première Communion à La Chapelle de King Street, Portman-Square.* London: Baylis.

Bolton, Mother, Religious of the Cenacle 1931: *A Little Child's First Communion: Introduction to the Spiritual Way.* London: George G. Harrap and Co. Ltd.

Bossy, John 1975: *The English Catholic Community 1570–1850.* London: Darton, Longman and Todd.

Botte, Bernard 1963: *La Tradition Apostolique de Saint Hippolyte: Essai de Reconstitution*. Münster: Aschendorff.

Bouscaren, T. Lincoln, and Adam C. Ellis 1946: *Canon Law: a Text and Commentary*. Milwaukee, WI: The Bruce Publishing Company.

Boyce, Frank 1999a: 'Catholicism in Liverpool's Docklands: 1950s–1990s', in Michael P Hornsby-Smith (ed.), *Catholics in England 1950–2000: Historical and Sociological Perspectives*. London: Cassell, pp. 46–66.

Boyce, Frank 1999b: 'From Victorian "Little Ireland" to Heritage Trail: Catholicism, Community and Change in Liverpool's Docklands' in Swift and Gilley (eds.), pp. 277–97.

Bradshaw, Paul 2002: *The Search for the Origins of Christian Worship: Sources and Methods for the Study of Early Liturgy*. Second edition. London: SPCK.

Brothers, Joan 1964: *Church and School: A Study of the Impact of Education upon Learning*. Liverpool: Liverpool University Press.

Brown, Callum G. 2001: *The Death of Christian Britain: Understanding Secularisation 1800–2000*. London: Routledge.

Bruce, Steve 1995: *Religion in Modern Britain*. Oxford: Oxford University Press .

Bruce, Steve 2002: *God is Dead: Secularization in the West*. Oxford: Blackwell.

Brusselmans, C. and B. Haggerty 1986: *We Celebrate the Eucharist*. New Jersey: Silver Burdett.

Bryson, Anne 1992: 'Riotous Liverpool, 1815–1860',.in John Belchem (ed.), *Popular Politics, Riot and Labour: Essays in Liverpool History 1790–1940*. Liverpool: Liverpool University Press, pp. 98–134.

Bugnini, Annibale 1990: *The Reform of the Liturgy 1948–1975*. Collegeville, MN: The Liturgical Press.

Bullen, Anthony 1969: *Living and Believing: A Religious Programme for 7 to 11-Year-Old Children*. Second edition. Slough: St Paul Publications.

Burke, Thomas 1910: *Catholic History of Liverpool*. Liverpool: C. Tingling and Co.

Burton, Edwin 1909: *The Life and Times of Bishop Challoner (1691–1781)*. London: Longmans, Green and Co.

Burton, Katherine 1950: *The Great Mantle: The Life of Giuseppe Melchiore Sarto, Pope Pius X*. Dublin: Clonmore and Reynolds.

Byrne, Anne and Chris Malone 1992: *Here I Am: A Religious Education Programme for Primary Schools*. First edition. London: HarperCollins.

Byrne, Anne, Chris Malone and Anne White 2000: *Here I Am: A Religious Education Programme for Primary Schools*. Second edition. London: HarperCollins.

Cabié, Robert (ed.) 1986: *The Church at Prayer: An Introduction to the Liturgy. Vol II: The Eucharist*. London: Geoffrey Chapman.

Cabié, Robert 1987: 'Christian Initiation', in Aimé-Georges Martimort (ed.), *The Church at Prayer: An Introduction to the Liturgy. Volume III: The Sacraments*. London: Geoffrey Chapman, pp. 11–100.

Cafferata, Henry T. 1910: *The Catechism Simply Explained*. Seventh edition London: Art and Book Company.

Cafferata, Henry T. 1911a: *The Catechism Simply Explained for Little Children*. London: St Anselm's Society.

Cafferata, Henry T. 1911b: *The Little Child's First Communion Book*. London: St Anselm's Society.

Carnegy, James 1725: *Instructions and Prayers for Children*. Publisher and place of publication not stated.

Catechism for First Communicants; Or Instructions for the Worthy Making and Preserving the Fruits of First Communion. 1781. Second edition. London: J P Coghlan.

A Catechism for First Communion Translated from the French by a Member of the Order of Charity, and Revised by the Very Rev John Baptist Pagani. 1850. London: Richardson and Son.

The Catechism for the Curats, Compos'd by the Decree of the Council of Trent and Publish'd by Command of Pope Pius the Fifth Faithfully Translated into English. 1687. London: Publisher not stated; printed by Henry Hills.

Catechism of the Catholic Church. 1994. London: Geoffrey Chapman.

Chadwick, Owen 1998: *A History of the Popes 1830–1914*. Oxford: Clarendon Press.

Challoner, Richard 1737: *The Catholick Christian Instructed in the Sacraments, Sacrifice, Ceremonies and Observances of the Church By Way of Question and Answer By RC* .... London: publisher not stated.

Challoner, Richard 1759a: *An Abridgement of Christian Doctrine: Newly Revised and Enlarged by RC*. London: 1759.

Challoner, Richard 1759b: *The Garden of the Soul: Or, A Manual of Spiritual Exercises and Instructions for Christians, who (living in the world): aspire to devotion By Richard Challoner, DD From the London Copy, neatly corrected and enlarged The last Edition*. Dublin: Printed for the Executors of the late Widow Kelly, for the Benefit of her Children.

Chavasse, Antoine 1951: 'Histoire de l'Initation Chrétienne des Enfants, de l'Antiquité à nos Jours', *La Maison Dieu*, 28, pp. 26–44.

Chenu, M.D. 1962: 'Le Nouveau Rite du Baptême des Adultes', *La Maison Dieu*, 71, pp. 15–77.

Chiron, Yves 1999: *Saint Pie X: Réformateur de l'Église*. Versailles: Publications du Courrier de Rome.

Chupungco, Anscar J. (ed.) 1986: *Anàmnesis: Introduzione Storico-Teologica alla Liturgia, vol 3/1 La Liturgia, I Sacramenti: Teologia e Storia della Celebrazione*. Genoa: Marietti .

Chupungco, Anscar J. (ed.) 1997: *Handbook for Liturgical Studies volume 1: Introduction to the Liturgy*. Collegeville, MN: Pueblo.

Clancy, Thomas Hanley 1996: *English Catholic Books 1641–1700 A Bibliography*. Revised edition. Aldershot: Scholar Press.

The Code of Canon Law in English Translation 1983. London: Collins.

Collins, Henry 1861: *Life of the Revd Father Gentili, Priest of the Order of Charity and Sometime Pastor of the Missions of Gracedieu, Shepshed and Loughborough*. London: Burns and Lambert.

Collins, Peter 2002: 'Connecting Anthropology and Quakerism: Transcending the Insider/Outsider Dichotomy', in Elizabeth Arweck and Martin D Stringer (eds), *Theorizing Faith: The Insider/Outsider Problem in the Study of Ritual*. Birmingham: Birmingham University Press, pp. 77–96.

Colomb, Joseph 1958: 'The Catechetical Method of Saint Sulpice', in Gerard S. Sloyan (ed.), *Shaping the Christian Message: Essays in Religious Education*. New York: Macmillan, pp. 91–111.

Common Worship: Initiation Services 1998. London: Church House Publishing.

Communion Verses for Little Children by a Sister of Notre Dame 1912. London: R and T Washbourne.

Connolly, Sean J. 1982: *Priests and People in Pre–Famine Ireland, 1780–1845*. Dublin: Gill and Macmillan.

Cooke, Michael J.G. 1998: *Diocese of Salford Sacramental Programme Review*. Manchester: Diocese of Salford.

Crehan, Joseph 1952: *Father Thurston: A Memoir with a Bibliography of his Writings*. London: Sheed and Ward.

Crichton, James D. 1958: 'Religious Education in England in the Penal Days', in Gerard S. Sloyan (ed.), *Shaping the Christian Message: Essays in Religious Education*. New York: Macmillan, pp. 63–90.

Crichton, James D. 1978: 'Challoner's "Catechism"', *Clergy Review*, 63 (4), pp. 140–46.

Crichton, James D. 1981a: 'Challoner and the "Penny Catechism"', *Recusant History*, 15 (6), pp. 425–32.

Crichton, James D. 1981b: 'Richard Challoner: Catechist and Spiritual Writer', *Clergy Review*, 66 (8), pp. 269–75.

Crichton, James D., H.E. Winstone and J.R. Ainslie 1979: *English Catholic Worship: Liturgical Renewal in England since 1900*. London: Geoffrey Chapman.

Dal-Gal, Hieronimo 1954: *Pius X: The Life-Story of the Beatus*. Dublin: M H Gill and Son.

Davie, Grace 1994: *Religion in Britain since 1945: Believing Without Belonging*. Oxford: Blackwell.

Davie, Grace 2002: *Europe: The Exceptional Case Parameters of Faith in the Modern World*. London: Darton, Longman and Todd.

Davies, Charlotte Aull 1999: *Reflex Ethnography: A Guide to Researching Self and Others*. London: Routledge.

Decree "Ne Temere" on Marriage Instructions of the Archbishop and Bishops of England and Wales With the Latin text of the Decree of the S Congregation of the Council, 2nd August, 1907, a translation of the same, and a letter addressed to the Bishops, 5th March, 1908, by his Eminence, the Cardinal Prefect of Propaganda. 1908: London: Burns and Oates.

Delumeau, Jean (ed.) 1987: *La Première Communion: Quatre Siècles d'Histoire*. Paris: Desclée de Brouwer.

Denzinger, H .and A. Shönmetzer 1977: *Enchiridion Symbolorum, Definitionum et Declarationum de Rebus Fidei et Morum*. Barcelona: Herder.

Directory on Children's Masses 1975: in Flannery, pp. 254–70.

Doctrine Explanations: Holy Communion, Part 1 1899: Manchester: J B Ledsham.

Douglas, Mary 1975: *Implicit Meanings: Essays in Anthropology*. London: Routledge.

Douglas, Mary 2001: *Purity and Danger: An Analysis of the Concepts of Pollution and Taboo*. London: Routledge.

Douglas, Mary and Isherwood, Baron 1996: *The World of Goods: Towards an Anthropology of Consumption*. Second edition. London : Routledge.

Doyal, Len and Ian Gough 1991: *A Theory of Human Need*. Basingstoke: Macmillan.

Duchesne, Louis 1904: *Christian Worship: Its Origin and Evolution A Study of the Latin Liturgy up to the time of Charlemagne*. Translation of third French edition. London: SPCK.

Duffy, Eamon 1981: "Richard Challoner 1691–1781: A Memoir", in Eamon Duffy (ed.), *Challoner and his Church: A Catholic Bishop in Georgian England*. London: Darton, Longman & Todd, pp. 1–26.

Dujarier, Michel 1979: *The Rites of Christian Initiation: Historical and Pastoral Reflections*. New York: Sadlier.

Durkheim, Émile 2001: *The Elementary Forms of Religious Life*. Oxford: Oxford University Press.

Dykstra, C. and Sharon Daloz Parks (eds) 1986: *Faith Development and Fowler*. Birmingham, AL: Religious Education Press.

Eucharistic Prayers for Masses with Children and Masses of Reconciliation (1975): Great Wakering, Essex: Mayhew-McCrimmon.

Evans-Pritchard, E.E. 1965: *Theories of Primitive Religion*. Oxford: Clarendon Press.

Evennet, H.O. 1950: 'Catholics and the Universities', in Beck, pp. 291–321.

Falconi, Carlo 1967: *The Popes in the Twentieth Century: From Pius X to John XXIII*. London: Wiedenfield and Nicholson.

First Communion: A Series of Letters to the Young 1848. Translated by John Battisti Pagani. London: James Burns.

Fisher, J.D.C. 1965: *Christian Initiation: Baptism in the Medieval West A Study of the Disintegration of the Primitive Rite of Initiation* (Alcuin Club Collections no. 47). London: SPCK.

Flannery, Austin (ed.) 1975: *Vatican Council II: The Conciliar and Post Conciliar Documents*. Leominster: Fowler Wright.

Foucault, Michel 1977: *Discipline and Punish: The Birth of the Prison*. London: Penguin Books.

Fowler, James R. 1981: *Stages of Faith: The Psychology of Human Development and the Quest for Meaning*. New York: HarperCollins.

Fowler, James R. 2000: *Becoming Adult, Becoming Christian: Adult Development and Christian Faith*. San Francisco, CA: Jossey–Bass.

Gallagher, Jim 1986: *Guidelines*. London: Collins.

Gallagher, Jim 2001: *Soil for the Seed: Historical, Pastoral and Theological Reflections on Educating to and in the Faith*. Great Wakering, Essex: McCrimmons.

Gallagher, Tom 1985: 'A Tale of Two Cities: Communal Strife in Glasgow and Liverpool before 1914', in Swift and Gilley, pp. 106–29.

Garrone, G.M. 1951: 'L'Enseignenement religieux des enfants dans une perspectif d'initiation chrétienne', in *La Maison Dieu* (28), pp. 45–51.

Gaupin, Linda Lee 1985: 'First Eucharist and the Shape of Catechesis Since *Quam Singulari*'. Unpublished PhD thesis. Catholic University of America, Washington, DC.

General Directory for Catechesis (1997): London: Catholic Truth Society.

Gibergues, de, L'Abbé 1911: *For Little Children: Acts Before and After Holy Communion*. London: R. and T. Washbourne.

Gibson, Henry 1877: *Catechism Made Easy, Being a Familiar Explanation of the Catechism of Christian Doctrine, in Three Volumes*. Liverpool: Rockliff Brothers.

Gibson, Henry 1892: *Instructions on First Communion*. London: Catholic Truth Society.

Gilley, Sheridan 1999: 'A Tradition and Culture Lost, to be Regained?' in Michael P. Hornsby-Smith (ed.). *Catholics in England 1950–2000: Historical and Sociological Perspectives*. London: Cassell, pp. 29–45.

Gillow, Joseph 1969: *A Literary and Biographical History, or Biographical Dictionary of the English Catholics from the Breach with Rome in 1534 to the Present Time*. New York: Burt Franklin.

Giordani, Igino 1952: *Pius X: A Country Priest*. Milwaukee, WI: Bruce.

Gobinet, Charles 1689: *Instructions Concerning Penance and Holy Communion; the Second Part of the Instructions of Youth, Containing the Means how we may return to God By CHARLES GOBINET, doctor of Divinity of the House and Society of the Sorbon, [sic] Principal of the College of PLESSIS-SORBON The Last Edition in French now render'd into English*. London: publisher not stated; printed by J B.

Gother, John 1698: *Instructions for Youth*. Place of publication and publisher not stated

Gother, John 1700: *Instructions for Confession and Communion*. Place of publication and publisher not stated.

Gother, John 1704: *Instructions for Children*. Place of publication and publisher not stated

Goubet-Mahé, Maryvonne 1987: 'Le Premier Rituel de la Première Communion XVIᵉ–XVIIᵉ Siècle', in Delumeau, pp. 51–76.

Gresillon, Sylviane 1987: 'De la Communion Solennelle aux Fêtes de la Foi', in Delumeau, pp. 217–53.

Grubb, Edward L. and Harrison L. Grathwohl 1967: 'Consumer Self-Concept, Symbolism and Market Behavior: A Theoretical Approach', *Journal of Marketing*, 31 (4), pp. 22–7.

Guest, Matthew, Karin Tusting and Linda Woodhead (eds) (2004): *Congregational Studies in the UK: Christianity in a Post-Christian Context*. Aldershot: Ashgate.

Gwynn, Denis 1951: *Father Luigi Gentili and His Mission (1801–1848)*. Dublin: Clonmore and Reynolds.

Gy, Pierre-Marie 1977: 'La Notion Chrétienne d'Initiation: Jalons pour une Enquête', *La Maison Dieu*, 132, pp. 33–54.

Haggerty, Brian A. 1973: *What did Quam Singulari Really Say? A Study Document on the Practices of First Communion and First Confession*. W. Mystic, CT: Twenty-Third Publications.

Haile, Martin and Edwin Bonney 1912: *Life and Letters of John Lingard 1771–1851*. London: Herbert and Daniel.

Hammersley, Martyn 1992: *What's Wrong with Ethnography? Methodological Explorations*. London: Routledge.

Hammersley, Martyn and Paul Atkinson 1995: *Ethnography: Principles in Practice*. Second edition. London: Routledge.

Harty, M. 1908: 'The New Marriage Legislation: Sponsalia – Celebration of Marriage – Formality of Registration', *Irish Ecclesiastical Record*, 23 (January–June), pp. 415–25.

Hedley, John Cuthbert 1912: *The Communion of Children: A Pastoral Letter*. London: Catholic Truth Society.

Heelas, Paul and Linda Woodhead 2004: *The Spiritual Revolution: Why Religion is Giving Way to Spirituality*. Oxford: Blackwell.

Heimann, Mary 1995: *Catholic Devotion in Victorian England*. Oxford: Clarendon Press.

Henchal, Michael (ed.) 2002: *Celebrating Confirmation Before First Communion: A Resource Kit for Restoring the Order of the Initiation Sacraments*. San Jose, CA: Resource Publications.

Hérault, Laurence 1996: *La Grande Communion*. Paris: Éditions du Comité des Travaux Historiques et Scientifiques.

Hérault, Laurence 1999: 'Learning Communion', *Anthropology Today*, 15 (4), pp. 4–8.

Hervé, J.M. 1946: *Manuale Theologiae Dogmaticae*. Westminster, MD: The Newman Bookshop.

Hickman, Mary J. 1999: 'The Religio-Ethnic Identities of Teenagers of Irish Descent', in Michael P. Hornsby-Smith (ed.). *Catholics in England 1950–2000: Historical and Sociological Perspectives*. London: Cassell, pp. 182–98.

Hirschman, Elizabeth C. and Morris B. Holbrook (eds) 1980: *Symbolic Consumer Behavior: Proceedings of the Conference on Consumer Esthetics and Symbolic Consumption*. Ann Arbor, MI: Association for Consumer Studies.

Holbrook, Morris B. and Elizabeth C. Hirschman 1980: 'Symbolic Consumer Behavior: An Introduction', in Hirschman and Holbrook, pp. 1–2.

Holbrook, Morris B. and John O'Shaughnessy 1988: 'On the Scientific Status of Consumer Research and the Need for an Interpretive Approach to Studying Consumption Behavior', *Journal of Consumer Research*, 15 (December), pp. 398–402.

Holman, Rebecca H. 1980: 'Apparel as Communication', in Hirschman and Holbrook, pp. 7–15.

Hornihold, John Joseph 1814: *The Sacraments Explained: in Twenty Discourses*. Dublin: Richard Coyne.

Hornsby-Smith, Michael P. 1987: *Roman Catholics in England: Studies in Social Structure Since the Second World War*. Cambridge: Cambridge University Press.

Hornsby-Smith, Michael P. 1989: *The Changing Parish: A Study of Parishes, Priests and Parishioners after Vatican II*. London : Routledge.

Hornsby-Smith, Michael P. 1999a: 'A Transformed Church', in ibid. (ed.), *Catholics in England 1950–2000: Historical and Sociological Perspectives*. London: Cassell, pp. 3–25.

Hughes, Philip 1950: 'The English Catholics in 1850', in Beck, pp. 116–50.

Hull, Lawrence CSsR 1937: *A First Communion Catechism*. Dudley: The Wellington Press.

Hymns and Benediction Sung for the First Communion of the Pupils of Notre Dame Kindergarten Class, Clapham; May 29th 1924. Privately published. Bound in British Library F274v3.

Instructions for First Communion, containing a Preparation for Confession Revised and Corrected by a Catholic Priest 1860. London: Richardson and Son.

Huguet, R.P., SM 1902: *Le Bonheur d'une Bonne Première Communion et le Malheur d'une Première Communion Sacrilege: Exemples et Conseils Offerts a l'Enfance*. Lille: Maison Saint-Joseph.

Johnson, Maxwell E. 1999: *The Rites of Christian Initiation: Their Evolution and Interpretation*. Collegeville, MN: Pueblo.

Jones, John 1822: *An Explanation of the First Catechism in Four Parts*. Newcastle: Prestom and Heaton.

Jones, Simon and Phillip Tovey (2001): 'Initiation Services', in Paul Bradshaw (ed.), *Companion to Common Worship* vol. 1, (Alcuin Club Collections no 78). London: SPCK, pp. 148–78.

Jungmann, Joseph A. 1959: *The Mass of the Roman Rite: Its Origins and Development (Missarum Sollemnia)*. London: Burns and Oates.

Kavanagh, Aidan 1991: *The Shape of Baptism: The Rite of Christian Initiation*. Collegeville, MN: The Liturgical Press.

Kelly, Revd William R. 1925: *Our First Communion Instructions in Story Form with Coloured Drawings Accompanying Text According to Modern Educational Methods Based on Essential Requirements of Canon 854 of the New Code of Canon Law*. London: Burns Oates and Washbourne.

Kerr, Madeline 1958: *The People of Ship Street*. London: Routledge and Kegan Paul.

Klauser, Theodor 1979: *A Short History of the Western Liturgy: An Account and Some Reflections*. Second edition. Oxford: Oxford University Press.

Kuhn, Annette 1995: *Family Secrets Acts of Memory and Imagination*. London : Verso.

Larkin, Emmet 1976, 1984: *The Historical Dimensions of Irish Catholicism*. Washington, DC: Catholic University of America Press.

Launay, Marcel 1997: *La Papauté à l'aube du XXᵉ Siècle: Léon XIII et Pie X (1878–1914)*. Paris: Les Éditions du Cerf.

Leetham, Claude 1965: *Luigi Gentili: A Sower for the Second Spring*. London: Burns and Oates.

Leichner, Jeannine Timko 1992: *Called to His Supper: A Preparation for First Holy Communion*. Huntington, IN: Our Sunday Visitor.

Lemaitre, Nicole 1987: 'Avant la Communion Solennelle', in Delumeau, pp. 15–31.

Leonard, Ellen 1982: *George Tyrrell and the Catholic Tradition*. London: Darton, Longman and Todd.

Levy, Sydney J. 1959: 'Symbols for Sale', *Harvard Business Review*, 37 (4), pp. 117–24.

Levy, Sydney J. 1978: 'Hunger and Work in a Civilized Tribe; or the Anthropology of Market Transactions', *American Behavioral Scientist*, 21 (4), pp. 557–70.

Levy, Sydney J. 1981: 'Interpreting Consumer Mythology: A Structural Approach to Consumer Behavior', *Journal of Marketing*, 45 (3), pp. 49–61.

Lewis de Granada 1688: *A Memorial of a Christian Life, Compendiously Containing all, that a Soul, Newly converted to GOD, Ought to do, That it may Attain to the Perfection, After which it ought to aspire Divided into Seven Books Written in Spanish by the R F LEWIS DE GRANADA of the Order of St Dominick Translated anew into English THE FIRST PART, Containing the four first BOOKS, which concern the DOCTRINE*. London: publisher not stated; printed for Mat Turner, at the Lamb in High Holborn.

Leys, M.D.R. 1961: *Catholics in England 1559–1829: A Social History*. London: Longmans.

Lingard, John 1840: *Catechetical Instructions on the Doctrines and Worship of the Catholic Church*. London: Charles Dolmen.

Livesey, Lowell W (ed.) 2000: *Public Religion and Urban Transformation: Faith in the City*. New York and London: New York University Press.

Lodge, Anne (1999): 'First Communion in Carnduffy: A Religious and Secular Rite of Passage', *Irish Educational Studies*, 18 (Spring), pp. 210–22.

Lukes, Stephen 1973: *Émile Durkheim, his Life and Work: A Historical and Critical Study*. Harmondsworth: Penguin Books.

McAuley, James White 1996: 'Under an Orange Banner: Reflections on the Northern Protestant Experiences of Emigration', in Patrick O'Sullivan (ed.), *Religion and Identity*. London: Leicester University Press.

McCallion, Michael J., David R. Maines and Steven W. Wolfel 1996: 'Policy as Practice: First Holy Communion in a Contested Situation', *Journal of Contemporary Ethnography*, 25 (3), pp. 300–26.

McClelland, V. Allan and Michael Hodgetts (eds) 1999: *From Without the Flaminian Gate: 150 Years of Roman Catholicism in England and Wales 1850–2000*. London: Darton, Longman and Todd.

McCracken, Grant 1986: 'Culture and Consumption: A Theoretical Account of the Structure and Movement of the Cultural Meaning of Consumer Goods', *Journal of Consumer Research*, 13 (September), pp. 71–85.

McCracken, Grant 1988: *Culture and Consumption: New Approaches to the Symbolic Character of Consumer Goods and Activities*. Bloomington and Indianapolis: Indiana University Press.

McCracken, Grant and Victor D. Roth 1989: 'Does Clothing Have a Code? Empirical Findings and Theoretical Implications in the Study of Clothing as a Means of Communication', *International Journal of Research in Marketing*, 6 (1) pp. 13–33.

McGrail, Peter 2004: 'Display and Division: Congregational Conflict among Roman Catholics', in Matthew Guest and Karin Tusting (eds), *Congregational Studies in the UK*. Aldershot: Ashgate.

McLeod, Daphne 2003: 'Go Therefore Teach', *Newsletter of the Latin Mass Society* (August): Online copy at <www.latin-mass-societyorg/catholiceducationhtm>.

McLeod, Hugh 1974: *Class and Religion in the Late Victorian City*. London: Croom Helm.

McPartlan, Paul 1995: *Sacrament of Salvation: An Introduction to Eucharistic Ecclesiology*. Edinburgh: T & T Clark.

Martin, David 2005: *On Secularization: Towards A Revised General Theory*. Aldershot: Ashgate.

Mary Loyola, Mother 1896: *First Communion Edited by Fr Thurston S J*. London: Burns and Oates.

Mary Loyola, Mother 1911: *The Children's Charter Talks with Parents and Teachers on the Preparation of the Young for First Communion Edited by Fr Thurston S J*. London: Burns and Oates.

Mauss, Marcel 1990: *The Gift: The Form and Reason for Exchange in Archaic Societies*. London: Routledge.

Mazure, H. 1910: *First Communion of Children and its Conditions*. Translated F.M. de Zulueta. London and Edinburgh: Sands and Co.

The Method of S Sulpice for the Organising of Catechisms with Plans of Instruction for the Various Catechisms 1896. London: Griffith Farran Browne and Co.

Metzger, Marcel 1988: 'Nouvelles Perspectives pour la Pretendue Tradition Apostolique', *Ecclesia Orans*, 5 (3), pp. 241–59.

Mick, David Glen 1986: 'Consumer Research and Semiotics: Exploring the Morphology of Signs, Symbols and Significance', *Journal of Consumer Research*, 13 (September), pp. 196–213.

Mohlberg, L.C., L. Eizenhöfer and P. Siffrin 1981: *Liber Sacramentorum Romanae Aeclesiae Ordinis Anni Circuli (Cod Vat Reg lat 316/Paris Bibl Nat 7193, 41/56): (Sacramentarium Gelasianum)*. Rome: Herder.

Moran, Gabriel 1983: *Religious Education Development: Images for the Future*. Minneapolis, MN: Winston Press.

Mullett, Michael A. 1998: *Catholics in Britain and Ireland, 1558–1829*. Houndhills, Basingstoke: Macmillan.

Neal, Frank 1988: *Sectarian Violence the Liverpool Experience, 1819–1914: An Aspect of Anglo-Irish History*. Manchester: Manchester University Press.

Neal, Frank 1997: 'The Famine Irish in England and Wales', in Patrick O'Sullivan (ed.), *The Meaning of the Famine*. London: Leicester University Press, pp. 56–80.

Neuner, J. and J. Dupuis 1978: *The Christian Faith in the Doctrinal Documents of the Catholic Church*. Third edition. Bangalore: Theological Publications in India.

Nist, James 1914: *Private First Communion Instructions for Little Children*. St Louis, MO, Freiburg, London: Herder.

Nocent, Adrian 1986: 'I Tre Sacramenti dell'Iniziazione Cristiana', in Chupungco, pp. 11–131.

Norman, Edward 1984: *The English Church in the Nineteenth Century*. Oxford: Clarendon Press.

Norman, Marion 1972: 'John Gother and the English Way of Spirituality', *Recusant History*, 11 (6), pp. 306–19.

O'Brien, Susan 1999: 'Religious Life for Women', in McLelland and Hodgetts, pp. 108–41.

O'Mara, Pat 1933: *The Autobiography of a Liverpool Slummy*. Liverpool: The Bluecoat Press.

Ordo Confirmationis 1973. Rome: Typis Polyglottis Vaticanis.

Padgett, D.K. 1998: *Qualitative Methods in Social Work Research: Challenges and Rewards*. Thousand Oaks, CA: Sage Publications, Inc.

Pagani, Giovanni Battista 1851: *Life of the Rev Aloysius Gentili, LLD Father of Charity and Missionary Apostolic in England*. London: Richardson and Son.

Parks, Sharon Daloz 1991: 'The North American Critique of James Fowler's Theory of Faith Development', in James Fowler, Karl Ernst Nipkow and Friedrich Schweitzer (eds), *Stages of Faith and Religious Development: Implications for Church, Education and Society*. London: SCM Press, pp. 101–15.

Pecklers, Keith F. 1997: 'History of the Roman Ritual from the Sixteenth until the Twentieth Centuries', in Chupungco, pp. 153–78.

Pickering, Bernard 1980: 'Bishop Challoner and Teaching the Faith', *Clergy Review*, 65 (1), pp. 6–15.

Police (Liverpool Inquiry): Act 1909 Before Mr Arthur J Ashton, KC Commissioner January 31st–February 26th 1910 Transcript of Shorthand Notes of Proceedings. Liverpool: Lee and Nightingale.

Plumb, Brian 1986: *Found Worthy: a Biographical Dictionary of the Secular Clergy of the Archdiocese of Liverpool (Deceased): since 1850*. Privately published.

de Puniet, P. 1910: 'Baptême', in *Dictionnaire d'Archéologie chrétienne et de Liturgie*, Vol 2, 1. Paris: Letouzey et Amé, pp. 251–346.

de Puniet, P. 1914: 'Confirmation' in *Dictionnaire d'Archéologie chrétienne et de Liturgie*, Vol 3, 2. Paris, Letouzey et Amé, pp. 2515–43

Purnell, A. Patrick 1985: *Our Faith Story: Its Telling and its Sharing*. London: Collins.

Ranchetti, Michele 1969: *The Catholic Modernists: A Study of the Religious Reform Movement 1864–1907*. London: Oxford University Press.

Raughel, Alfred 1951: 'Comment orienter les retraites de Communion Solennelle et de Confirmation' in *La Maison Dieu* (28), pp. 52–62.

Reardon, Bernard M.G. 1970: *Roman Catholic Modernism*. London: Adam and Charles Black.

Richards, J.B. 1883: *A Catechism of First Communion With Preparation and Thanksgiving*. London: Burns and Oates.

Rite of Christian Initiation of Adults (1987): London: Geoffrey Chapman English.

Robert, Odile 1987: 'Fonctionnement et Enjeux d'une Institution Chrétienne au XVIIIᵉ Siècle', in Delumeau, pp. 77–113.

Robert, Patrick 1951: 'Une Cérémonial de Communion Solennelle' in *La Maison Dieu* (28), pp. 107–13.

Rochberg-Halton, Eugene 1984: 'Object Relations, Role Models, and Cultivation of the Self', *Environment and Behavior*, 16 (3), pp. 335–68.

Roche, Arthur and Tom Horwood (eds) 2000: *150 Years: Anniversary of the Restoration of the Catholic Hierarchy in England and Wales*. London: Catholic Media Office.

The Roman Missal Revised by Decree of the Second Vatican Council and Published by Authority of Pope Paul VI Official English Texts 1975. Alcester and Dublin: Goodliffe Neale.

Rook, Dennis W. 1984: 'Ritual Behavior and Consumer Symbolism', *Advances in Consumer Research*, 11, pp. 279–83.

Rook, Dennis W. and Sydney J. Levy 1983: 'Psychological Themes in Consumer Grooming Rituals', *Advances in Consumer Research*, 10, pp. 329–33.

Rosenbaum, Catherine 1987: 'Images-Souvenirs de Première Communion', in Delumeau, pp. 113–69.

Rowlands, Marie 1969: 'The Education and Piety of Catholics in Staffordshire in the Eighteenth Century', *Recusant History*, 10 (2), pp. 67–78.

Rowlands, Marie (ed.) 1999: *The English Catholics of Parish and Town 1558–1778*. London: Catholic Record Society.

Sagovsky, Nicholas 1990: *'On God's Side': a Life of George Tyrrell*. Oxford: Clarendon Press.

Saris, Wim 1982: *Together We Communicate*. London: Collins.

Sauzet, Robert 1987: 'Aux Origenes', in Delumeau, pp. 33–50.

Sawyer, Kieran 2002: 'Sealed with the Spirit', *National Catholic Reporter*, 22 March 2002 <http://www.natcath.com?NCR_Online/archives/032202/032202s.htm>.

Schenk, Carolyn Turner and Rebecca H. Holman 1980: 'A Sociological Approach to Brand Choice: The Concept of Situational Self Image', *Advances in Consumer Research*, 7, pp. 610–14.

Schroeder, H.J. 1941: *Canons and Decrees of the Council of Trent: Original Text with English Translation*. London and St Louis, MO: Herder.

Schuster, Ildefonso 1924: *The Sacramentary (Liber Sacramentorum): Historical and Liturgical Notes on the Roman Missal*. Vol. 1. London: Burns Oates and Washbourne.

Schwartz, Barry 1967: 'The Social Psychology of the Gift', *The American Journal of Psychology*, 73 (1), pp. 1–11.

Ségur, Louis Gaston Adrien de 1887: *To Children Practical Counsels for Holy Communion With Introduction by his Lordship the Right Rev Dr Furlong*. Fifth edition. London: Burns and Oates Ltd.

Sheehey, Gerard, Ralph Brown, Donal Kelly and Aidan Mcgrath (eds) 1983: *The Canon Law: Letter and Spirit A Practical Guide to the Code of Canon Law*. London: Geoffrey Chapman.

Sherry, John F. Jr 1983: 'Gift Giving in Anthropological Perspective', *Journal of Consumer Research*, 10 (September), pp. 156–68.

Sirgy, M. Joseph 1982: 'Self-Concept in Consumer Behavior: A Critical Review', *Journal of Consumer Research*, 9 (1), pp. 287–300.

Slater, Don 1997: 'Consumer Culture and the Politics of Need', in M. Nava, A. Blake, I. Macrury and B. Richards (eds), *Buy This Book: Studies in Advertising*. London: Routledge, pp. 51–63.

Solomon, Michael R. 1983: 'The Role of Products as Social Stimuli: A Symbolic Interactionist Perspective', *Journal of Consumer Research*, 10 (3), pp. 319–29.

Soper, Kate 1981: *On Human Need: Open and Closed Theories in a Marxist Perspective*. Sussex: The Harvester Press.

Speiaght, Robert 1957: *The Life of Hilaire Belloc*. London: Hollis and Carter.

Stanner, W.E.H. 1967: 'Reflections on Durkheim and Aboriginal Origins', in Maurice Freedman (ed.), *Social Organization: Essays Presented to Raymond Firth*. London: Frank Cass, pp. 216–40 .

Steven, James H.S. 2002: *Worship in the Spirit: Charismatic Worship in the Church of England*. Carlisle: Paternoster Press.

Stringer, Martin D. 1999: *On the Perception of Worship: The Ethnography of Worship in Four Christian Congregations in Manchester*. Birmingham: Birmingham University Press.

Swatos, William H. and D.V. Olson (eds) 2000: *The Secularization Debate*. Lanham, MD: Rowman & Littlefield.

Sweeney, Morgan V. 1950: 'Diocesan Organisation and Administration', in Beck, pp. 116–50.

Swift, Roger and Sheridan Gilley (eds) 1999: *The Irish in Victorian Britain: the Local Dimension*. Dublin: Four Courts Press.

Torres, Carlos Alberto 1992: *The Church, Society and Hegemony: a Critical Sociology of Religion in Latin America*. London, Westport, CT: Praeger.

Tozzi, Eugene Vincent 1994: 'Parent and Family Religious Education: A Case Study Based on an Ecological Theory of Human Development', Unpublished PhD thesis, Fordham University, New York.

Turberville, Henry 1685: *An Abridgement of Christian Doctrin [sic] With Proofs of Scripture for Points Contraverted Catechetically explain'd, by way of Question and Answer*. London: publisher not stated; printed by Henry Hills.

Turner, Paul 1995: 'The Challenge of the Confirmation Praxis', *Federation of Diocesan Liturgical Commissions Newsletter*, 22/6 (December): 45–8.

Turner, Paul 2000: *Ages of Initiation: The First Two Christian Millennia*. Collegeville, MN: The Liturgical Press.

Turner, Victor 1967: *The Forest of Symbols: Aspects of Ndembu Ritual*. Ithaca, NY and London: Cornell University Press.

Turner, Victor 1969: *The Ritual Process: Structure and Anti–Structure*. New York: Aldine de Gruyter.

Van Gennep, Arnold 1960 [1909]: *The Rites of Passage*. Chicago, IL: University of Chicago Press.

Vaux, Laurence 1568: *A Catechisme, Or a Christian Doctrine Neccessarie for Chyldren and the Ignorant People*. Louvain: publisher not stated.

Walkerdine, Valerie 1997: *Daddy's Girl: Young Girls & Popular Culture*. Cambridge, MA: Harvard University Press.

Waller, P.J. 1981: *Democracy and Sectarianism: a Political and Social History of Liverpool 1868–1939*. Liverpool: Liverpool University Press.

Wagner, R. 1981: *The Invention of Culture*. Chicago, IL: University of Chicago Press.

Ward, Bernard 1909: 'English Catholics in the XVIIIth Century', *Dublin Review*, Jan., pp. 53–66.

Ward, Bernard 1915: *The Sequel to Catholic Emancipation: The Story of the English Catholics Continued Down to the Re–Establishment of their Hierarchy in 1850*. London: Longmans, Green and Co.

Ward, Connor 1965: *Priests and People: A Study in the Sociology of Religion*. Liverpool: Liverpool University Press.

Wedam, Elfriede 2000: 'Catholic Spirituality in a New Urban Church', in Liveszey, pp. 213–37.

Westerhoff, John H. III 2000: *Will Our Children Have Faith?* Revised edition. Harrisburg, PA: Morehouse Publishing.

Williamson, Catherine E. 1999: 'Passing on the Faith: The Importance of Parish-Based Catechesis in a Roman Catholic Diocese', Unpublished Ph D Thesis. University of Brighton, England.

Yarnold, Edward 1994a: *The Awe-Inspiring Rites of Christian Initiation: The Origins of the RCIA*. Edinburgh: T and T Clark.

Yarnold, Edward 1994b: 'The Sacraments of Christian Initiation', in Michael Walsh (ed.), *Commentary on the Catechism of the Catholic Church*. London: Geoffrey Chapman, pp. 242–58.

Zulueta, F.M. de 1911: *Early First Communion A Commentary upon the Decree* 'Quam Singulari'. London: R & T Washbourne.

Zulueta, F. M. de 1920: *Gathered Fragments Or Stray Leaves on Frequent and Daily Communion*. London: The Manresa Press.

Section B: Archival Sources

1 Newspapers

The Catholic Times New Series 1907, 1908, 1910, 1911 passim. Accessed in the library of Heythrop College, London.

The Liverpool Catholic Herald 1907, 1908, 1910, 1911 passim. Microfilm Collection in Liverpool Public Library.

The Tablet 1907, 1908, 1910, 1911 passim. Accessed in the Gradwell collection at Liverpool Hope University.

2 Liverpool Archdiocesan Archives

Most circular letters and reports from the early twentieth century have been bound in a series of volumes entitled *Liverpolitana*. Each individual document had its own page numbering; in the binding process they were additionally numbered by hand across the entire volume. In this list the global page numbers are given. Within the text, the original page numbers are cited. Unbound documents are stored in a series of numbered boxes.

a Formal Documents of Bishop Thomas Whiteside

Whiteside CXXV: *Ad Clerum* letter, 12 November 1907, RCAL Archives S1 VIII C/2. Forwards a copy of *Pascendi* to the clergy.

Whiteside CLIX: *Report on the Liverpool Archdiocese Mission Fund for the Year 1909* (21 November 1910): Liverpool, Rockliffe Brothers. Bound in *Liverpolitana III*, pp. 443–56. Forwards a copy of *Quam Singulari* to the clergy, instructing them to take steps towards its implementations.

Whiteside CLX: *Ad Clerum* letter, 8 December 1910. Bound in *Liverpolitana III*, p. 467. Outlines arrangements for the taking of the anti–modernist oath.

Whiteside CLXIII: *Report on the Ecclesiastical Education Fund for the Year Ending January 3st 1911* (2 March 1911): Liverpool: Rockliffe Brothers. Bound in *Liverpolitana IV*, pp. 27–33. Includes the text of a Pastoral Letter on *Quam Singulari,* to be read in all churches on Sunday, 12 March 1911.

Whiteside CLXXV: *Report of the Liverpool Diocesan Mission Fund for the Year 1911* (28 November 1912): Liverpool: Rockliffe Brothers. Bound in *Liverpolitana IV*, pp. 239–262. Includes Whiteside's initial analysis of the implementation of *Quam Singulari.*

Whiteside CLXXVII: *Report of the Ecclesiastical Education Fund For the Year Ending January 31, 1914* (27 February 1914): Liverpool: Rockliffe Brothers. Bound in *Liverpolitana IV*, pp. 445–54. Contains a detailed statistical analysis of the impact Whiteside claims for *Quam Singulari* in the diocese.

b Liverpool Diocesan Synods

Synodus Diocesana Liverpolitana Duodevicesima Anno 1911 (1911): Liverpool: Rockliffe Brothers. Bound in *Liverpolitana IV*, pp. 113–24.

Synodus Diocesana Liverpolitana Undevicesima Anno 1914 (1914): Liverpool: Rockliffe Brothers. Bound in *Liverpolitana IV*, pp. 527–40.

c Acta and Minutes of the Bishops' Meetings

The box Early Bishops' Collection: Brown–Whiteside: Series 1 VII B/2 contains documents relating to meetings of the Bishops of England and Wales held on the following dates: 10 October 1907; 4 February 1908; 3 November 1910; 29 April 1919.

Section C: Internet Sources

These are listed in alphabetical order of the URL, with a brief definition of what was to be found at the address on 9 April 2006, the date when each was last checked.

Aquila, Samuel 2002: *Send Forth Your Spirit: Pastoral Letter to the People of Eastern North Dakota on the Sacrament of Confirmation.* <http://www.fargodiocese.org/ EducationFormation/Evangelization/Confirmation/confirmation.pdf>.

McLeod, Daphne 2003: Go Therefore Teach. *Newsletter of the Latin Mass Society* (August): Online copy at <www.latin-mass-societyorg/catholiceducation.htm>.

English translation of *E Supremi* (1903). <http://www.vatican.va/holy_father/pius_ x/encyclicals/documents/hf_p-x_enc_04101903_e-supremi_en.html>.

Index